Crimes of Reason

Crimes of Reason

On Mind, Nature, and the Paranormal

Stephen E. Braude

ROWMAN & LITTLEFIELD
Lanham • Boulder • New York • London

Published by Rowman & Littlefield
A wholly owned subsidiary of The Rowman & Littlefield Publishing Group, Inc.
4501 Forbes Boulevard, Suite 200, Lanham, Maryland 20706
www.rowman.com

16 Carlisle Street, London W1D 3BT, United Kingdom

Copyright © 2014 by Rowman & Littlefield
First paperback edition 2016

All rights reserved. No part of this book may be reproduced in any form or by any electronic or mechanical means, including information storage and retrieval systems, without written permission from the publisher, except by a reviewer who may quote passages in a review.

British Library Cataloguing in Publication Information Available

Library of Congress Cataloging-in-Publication Data
The hardback edition of this book was previously cataloged by the Library of Congress as follows:

Braude, Stephen E., 1945-
Crimes of reason : on mind, nature, and the paranormal / Stephen E. Braude.
p. cm.
Includes bibliographical references and index.
1. Philosophy of mind. 2. Extrasensory perception. I. Title.
BD418.3.B728 2014
128'.2--dc23
2014016155
ISBN 978-1-4422-3575-5 (cloth : alk. paper)
ISBN 978-1-4422-7590-4 (pbk : alk. paper)
ISBN 978-1-4422-3576-2 (electronic)

∞™ The paper used in this publication meets the minimum requirements of American National Standard for Information Sciences Permanence of Paper for Printed Library Materials, ANSI/NISO Z39.48-1992.

Printed in the United States of America

For Gina,
One of life's miracles

Contents

Preface ix

1 Memory without a Trace 1
2 Radical Provincialism in the Life Sciences: A Review of Rupert Sheldrake's *A New Science of Life* 27
3 In Defense of Folk Psychology: Inner Causes versus Action Spaces 49
4 The Creativity of Dissociation 81
5 Multiple Personality and Moral Responsibility 103
6 Parapsychology and the Nature of Abilities 141
7 Some Thoughts on Parapsychology and Religion 181
8 Credibility under Fire: Advice to the Academically Marginalized 197

Index 217

Preface

This volume brings together expanded and updated versions of previously published essays that I continue to feel have some merit, along with new essays written specifically for this book. Although the essays deal with a variety of topics, they all hover around a set of interrelated general themes. These are (1) the poverty of mechanistic theories in the behavioral and life sciences, (2) the nature of psychological explanation and (at least within the halls of the academy) the unappreciated strategies required to understand behavior, (3) the nature of dissociation, and (4) the nature and limits of human abilities. Although the topics are often abstract and the issues are deep, their treatment in this book is accessible, and the tone of the book is both light and occasionally combative. Moreover, although some of the essays are previously published, the new versions should be easier to read, shorn of much of their former obligatory and ponderous scholarly prose. I've also added new material to each, sometimes quite a lot of it, and brought the essays up to date when necessary. The individual essays remain self-contained, but they now mutually reinforce one another in a way that would have been difficult to manage (or discern) in their previous and widely scattered incarnations. Moreover, the philosophical threads running through the earlier essays are explored further in the new material written explicitly for this volume.

The title *Crimes of Reason* has a dual meaning. On the one hand, it refers to the often egregious conceptual errors underlying mechanistic thinking in the behavioral sciences as well as to the shoddy—and sometimes flagrantly dishonest—dialectical tactics adopted by critics of both parapsychology and the study of dissociation. On the other hand, it alludes to the charges leveled against my principal research agendas over the past several decades, all of which have been branded at one time or another either as forms of pseudoscience or demonstrations of irrationality.

The outline of the book is as follows.

Chapter 1: "Memory without a Trace." This chapter takes a close and critical look at the customary view of memory as something that is stored (presumably in the brain) in the form of memory traces or "engrams." As familiar and seductive as that view is, I argue that it's disguised nonsense and no more plausible than an ancient position from which it's philosophically indistinguishable—namely, Plato's clearly naive view that memory works by means of a process analogous to creating impressions in wax. This is one of several chapters that illustrate the underlying flawed assumptions behind mechanistic analyses of the mental.

Chapter 2: "Radical Provincialism in the Life Sciences." This chapter is a review of Rupert Sheldrake's *A New Science of Life*, a work that has received considerable attention from both scientists and laypersons. Some hail the book as a radically new and viable approach to a vast range of scientific issues. Its opponents, on the other hand, either dismiss it mildly as merely a wrongheaded theoretical program or else denounce it strongly as a work of indefensible eccentricity. Although Sheldrake conceived his theory of morphogenetic fields as a revolutionary but feasible alternative to mechanistic theories in the life sciences, I show that the theory is (ironically) flawed for essentially the same reasons as other mechanistic theories. So one reason this chapter is important is that by seeing how mechanistic confusions manifest in Sheldrake's theorizing about formative causation, readers will be better able to appreciate both the nature of those errors and the extent to which they permeate received scientific thinking generally. And then, hopefully they'll be better able to detect inevitable new versions of the errors when those errors appear.

Chapter 3: "In Defense of Folk Psychology: Inner Causes versus Action Spaces." This is one of the new chapters for the book. Perhaps the biggest problem facing criticisms of mechanistic theories of the mental (or of behavior) is that they fail to provide an alternative theoretical program. Here, I make an effort in that direction, principally by taking a fresh look at what it means to explain and understand a person's behavior. This requires, first, surveying the usual (but flawed) approaches to explaining behavior and then considering examples typically ignored in the literature, which demonstrate both the limitations of those usual approaches and the need for the quite different strategy I recommend.

Chapter 4: "The Creativity of Dissociation." This is the first of two chapters focusing exclusively on both dissociation generally and dissociative identity (formerly multiple personality) disorder, or DID, in particular. It examines the creative maneuvering required to maintain a state of profound dissociation—a topic that researchers in the field have surprisingly neglected. I examine this first in connection with the hypnotic phenomena of negative hallucination and systematized anesthesia, and then I look at more complex and clinically substantive cases of DID. Those latter cases also require a closer look at the nature and organization of both human abilities and character traits, topics that connect with several other chapters in the book.

Chapter 5: "Multiple Personality and Moral Responsibility." For the most part, the philosophical literature on multiple personality has focused on that pathology's relevance to traditional problems concerning the nature of persons, personal identity, and psychological explanation. But philosophers have paid relatively little attention to problems of responsibility in these cases. And perhaps the most vexing and peculiar of those questions is this: In what respect(s) and to what extent should a multiple be held responsible for the actions of his or her alternate personalities (or *alters*)? That's the issue I examine, first by considering whether we should hold individuals responsible for things experienced or actions taken during a dream, and then by examining the tangled snarl of legal issues involved when a multiple faces prosecution for a crime committed by an alter. This chapter also connects with the previous chapter's focus on the adaptational nature of dissociation.

Chapter 6: "Parapsychology and the Nature of Abilities." This chapter is one of several in the book that examine unusual forms of human creativity, performance, and expertise, either in connection with the evidence from parapsychology or as manifested in cases of savantism, prodigies, and either dissociation generally or DID in particular. These matters connect as well to my long-standing concern with more general problems of psychological explanation, particularly in light of the gross inadequacies of trendy computational theories of the mind (a topic addressed more directly in chapters 1 and 3). This chapter focuses specifically on savants, prodigies, and dissociative virtuosi, who have much to teach us about the distribution, limits, and perhaps also the latency of human talent. It also focuses on the evidence for postmortem survival, which forces us to look closely at the analysis and relations between various skills or abilities. Moreover, the chapter examines some important issues concerning memory, a topic considered in great detail, and from a different angle, in chapter 1.

Chapter 7: "Some Thoughts on Parapsychology and Religion." This admittedly speculative chapter considers how atheists or agnostics sympathetic to parapsychology might make sense of the claim that you can't fool God. One intimidating way of understanding the evidence for ESP and psychokinesis (PK) is that we have more than the normal ways of gaining information about and affecting—even taking action against—one another. So the data of parapsychology suggest that people might sometimes pay for their wrongdoings through psychic interventions. If telepathic interactions occur, then perhaps our real motives can't be as easily concealed as we like to think. And if

PK occurs, then perhaps psychic vendettas are a genuine option. In that case, then, we can apparently interpret the claim that you can't fool God in a way consistent both with deism and nondeism. And on a related but somewhat less sinister (or at least less unsettling) note, I consider how the data of parapsychology might also help us understand the apparent (if only sporadic) efficacy of prayer.

Chapter 8: "Credibility under Fire: Advice to the Academically Marginalized." I think of this new chapter as a kind of curmudgeonly (and I hope amusing) and provocatively polemical postscript. It's a consideration of the similarly suspicious and often dishonest tactics adopted by critics of research into both parapsychology and dissociation. I also offer some very personal reflections on the attacks leveled against me as well as advice and words of encouragement to other researchers in these areas. This essay, too, reviews widely held but flawed assumptions prevalent in the physical and behavioral sciences.

Several friends and colleagues have generously offered very helpful comments and criticisms as I put this volume together. In particular, I'd like to thank Ed Kelly, Alan Gauld, Gerald Barnes, Stan McDaniel, Scott Davison, Dick Bierman, and Peter Barach.

Sections of chapter 1 appeared first in "The Misuse of Memory in Psi Research," in *Aquém e Além do Cérebro (Behind and Beyond the Brain): Proceedings of the 6th BIAL Foundation Symposium* (Porto, Portugal: BIAL Foundation, 2006): 199–219, and then as "Memory without a Trace," *European Journal of Parapsychology* 21, special issue (2006): 182–202. Chapter 2's precursor appeared originally in the *Journal of the American Society for Psychical Research* 77 (1983): 63–78. Chapter 4 was published originally in the *Journal of Trauma and Dissociation* 3 (2002): 5–26. Chapter 5 first appeared in *Philosophy, Psychiatry, & Psychology* 3.1 (1996): 37–54. Copyright © 1996 The Johns Hopkins University Press. Reprinted with permission by Johns Hopkins University Press. A very early version of chapter 6 served as the presidential address for the Parapsychological Association and was published in the *Journal of Parapsychology* 56 (1992): 205–28. And an ancestor of chapter 7 appeared in C. Tart, ed., *Body, Mind, Spirit* (Charlottesville, VA: Hampton Roads, 1997), 118–27. My sincere thanks to the editors and publishers of these publications for permission to reuse the material here.

Chapter 3 began life as a joint project with my colleague Bruce Goldberg. However, other projects and life issues intervened, and at the time of Bruce's untimely death the essay remained far from completed. Bruce had made it clear in any case that he was ready for me to carry on with what we'd already done, and I can only hope that he would have approved of the final result.

Chapter One

Memory without a Trace

One of the most persistent conceptual errors in philosophy, psychology, and neurophysiology is the attempt to explain memory by means of memory traces (sometimes called "engrams"). The underlying problems are very deep and difficult to dispel, and as a result, trace theories are quite seductive. In fact, in the cognitive sciences, this approach to memory is ubiquitous and is almost never seriously questioned.[1] If doubts are raised at all, they typically concern how trace mechanisms are implemented or what the physical substrate of traces might be, not whether something is profoundly wrongheaded about the very idea of a memory trace. Moreover, positing memory traces is one aspect of a larger explanatory agenda that prevails in the behavioral sciences—namely, the tempting but ultimately fruitless strategy of explaining human behavior as if it's emitted by, and wholly analyzable in terms of, processes occurring within an agent (typically, inside the agent's brain). And one reason that agenda is so difficult to overturn is that in order to present a viable alternative, one must outline a very different approach to the explanation and understanding of human behavior.

Not surprisingly, that last task is a big one, and I'll make at least a modest introductory stab at it in chapter 3. For this chapter, I have an even more modest (though no less important) goal—namely, to summarize the main reasons for thinking that the concept of a memory trace is not simply useless but actually nonsensical. At the end of the chapter, I'll also show, only briefly, how analogous concepts have crept insidiously into various areas of parapsychological theorizing, especially in connection with the evidence for postmortem survival—for example, speculations about cellular memory in transplant cases and genetic memory in reincarnation cases.[2]

WHY TRACES?

Suppose I meet my old friend Jones, whom I haven't seen in twenty-five years. How is it, we wonder, that I'm able to remember him? Many believe that I couldn't possibly remember Jones without there being something *in* me, a trace (presumably a modification in my brain) produced in me by my former association with Jones. Without that trace, that persisting structural modification in my brain, we'd apparently have causation over a temporal gap. We'd have to suppose that I remember Jones now simply because I used to know him. And to many, that looks like magic. How could something twenty-five years ago produce a memory now, unless that twenty-five-year gap is somehow bridged? So when I remember Jones after twenty-five years, we're tempted to think it's because something in me now closes that gap, linking my present memory to my past acquaintance with Jones.

Now parenthetically, I have to say that it's at least controversial (and in many instances rather naive) to suppose there's something wrong with the idea of causation over a temporal gap. Gappy causation is a problem only on the assumption that the only real causes are proximate causes (i.e., that cause and effect must be spatiotemporally contiguous). But that's a thread I can't pursue here. Positing memory traces is problematic enough quite apart from its underlying questionable picture of causation.

So, let's return to the motivation for asserting the existence of memory traces. Notice that traces aren't posited simply to explain how I happen to be in the particular states we identify as instances of remembering—for example, my experiencing a certain mental image of Jones. They're supposed to explain how memory is *possible* in the first place. The idea is that without a persisting structural modification in me caused by something in my past—in this case, presumably, a physiological representation of Jones—no state in me *could* be a memory of Jones. So if after twenty-five years I have a mental image of Jones, the only way that image could count as a memory of Jones would be if it had the right sort of causal history. And the right sort of causal history, allegedly, is one that spatially and temporally links my present experience with my past acquaintance with Jones. So my image of Jones counts as a memory of Jones only if (1) there's a trace in me, caused by my previous acquaintance with Jones, and (2) the activation of that trace is involved in producing my present image of Jones. So mental images of Jones might be possible without that sort of causal history, but they wouldn't then be instances of remembering.

History has proved that this general picture of remembering is initially very attractive. But it gets very ugly very quickly, as soon as one asks the right sorts of questions. (In my view, this is where philosophy is most useful and often the most fun: showing how claims which seem superficially plausible crumble as soon as their implications or presuppositions are exposed.)

What eventually becomes clear is that the idea of memory as involving *storage* is deeply mistaken and that the mechanism of storage, memory traces conceived as representations of some kind, can't possibly do the job for which they're intended. This is actually an enormous topic and one of the most interesting subjects in the philosophy of mind. But since this issue is both vast and only part of what I want to discuss, I can't do more here than outline a few of the problems with the concept of a memory trace and indicate where one might look for additional details.[3]

MORE PRELIMINARIES

The first thing to note is that the problems with the concept of a memory trace are *hardware independent*. It doesn't matter whether traces are conceived as mental or physical, or more specifically as static, dynamic, neurological, biochemical, atomic, subatomic, holographic (à la Pribram), nonspatial mental images, or (as Plato suggested) impressions in wax. No matter *what* memory traces are allegedly composed of or how they're purportedly configured, they turn out to be impossible objects. Memory-trace theory requires them to perform functions that nothing can fulfill. So my objections to trace theory have nothing to do specifically with the fact that those theories are typically physiological or physical. Rather, it's because they're *mechanistic* and (in particular) because the mechanisms they posit can't possibly do what's required of them.

Before getting into details, I must deflect a certain standard reaction among scientists to the sort of criticisms I'm making here. Many have complained to me that as scientists, they're merely doing empirical research, and so it's simply beside the point to argue, a priori, that their theories are unintelligible or otherwise conceptually flawed. However, I'm afraid that this response betrays a crucial naiveté about scientific inquiry. There's no such thing as a purely empirical investigation. Every branch of science rests on numerous, often unrecognized, abstract (i.e., philosophical) presuppositions, both metaphysical and methodological. These concern, for example, the nature of observation, properties, or causation, the interpretation, viability, and scope of certain rules of inference, and the appropriate procedures for investigating a given domain of phenomena. But that means that the integrity of the discipline as a whole hinges on the acceptability of its root philosophical assumptions. If those assumptions are indefensible or incoherent, that particular scientific field has nothing to stand on, no matter how attractive it might be on the surface. And I would say that several areas of science, as a result, turn out simply to be bad philosophy dressed up in obscurantist technical jargon so that the elementary nature of their mistakes remains well hidden. Memory-trace theory is just one example of this. And I'd argue that today's trace theories of memory, for all their surface sophistication, are at bottom as wrongheaded and simplistic as Plato's proposal that memories are analogous to impressions in wax. In short, I'd say they're disguised nonsense.

Two more disclaimers, before outlining my objections to trace theory. First, when I say that the concept of a memory trace is nonsensical or that trace theory is conceptually naive in certain respects, I'm not saying that trace theories—or the scientists who hold them—are stupid. To say that a proposal or concept is nonsensical or incoherent is simply to say it makes no sense. Now although the world isn't suffering a shortage of stupidity, not all nonsense is stupid. In fact, the most interesting nonsense is *deep* nonsense, and it's something which can all too easily deceive even very smart people. That's because the problematic assumptions are buried well below the surface and require major excavation.

Second, I've learned over the years that when I outline my objections to trace theory, many hear me as suggesting that the brain has nothing to do with memory. I'll say a bit more about this later, but for now I'll just note that I'm saying nothing of the kind. Although evidence for postmortem survival *would* seriously challenge this, we can overlook for now complications to all physiological cognitive theories posed by the evidence for postmortem survival and restrict our attention to embodied humans. In those cases, clearly, the capacity to remember is causally dependent not simply on having a functioning brain, but probably also on changes to specific areas of the brain. However, it's one thing to say that the brain *mediates* the capacity to remember and another to say it *stores* memories. The former view (more likely the correct one) takes the brain to be an instrument involved in the expression of memory; the latter view turns out to be deeply unintelligible.

THE HORNS OF A DILEMMA

So why is the concept of a memory trace fundamentally nonsensical? Let's begin with an analogy drawn from John Heil's outstanding critique of trace theory.[4] Suppose I invite many guests to a party, and suppose I want to remember all the people who attended. Accordingly, I ask each guest to leave behind something (a trace) by which I can remember them. Let's suppose each guest leaves behind a tennis ball. Clearly, I can't use the balls to accomplish the task of remembering my party guests. For my strategy to work, the guests must deposit something reliably and specifically linked to them, and the balls obviously aren't differentiated and unambiguous enough to establish a link only with the person who left it.

So perhaps it would help if each guest signed his or her own tennis ball or perhaps left a photo of himself or herself stuck to the ball. Unfortunately, this threatens an endless regress of strategies for remembering who attended my party. Nothing reliably (much less uniquely and unambiguously) links the signature or photo to the guest who attended. A guest could mischievously have signed someone else's name or left behind a photo of another person. Or maybe the signature was illegible (most are), or perhaps the only photo available was of the person twenty-five years earlier (e.g., when he still had hair, or when he had a beard, wore eyeglasses, and was photographed outdoors, out of focus, and in a thick fog), or when he was dressed in a Halloween costume or some other disguise.

But now it looks like I need to remember in order to remember. A tennis ball isn't specific enough to establish the required link to the person who left it. What the situation requires is an *unambiguous representational calling card*, and the tennis ball clearly doesn't do the job. So we supposed that something else might make the tennis ball a more specific link—a signature or a photo. That is, we tried to employ a secondary memory mechanism (trace) so that I could remember what the original trace (the tennis ball) was a trace of. But the signature and photo are equally inadequate. They, too, can't be linked unambiguously to a specific individual. Of course, if I could simply *remember* who wrote the signature or left behind the photo, then it's not clear why I even needed the original tennis balls. If no memory mechanism is needed to make the connection from photo to photo donor or from illegible signature to its author, then we've conceded that remembering can occur without corresponding traces, and then no trace was needed in the first place to explain how I remember who attended my party. So in order to avoid that fatal concession, it looks like yet another memory mechanism will be required for me to remember who left behind (say) the illegible or phony signature or the fuzzy photo. And off we go on a regress of memory processes. It seems that no matter what my party guests leave behind, nothing can be linked only to the guest who left it. We'll always need something else, some other mechanism, for making the connection between the thing left behind and the individual who left it.

In fact, it seems that the only way to stop the regress is for a guest to leave behind something that is *intrinsically* and exclusively linked to only one individual. That's why Wolfgang Köhler, for example, proposed that traces must be *isomorphic* with (i.e., inherently and structurally similar to) the things of which they're traces—that is, the things they represent.[5] But what Köhler and others have failed to grasp is that this kind of intrinsic connection is impossible, because nothing can function in one and only one way. As I'll argue shortly, this is especially clear when the function in question is one of representation or meaning. Nothing can represent unambiguously (or represent one and only one thing); representing is not something objects can do all by themselves; and representation can't be an intrinsic or inherent relation between the thing represented and the thing that represents it.

Interestingly, although Köhler failed to see why trace theory is doomed to fail, he was remarkably clear about what trace theory requires. Köhler understood that a major hurdle for trace theory is to explain trace *activation*—that is, how something present triggers my trace of Jones rather than the trace of someone else. And that's a serious problem, because what triggers a memory (or activates a trace) can be quite different from what established it in the first place. So Köhler wrote,

> recognition . . . means that a present fact, usually a perceptual one, makes contact with a corresponding one in memory, a trace, a contact which gives the present perception the character of being known or familiar. But memory contains a tremendous number of traces, all of them representations of previous experiences which must have been established by the processes accompanying such earlier experiences. Now, why does the present perceptual experience make contact with the *right* earlier experience? This is an astonishing achievement. Nobody seems to doubt that the *selection* is brought about by the similarity of the present experience and the experience of the corresponding earlier fact. But since this earlier experience is not present at the time, *we have to assume that the trace of the earlier experience resembles the present experience, and that it is the similarity of our present experience (or the corresponding cortical process) and that trace which makes the selection possible.*[6]

By the way, this passage reveals another serious limitation of trace theory, one I can only mention in passing here. If trace theory has any plausibility at all, it seems appropriate only for those situations where remembering concerns past *experiences*, something which apparently could be represented and which also could resemble certain triggering objects or events later on. But we remember many things that aren't experiences at all, and some things that aren't even past—for example, the day and month of my birth, the time of a forthcoming appointment, that the whale is a mammal, the sum of a triangle's interior angles, the meaning of "anomalous monism." Apparently, then, Köhler's point about trace activation and the need for similarity between trace, earlier event, and triggering event, won't apply to these cases at all. So even if trace theory were intelligible, it wouldn't be a theory about memory generally.

In any case, trace theory is not intelligible, and Köhler's observation reveals why. To avoid the circularity (and regress) of positing the ability to remember in order to explain my ability to remember (e.g., by requiring further trace mechanisms to enable the previous trace do its job), we must suppose that some trace uniquely and unambiguously represents or connects to the original experience. And because unambiguous representation is an impossible process, trace theory is caught between two fatal options. I'll explain in a moment why unambiguous representation is impossible, but first, we need to observe that the tennis ball/party example hides a further complication noted in the passage from Köhler.

Traces are usually supposed to be brain processes of some sort, some physiological representation produced, in this case, by a party guest. But what *activates* this trace later can be any number of things, none of which need to resemble the experience, object, or event that produced the original trace. Suppose Jones attended my party. Trace theory requires my experience of Jones at the party to produce a representation in me of Jones (or my experience of him) so that I can later remember that he was at the party. But what will eventually activate that trace? It could be Jones himself, or an image of Jones, or the lingering smell of someone's cologne, or a telltale stain on the carpet, or perhaps someone asking, "Who was at the party?"

Of course, some of these potential triggering objects or events might plausibly be said to resemble the thing that originally produced the trace. But how can (say) the smell of cologne, a stain, or the words "Who was at the party?" trigger the trace of Jones created by his presence at the party? These things aren't obviously similar to Jones himself. If we posit another memory *mechanism* to explain how I draw the connection between the cologne and Jones (e.g., he may have worn it, spilled it, or simply talked about it) or how the question "Who was at the party?" leads me to the right party and not some other party, *or even how I remember what the word "party" means*, we're starting a regress of memory mechanisms. But if we say it's because I can simply *remember* who wore (or perhaps mentioned) the cologne, who stained the carpet, or who my party guests were, or what "party" means, then we're still reasoning in a circle. We're still explaining memory by appealing to the ability to remember. Moreover, if I can remember these things without some further trace, then we didn't need a trace in the first place to explain my ability to remember that Jones was at the party. However, if we follow Köhler's lead, then we have to assert some kind of intrinsic similarity or resemblance, some kind of psychophysical *structural isomorphism*, between three—potentially quite different—things: the original experience or event, the trace produced on that occasion, and the subsequent triggering events.

Furthermore, if (like me) you believe that the meanings of sentences or words aren't things that have a structure, something whose parts and relations between them can correspond to another structure in the brain (or somewhere else), a trace theory of memory can't appeal to a system of representations and structural isomorphism or similarity to explain how one remembers the meanings of words. But then trace theory has to be *completely mute* on the question: How does the sentence "Who was at the party?" trigger my memory that Jones was at the party?

If nothing else, these considerations should make you suspicious that an inner (brain) representation of Jones at the party can be isomorphic both to Jones (or my experience of him) and to the innumerably many and quite different things that can later activate the trace—for example, a particular scent or a sequence of sounds. What kind of similarity could this be? The answer is that it can't be any kind of similarity and that Köhler's proposal is literally meaningless. As tempting as it is to continue for a while enumerating the problems with trace theories, I'll restrict myself now to two more points, to explain perhaps the deepest confusion underlying these theories.

The first problem is with the very idea of structural isomorphism. The term "structural isomorphism" sounds impressive and scholarly, but in trace theories, the appeal to structural isomorphism is really just the appeal to an *inherent similarity* between two things, *determined solely by their respective structures*. It's merely a kind of copying, and perhaps if trace theorists spoke only of copying rather than isomorphism, their theories would appear as silly as they really are. That's why nobody takes seriously the theoretically identical position that Plato proposed—namely, that memories are like impressions in wax. It sounds much more impressive to speak instead of isomorphism, and it's also much more effective than speaking of wax impressions, because it drives the confusions and theoretical silliness underground. But the unavoidable nonsense of trace theory remains, and the crucial point is this: traces must be produced in a way that relates them structurally to the things of which they're traces, and they must be activated only by things having the right underlying structure. Moreover, that activation must be determined solely by intrinsic relations between the structures of the trace and the things that activate them. Otherwise, we'd need another mechanism to explain how the *right* trace is activated in the presence of a trigger that could just as well have been isomorphic with (or mapped onto) something else. And that raises the circularity or regress problem noted earlier.

But the alternative, inherent similarity, makes no more sense than saying that a square is a circle. Inherent similarity is a *static* relation obtaining only between the similar things. And it must hold between those things *no matter what*. If, for example, context could alter whether two things count as similar, then those things are not similar merely in virtue of intrinsic relations holding between their respective structures. But that's why intrinsic similarity is nonsense. Context *does* matter; in fact, it's indispensable. Things are never similar solely in virtue of static relations between them or in virtue of properties inherent in them. Things must *count* or *be taken as* similar or dissimilar relative to some context of inquiry and criteria of relevance. For example, the movements of an elephant aren't inherently similar or dissimilar to those of a flea. They might count as similar in a situation where the size of an organism isn't relevant but dissimilar in a context where size is a major concern. Or suppose I try to tell the same joke I heard someone tell the day before. Is the joke I told similar or not to the one I heard earlier? Obviously, it depends on what's relevant to our answering that question, and no criteria of relevance are inherently privileged over the others. Depending on the situation, we might focus on whether my joke made the audience laugh, whether the words were exactly the same, whether they were delivered at the same speed, or with the same accent or timing, or with the same inflection, or whether my voice had the same timbre as that of my predecessor. Although cognitive scientists and memory theorists seem to ignore it all the time, the point is painfully clear: similarity exists *only* with respect to variable and shifting criteria of relevance. It can only be a dynamic relation holding between things at a time and within a context of needs and interests.

Another example, this time from geometry, should make the point even more clearly. Consider the triangle (A) in figure 1. Then, compare it to the geometric figures (B)–(E). Now consider the question: To which of the last four figures is (A) similar? The proper response to that question should be puzzlement; you shouldn't know how to answer it. Without further background information, without knowing what matters in our comparison of the figures, the question has no answer at all. Mathematicians recognize this, although instead of the term "similarity" they use the expression "congruence." In any case, mathematicians know that in the absence of some specified or agreed-upon rule of projection or function for mapping geometric figures onto other things, no figure is congruent with (similar to) anything else.

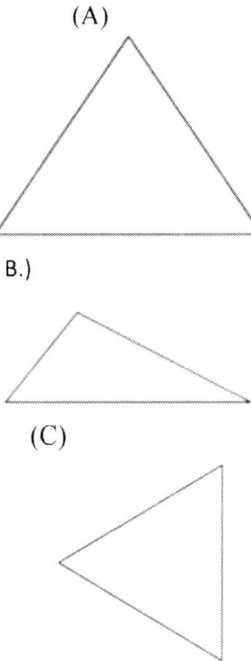

(A)

B.)

(C)

D.)

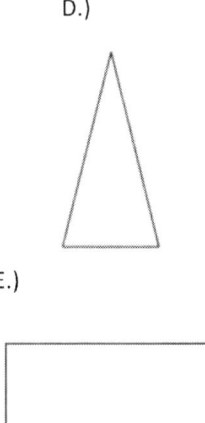

E.)

Mathematicians recognize that there are different standards of congruence appropriate for different situations. But no situation is *intrinsically basic*, and so no standard of congruence is inherently privileged or more fundamental than others. For example, engineers might sometimes want to adopt a fairly strict mapping function according to which (A) is congruent only with other figures having the same interior angles and the same horizontal orientation. In that case, (A) would be congruent with none of the other four figures. Of course, only in very specialized contexts are we likely to compare figures with respect to their horizontal orientation. In many situations it would be appropriate to adopt a different standard of congruence, according to which sameness of interior angles is all that matters. And in that case we'd say that figures (A) and (C) are congruent but that (A) is not congruent with the other figures. However, there's also nothing privileged about sameness of interior angles. Perhaps what matters is simply that (A) is congruent with any other three-sided enclosed figure, in which case we could say it's congruent with the three triangles (B)–(D) but not with the rectangle (E). But even that criterion of congruence can be modified or supplanted. Mathematicians have rules of projection that map triangles onto any other geometric object, but not (say) to apples or oranges. Of course, the moral here is obvious. If simple geometric figures aren't intrinsically similar—that is, if they count as similar only against a background of assumptions about which of their features matter (i.e., are relevant), then we certainly won't find intrinsic similarity with much more complex objects—in particular, memory traces and the various objects or events that allegedly produce and activate them.

But maybe you're still not convinced. Perhaps you think that there *is* a fundamental principle of congruence for this geometric example. You might think that, first and foremost, (A) is similar to just those figures with sides of *exactly* the same length, the same horizontal orientation, and exactly the same interior angles. And perhaps you'd want to call that something like "strict congruence (or identity)." But there are at least three serious problems with that position.

First, even if this sort of congruence counted as more fundamental than other forms of geometric similarity, that could only be in virtue of a kind of historical accident. The primacy of that standard of congruence would reveal more about us, our conventions and values—in short, what merely happens to be important to us—than it does about the figures themselves. In fact, it's a standard appropriate for only a very narrow range of contexts in which we consider whether things are similar. Second (and as an illustration of that first point), it's easy to imagine contexts in which two triangles have exactly the same interior angles, horizontal orientation, and sides but don't count as similar. If we're interior designers, for example, it might also matter whether the triangles are of the same color, or whether they're placed against the same colored background, or whether they're made of the same material. If we're graphic artists, it might matter whether the triangles were both original artworks or whether one was a print. Or if we're librarians or archivists, it might matter whether the triangles occur on the same page of different copies of the same book. And third, even if we could decide on some very strict sense of congruence (or identity) that would count as privileged over all other forms of similarity, it would be useless in the present context. Memory traces are never strictly identical either with the things that produce them or with the things that activate them. The looser and more complex forms of similarity at issue in trace theories are classic examples of the sorts of similarities that can't possibly be inherent, static relations between things.

And as if that weren't enough, another aspect of this general confusion about similarity is the requirement that traces and other things have intrinsic or inherent *structures*—that is, some context-independent parsing into basic elements. Because isomorphism (mapping) is tied to structural elements of the isomorphic things, that's a necessary condition for intrinsic isomorphism to hold between the trace and the things it represents. After all, if what counted as structure depended on context—that is, if a trace could just as well have been parsed differently and assigned alternative structures—then it could be mapped onto (or count as similar to) different things. And, unfortunately for trace theory, objects and events can always be parsed in an indefinite number of ways, and whatever parsing we select can only be conditionally, and never categorically or intrinsically, appropriate. We always determine a thing's components relative to a background against which certain features of the things (but not others) count as relevant. But then it's only against shifting and nonprivileged background criteria of relevance that we take two things to have the same structure; they're never isomorphic *simpliciter*—that is, intrinsically or inherently.

So the trace theorist's inevitable appeal to privileged, inherent structures and intrinsic mappings is literally absurd. It's on a par with claiming that a pie has a basic or privileged division into slices or elements—that is, a context-independent answer to the question "How many pieces are there to this (unsliced) pie?" as if the number of potential pie eaters were irrelevant to our answer. Similarly, it's as absurd as claiming that there's an absolutely context-independently correct and privileged answer to the questions "How many events were there in World War II?" and "How many things are in this room?" If we consider the first of those questions, it's clear that our answer depends on how much of a bird's-eye view we're taking on World War II, and that depends entirely on the purpose of the discussion in which the question arises. In a broad discussion of military history generally, it might be enough to parse the war into just the European and Pacific campaigns. But in more specialized discussions, finer-grained parsings are likely to be more appropriate—say, into particular battles alone, or battles plus relevant meetings and decisions of world leaders and military commanders. Independent of some such context, the question "How many events were there in World War II?" has no answer at all; there's simply no basis for dividing it into certain parts rather than others.

CONFUSIONS ABOUT REPRESENTATION

The appeal to inherent similarity or structure is merely a specific form of a more pervasive problem in the so-called cognitive sciences—namely, confusions about and equivocations on the term "representation." Traces are supposed to represent their causes, the objects, events, or experiences that produced them, and they must be internally and structurally differentiated in ways that correspond to the different things we remember. In other words, the trace of (or the internal state that represents) Jones at the party must differ structurally from the trace of (or the internal state that represents) Smith at the party, or Jones at some other party, or my dissertation defense, or the joke someone told the previous evening. And those traces (or internal states) must differ structurally from one another in ways corresponding to the respects in which their causes differ structurally. After all, if my trace of last night's joke wasn't uniquely and structurally distinct from my trace of Jones at the party, then trace theorists would have no way to explain how activation of a trace produces one memory rather than another—and the right one at that. So trace theory is one version of the general view that particular mental states are caused by (or are identical to) certain corresponding distinct internal brain states, and that what those different internal states *are* (i.e., what they represent) is explainable wholly in terms of their distinctive structural features. At this point, cognitive scientists typically do a lot of hand waving and say something like, "We may not currently know all the details, but presumably some psychologist in the future (or perhaps God) would be able to look inside our heads and know, from the way we're configured, what we're thinking."

However, this general picture rests on the utterly false assumption that a thing's representational properties can be determined solely by its structural or topological features. I've examined this error in considerable detail elsewhere.[7] For now, a few brief remarks will have to suffice.

To see what's wrong, we need to appreciate that *anything can represent anything*. In fact, a thing's representational options are limited only by the situations into which it can be inserted. And that set of situations is as indefinite and vast as the set of possible twists and turns human life can take. But if that's the case, then what something represents can't simply be a function of how it's configured. Things must be *made* to represent or mean something. Suppose I'm trying to teach a child the alphabet. I show him a picture of a dog and I say, "*D* is for dog." In that case, we might say that the picture represents the class of dogs. But I could have said, "*C* is for collie," and in that case, the picture would have represented a subset of the set of dogs. Similarly, I could have said "*L* is for Lassie," in which case the picture would have represented an even smaller subset of dogs. I could also have said "*Z* is for Ziggie," referring to the child's pet collie. And notice, these changes in what the picture represents have nothing whatever to do with corresponding changes in the arrangement of pixels, or atoms, or anything else in the picture. Those structural features of the pictures remained the same in all cases. What the picture represents depended instead on how it was used.

In fact, the picture's representational properties could be changed even more dramatically. My disgruntled students could make the picture represent me and symbolically express their hostility toward me by using it as a target for darts. Or I could jokingly point to the picture and say, "This was Joan Rivers before plastic surgery." Or suppose I'm trying to give directions to someone without the aid of a map. I could place the picture on a table and say, "This is the shopping center, this [a tuna sandwich] is the hospital, this [my fork] is the access road, and this [a salt shaker] is the water tower."

Of course, contexts in which (say) a sandwich represents a building or in which a picture of a dog represents a distinguished philosopher (or over-the-hill comedienne) are atypical in some respects. But those situations are unusual *only* with respect to what the objects represent. They aren't at all unusual with respect to how representational properties are acquired. And it doesn't matter whether we're talking about images, words, or (say) synaptic connections. In every case (familiar and offbeat), what a thing represents depends ultimately on the way we place it in a situation, against an enormously rich background of needs and interests and both local and global traditions and assumptions about the way the world is and which things matter. *There are no purely structural or context-independent forms of representation or meaning.* So when it comes to examples like the picture of a dog or the tuna sandwich, the mistake many make is to think that some representational properties—the familiar and apparently default ones—are inherently fundamental and that others are anomalous. That is, they believe that representation in familiar cases is somehow built into or hardwired into the representing objects and that this inherent function simply gets *overridden* in the more unusual cases. But in fact, the familiarity of certain contexts reveals more about us, about our patterns of life and our interests, than it does about the objects themselves. If our form of life were radically different, the ostensibly default or familiar representational properties of objects could change accordingly.

But then, if a brain structure (say) is to represent something past and function as a memory trace, it can't do so solely in virtue of its structural features. Nothing represents or means what it does on topological grounds alone. However, the whole point of Köhler's principle of psychophysical isomorphism (or related hypotheses in the cognitive sciences) is to tie what a thing represents solely to its structure. That was the only way to avoid the equally fatal error of requiring a regress of mechanisms to explain how the original mechanism or state can do its job. So this, too, turns out to be a dead end.

TOKENS AND TYPES

But let's return more explicitly to trace theory. A related and equally unheralded problem with trace theory is its ontology. It posits an entity that's of a radically different kind from the concrete things in the world that are supposed to cause and activate memory traces. And that's a problem because the sort of thing this entity must be is something that many believe is a philosophical fiction. In fact, positing the existence of memory traces is more a philosophical move than a scientific move. Hopefully, one distinction and one more example will make this clear.

Trace theorists have always been tempted to regard traces as kinds of *recordings* of the things that produced them. In fact, some previous influential writings on memory compared traces to tape recordings or grooves and bumps in a phonograph record. The justification for that idea, as we've seen, is that traces must somehow capture essential structural features of the things that both produce and activate them. That's one of the keys to how trace theory is supposed to work. Allegedly, what links together and unifies traces both with their causes and their activators is a common underlying *structure*.

So the issue we must now address is: What sort of thing is this structure? I'll argue that the required structure is an impossible object.

Consider: one of the things I remember is Beethoven's Fifth Symphony (hereafter abbreviated as B5). Modern versions of trace theory require that my memory be explained in terms of a representation of B5, stored in some concrete physical form in my brain and (let's say) produced in me by an experience of hearing B5 in the past. This trace must have certain structural or topological properties that link it both to the thing(s) that caused it and also to those which later activate or trigger it. These must also be properties that distinguish the trace of B5 from traces of other pieces of music. So presumably, this B5 trace was produced by and captures specific features of a performance I heard of B5 which will enable activation of the B5 trace in the presence of subsequent items sharing those specific features.

But which features might these be? Tempo, rhythm, pitch, length of notes, instrumental timbre, dynamic shadings? You'd think so if my trace of B5 was produced by and represents or records a B5 performance and also if that trace is to differ (say) from my trace of Beethoven's Fourth (B4) or even "Yankee Doodle." But I (like many others) can remember B5 by recognizing a wide variety of musical performances as *instances* (or as philosophers would put it, *tokens*) of B5. And these tokens can differ from one another and from the original trace-producing instance of B5, with respect to *any* features of that original event. Even wild parodies of B5 are instances or tokens of B5. That's why I can tell what they're parodies *of*—that is, that they're B5 parodies. Obviously, that feat of identification is one form of remembering B5. For instance, I could recognize B5 when certain notes are held for an unusually long time, or when it's played with elaborate embellishments, or with poor pitch and many mistakes by an amateur orchestra. In fact, I could recognize truly outlandish musical events as instances of B5—for example, when it's played extremely slowly or rapidly, or with tempo changing every bar, or with arbitrary notes raised a major sixth, or when it's played with inverted dynamics or played only on kazoos, banjos, or tubas. Similarly, I could recognize a series of percussive taps as a pitch-invariant version of the opening bars of B5.

So what is it that the B5 trace has in common with the concrete events that can cause and trigger it? As we'll see, it must be a very unusual sort of entity. Whereas the remembered and triggering events are (typically) concrete instances of B5 (e.g., performances of one kind or another), and whereas the trace itself is also a specific, concrete thing—that is, some kind of persisting modification of the person (e.g., a brain state), this common unifying element must be a relentlessly abstract object—what philosophers call a *type*. Moreover, since memory-triggering instances of B5 can differ from the original trace-producing event with respect to *any* of the original event's features (e.g., rhythm, dynamics, timbre, tempo, pitch, absence or presence of embellishments, etc.), and since the B5 trace is presumably an even more radically different kind of *version* of B5 (say, a neurological version that itself has no pitch, tempo, timbre, etc.), the structure that they allegedly share must be so abstract that it contains *none of the concrete musical features* found in the events that produced it (e.g., precise rhythm, pitch, etc.). In fact, it can't have specific features found in any *possible* version or embodiment of B5.

Remember that the B5 trace is supposed to provide a unifying permanent structural link between the past's original trace-producing B5 token and all possible subsequent B5 tokens that activate the B5 trace. Trace theory requires that all those events and the trace are B5s because they share a common underlying structure. That's how Köhler's principle of psychophysical isomorphism works. It's supposed to help explain how the right trace, the B5 trace, gets picked out and activated by an event that could, in principle, be mapped onto (linked structurally to) something else. Although we've seen that this explanatory strategy relies on the incoherent notion of intrinsic similarity (or else falls victim to an endless regress of memory mechanisms), the outlines of the strategy are clear enough. We're supposed to believe that certain events activate the B5 trace because they share a deep structure with that trace, and also that the trace is a B5 trace because it shares that same structure with the instance of B5 that produced it.

But in that case, it's reasonable to ask the trace theorist: Which *specific* features, exactly, might these various tokens of B5 have in common—that is, which features count as parts of the underlying common structure? Notice, that question will be difficult to answer so long as any specific feature of any instance of B5 can be absent from some other token. This is easy to see even if we consider only musical performances. If one B5 token is at a certain pitch, or volume, or tempo, or whatever, some other token might be at a different pitch, volume, tempo, and so on. And then, of course, if the B5 trace is a brain state (as trace theorists usually suppose), it has neurological (biochemical, or whatever) properties that *represent* musical properties. It has no musical properties (such as pitch, tempo, etc.) itself. So it appears that the hypothetical common deep structure linking the B5 trace to all concrete instances of B5 has none of the specific features found in any actual instance of B5. That's why trace theorists have no choice but to posit a common *abstract* type (e.g., a B5 type) linking the indefinitely many and different possible B5 event tokens. The memory trace, the original trace-producing event, and later triggering events would all *exemplify* or embody this type, in virtue of sharing that type as their common underlying structure.

To see this more clearly, let's review some issues discussed earlier. Suppose that the only performance of B5 I ever heard—and thus, the performance that produced my trace—was a conventional and accurate modern orchestral performance. How, then, is that B5 trace picked out and activated by my hearing something radically different—for example, a thoroughly novel and (thank heaven) once-in-a-lifetime accordion-only performance of B5 played at quarter speed, transposed to another key, with many wrong notes, and embellished as only accordion players can? That is, how do I recognize that this nightmare musical event is a B5 and not (say) an anthem played at the unveiling of a central European monument? How does this nightmare musical event activate the B5 trace rather than one or more of the myriad other events we could consider similar to it? If we try to prevent a regress by saying that I can simply recognize that the accordion-only performance is an instance of B5, then we don't need to posit the trace of B5 at all. We've conceded that I can remember and thereby recognize B5 without recourse to a B5 trace. Again, that's one reason Köhler and others appealed to structural isomorphism—intrinsic similarity—between the original event that produced the trace, the memory trace itself, and the triggering event that activates the trace. As we've already seen, that's a fatal move because the very idea of intrinsic similarity is conceptually confused. Moreover, it clearly wouldn't work anyway in the sorts of cases we're considering now, where original and triggering events differ dramatically in their concrete properties. That's supposed to be one of the attractions of appealing instead to properties of a common abstract type (e.g., a B5 type) that cuts right through these concrete variations and links the different event tokens to one another and to the trace.

But now look at what's happened. We've seen that the common element linking all B5 tokens as B5s isn't something that has any particular features of any particular performance or instance of B5. But it's still supposed to be a kind of thing, *the structure* that all B5 tokens share and in virtue of which they're B5s rather than B4s or other tokens. However, that structure has to have *some* features in virtue of which it's a B5 structure and not that of (say) Beethoven's Fourth, the "Waldstein" Sonata, or "Yankee Doodle." But it can't have features found in any specific instances or tokens of B5, because for whatever feature we specify, some other instance of B5 might lack it. But then no specific feature of an instance of B5 can be necessary for something's being a B5. So although it can't be anything like any actual B5 performance, with specific pitches, dynamics, rhythm, and so on, the common B5 structure—that is, *the* thing that all B5s have in common—somehow needs to have features necessary for its being *the* B5 structure but also distinctive to its being the B5 (rather than, say, a B4) structure. In fact, it must *inherently* be the kind of structure it is. And it must inherently be a B5 structure, despite lacking all properties that B5 tokens might have.

We can't even say that, whatever sort of properties the B5 structure has, they must at least be—presumably abstract—*musical* features (pitch, rhythm, etc). For one thing (as we've noted), if a B5 trace in the brain counts as a B5, its neurological or biochemical (or whatever) properties would be of an entirely different sort. Morever, it's not clear what an abstract musical feature would be. A determinable property, like *some pitch or other*? Some tempo or other? That wouldn't enable the B5 structure to differ from a B4 structure. Those different common structures must differ with respect to determinate (i.e., actual, specific) properties, not determinable properties.

In short, the common B5 structure must have features *necessary and sufficient* for its being a B5 and not (say) a B4 but without having any specific features regarding pitch, tempo, dynamics, and so on, any of which might be absent from any concrete instance of B5. (Perhaps you can now see why many consider abstract types to be impossible objects.) So what allegedly links the B5 trace to both the remembered and triggering events is a shared, abstract, B5 structure, which—incredibly—is inherently that of a B5 (and not a B4) but which has no specific features of an actual instance of B5, no actual specifications or instances of pitch, dynamics, rhythm, and so on.

To avoid even further embarrassment to the trace theorist, we can conveniently ignore for now cases where what causes me to remember B5 (i.e., what activates the trace) is not another musical event but something that can't even remotely be considered to have the same underlying abstract structure as a concrete instance of B5—for example, a portrait of Leonard Bernstein, a hearing aid, or the question "Can you hum the first few bars of that symphony you heard last week?"

In any case, we've arrived at the point where we see the ultimately non-scientific nature of trace theory. It's committed to the view that a memory trace of B5 and all concrete instances of B5 have a structure that is essential to all things that are instances of B5 but none of the specific features that real, concrete versions of B5, including the trace itself and nightmare versions, can lack. This position is commonly called Platonic essentialism—the view that things are of the same kind in virtue of sharing a common underlying but abstract structure. And that's not a scientific view at all. It's a philosophical view, and a bad one at that.

RECENT MEMORY RESEARCH

A predictable rejoinder to the foregoing arguments against trace theory would be that memory research has progressed considerably since the days of Köhler. Some might even suggest that talk of memory traces is now passé. So perhaps the position I've defended is simply out of date and my arguments just don't apply to current memory theory.

Granted, there's been undeniable progress in thinking about the domain of memory—for example, taxonomic advances in identifying the varieties or types of memory. Likewise, increasingly advanced technology has enabled researchers to probe our neurophysiological systems in unprecedented detail.

Nevertheless, in a crucial respect, recent memory research shows no progress at all and remains defiantly superficial. It takes for granted that some form of storage and retrieval takes place in the brain, whether the putative physiological mechanism is a unitary engram or something distributed or diffuse—say, across a cell assembly, and whether what's stored in the brain is static or dynamic. But it never addresses the fundamental issues of how any physical modification can represent or stand for what is remembered and indeed how it can represent or stand for one thing rather than another. And trace talk is alive and well.

A full review here of the broad spectrum of recent memory work is out of the question, but the brief survey below should make the point handily. Consider, for example, the sorts of proposals that create flurries of excitement within the community of memory researchers. One recent innovation was to revise the long-held view that memories are initially labile and must be stabilized or consolidated before they become long-term memories. The innovation was to argue that long-term memories aren't as firmly rooted as once believed and that "memories, or parts of them, need to be restabilized after their expression in a manner analogous to the initial stabilization process."[8] In particular, some claimed that once memories are retrieved, they become labile again and need to be reconsolidated.[9] Another hotly debated proposal (first aired by Todd Sacktor) concerns the alleged importance of an enzyme named protein kinase M-zeta (or PKMζ) in sustaining long-term memories in the brain.[10] This is even described by Sacktor as "a candidate, persistent enzymatic molecular mechanism for the longterm memory trace."[11] However, more recent work seems to have successfully challenged this alleged role for PKMζ.[12]

Significantly, nowhere in any of this work will you find critical reflection on whether traces are possible objects or whether the concept of memory storage is tenable. In recent work it's simply taken for granted that information is stored somehow in the brain, as if the matter were settled a long time ago and all that we need to do now is to figure out what the correct hardware description of the process is. So that fundamental assumption is never defended or scrutinized, and the problems with it and with its associated reliance on the notion of representation apparently go unrecognized. But then, despite the technical and technological advances of the latest work on memory, that work is ultimately even less sophisticated conceptually than the old work of Köhler. Köhler at least realized that the very idea of storage and retrieval had an ineliminable philosophical component and that the posited memory mechanism—whatever its precise hardware realization—required an appeal to the principle of isomorphism, the defects of which we examined earlier.

As another example, consider how Karim Nader summarizes the thrust of his paper "Memory Traces Unbound" (and for that matter, much of his recent research): "The idea that new memories are initially 'labile' and sensitive to disruption before becoming permanently stored in the wiring of the brain has been dogma for > 100 years. Recently, we have revisited the hypothesis that reactivation of a consolidated memory can return it to a labile, sensitive state—in which it can be modified, strengthened, changed or even erased!"[13]

Notice, what's at issue here is only whether (or to what extent) the physiological storage of memories in the brain is permanent—not whether there's any kind of storage at all or whether storage of the kind required is even possible. Evidently, it never occurred to Nader that a more profound dogma is that memories can be "stored in the wiring of the brain."

This is by no means an isolated case. In a comprehensive four-volume set from 2008 intended to display the state of the art in research on memory and learning,[14] we find the following, all too typical, passages. (a) "The notion of a physical memory trace, independent of its use . . . is a central presumption in neuroscience."[15] (b) "A neuroscientist cannot help but assume that the knowledge stored in memory continues to exist during time periods when it is not retrieved."[16] Remarkably enough and significantly, these statements appear in the introductory essay to the entire four-volume set.

Some memory researchers believe they've made advances by supposing that there are different, or different kinds of, memory systems, corresponding to different kinds of memory—not simply (say) memory for past events—what is sometimes called episodic and autobiographical memory.[17] For example, John O'Keefe and Lynn Nadel write, "It appears that there are different types of memory, relating perhaps to different kinds of information, and that these are localized in many, possibly most, neural systems."[18] And later, "There is no such thing as the memory area. Rather, there are memory areas, each responsible for a different form of information storage.[19] Again, the process of memory storage is simply taken for granted, and it's uncritically assumed to be due to some kind of localized physiological change in the brain.

Similarly (from the Byrne four-volume set), Nadel concedes that all "memory systems" rely on the same fundamental presupposition: "It makes . . . sense to think about all neural systems as both processing and storing knowledge, with the differences between systems reflecting the nature of the knowledge being processed and stored, and the timescale of that storage."[20]

It's very easy to multiply examples. Raymond Kesner defends "a tripartite attribute-based theoretical model of memory that is organized into event-based, knowledge-based, and rule-based memory systems."[21] But "Each system is . . . mapped onto multiple neural regions and interconnected neural circuits."[22] And what does that talk of mapping mean? Well, for instance, "The event-based memory system provides for temporary representations of incoming data concerning the present" and the "knowledge-based memory system provides for more permanent representations of previously stored information in long-term memory and can be thought of as one's general knowledge of the world."[23]

But of course, this is just recourse to the old talk of representation and storage. No deep problems are solved by the recourse to multiple memory systems rather than one so long as the idea of physiological storage is retained. So this multiple-system position remains a house of cards. If the strategy for explaining memory of even just past events fails for the fundamental reasons discussed earlier, it undermines all the attempts to ground additional forms of memory "storage" in their respective neurophysiological systems. But even if some forms of memory—say, memory-how (procedural or skill memory)—escape the critique of this chapter, memory theory still suffers a colossal failure if it can't explain memory of past events in terms of storage and representation.

One final example. A recent study, admittedly involving only mice, explored the "optogenetic reactivation of hippocampal neurons activated during fear conditioning,"[24] and the results were taken to indicate that "activating a sparse but specific ensemble of hippocampal neurons that contribute to a memory engram is sufficient for the recall of that memory."[25] It's worth noting, again, how the authors describe the conceptual background against which their study should be viewed. They write, "An important question in neuroscience is how a distinct memory is formed and stored in the brain. Recent studies indicate that defined populations of neurons correspond to a specific memory trace, suggesting a cellular correlate of a memory engram."[26]

But this is simply old-fashioned trace theorizing centering on another candidate du jour for the locus of the trace. So I must reiterate a point made earlier in this essay. It doesn't matter what the hardware account of memory traces is—for example, whether it's static or dynamic, where in the brain it is, or how it's configured or localized. It doesn't even matter whether the trace is physical. The problem with trace theory is that traces, however they're conceived, are required in order to perform a function that no object can fulfill. And trace theory relies on a concept of similarity—intrinsic similarity—that literally makes no sense.

TRACE THEORY IN PARAPSYCHOLOGY

It's unfortunate enough that memory-trace theory is received dogma in the cognitive sciences. Almost no one seems to doubt that memories are somehow stored and encoded in us. So it's not surprising that this picture of memory has found its way to more overtly speculative or frontier areas of science, including parapsychology. No doubt it's very tempting for parapsychologists to posit trace-like processes in their own theories, because they can then at least appear to be reasoning along scientifically orthodox lines, even if the subject matter itself falls outside the scientific mainstream.

For example, William Roll proposed a "psi structure" theory of postmortem survival, modeled explicitly after memory-trace theory and according to which memory traces are left not simply in individual brains but in our environment as well.[27] Of course, this escapes none of the classic problems of trace theory, because in Roll's view, what certain structures represent (or are similar to) remains unintelligibly tied to inherent features of those structures. This is especially problematic when Roll suggests that an individual mind or personality is a system of such structures. That's no more plausible than saying that we can tell whether a person is thinking about his grandmother just by examining the state of his brain, or that a picture of a dog represents something specific independent of its use in a context. Roll's view requires brain or mental structures to mean or represent something simply in virtue of how they're configured, never mind their dynamic position within an equally dynamic life situation. Roll also proposes explaining ESP as the response to memory traces left on objects by previous guesses. But that seems no more credible than supposing that my ability to remember my party guests is simply a mechanical function of the tennis balls they left behind or the illegible signatures or photos they left along with the balls.

Trace theory also appears in other guises in connection with the evidence for postmortem survival. One is the suggestion that reincarnation cases can be explained in terms of genetic memory. However, I've found no serious researcher making that suggestion. It seems, instead, to be entertained simply as a real possibility, albeit one that can be rejected on empirical grounds.[28] That is, it's treated as if it's an intelligible position that happens merely to be inadequate to the data. Another application of trace theory to survival is the attempt to explain transplant cases by appealing to cellular memory.[29] No doubt the reason it's tempting here to posit genetic or cellular memory traces is that in reincarnation and transplant cases, complex psychological regularities seem to persist in the absence of the usual presumed bodily correlates. So to those for whom it's unthinkable that individuals can remember without their memories being stored somewhere, it might seem reasonable to propose that memories and personality traits can be encoded in a kind of hardware that has nothing to do with the brain. However, since the problems noted earlier with trace theories are hardware independent, it's an insignificant change merely to relocate the traces in different physical systems. It's still untenable to suppose that representation, meaning, or similarity are determined solely by a thing's topological features.

To me, it's interesting that when the usual suspect—the brain—isn't available as the locus of memory storage, some find it inevitable that memories must simply be located in a different place or perhaps in a modified form. It demonstrates just how deeply mechanistic assumptions have taken root, and in a way, it shows a profound lack of scientific imagination. The situation here closely parallels what happened in response to Karl Lashley's famous experiments in the 1920s.[30] When Lashley found that no matter how much of a rat's brain he surgically removed, trained rats continued to run their maze, some concluded that the rats' memories weren't specifically localized in their brains. Instead, they suggested that the memories were *diffusely* localized, much as information is diffusely distributed in holograms.[31] But to someone not antecedently committed to traditional mechanistic dogma, Lashley's experiments take on a different sort of significance, perhaps similar to that of the evidence for postmortem survival. They suggest that memories aren't located anywhere or in any form in the brain. And more generally, they suggest that the container metaphor (that memories and mental states in general are *in* the brain or in something else) was wrong from the start and also that memories (and mental states generally) aren't *things* or *objects* with distinct spatiotemporal coordinates. Of course, that's what my arguments in the preceding sections were intended to show.

Another variant of this general error emerges in Rupert Sheldrake's suggestion that morphic fields capture the essential structure of developmental forms and even behavioral kinds. Although Sheldrake thought he was escaping the evils of mechanistic theories with his view, in fact he retained the underlying errors of supposing that similarity is an intrinsic structural relation between things and that things of the same kind are of that kind because they share a common underlying structural essence. The claim that behavioral kinds, such as feeding behavior and courtship, can be captured in strictly structural terms is especially implausible. (For a detailed critique of Sheldrake's theory, see chapter 2.)

SUMMING UP

I realize that I'm pretty much a voice in the wilderness on these issues, and I find myself in the unenviable position of having to argue that many prominent and respected scientists actually don't know what they're talking about. I wish there were some other, less fundamentally upsetting, way to undercut trace theories of memory. But I believe that the problems really are that deep and that the theories really are that essentially confused.

However, as long as I'm being antagonistic, I see no compelling reason to stop where I left off. I might as well finish with a brief obnoxious coda. As I see it, both memory researchers and parapsychologists are missing an opportunity to be genuine scientific pioneers. Rather than boldly searching for new explanatory strategies (for memory specifically and for human behavior generally), they cling instead to familiar mechanistic presuppositions, which they've typically never examined in any depth but by means of which they can maintain the illusion that they're doing science according to the allegedly tough-minded methods exemplified in some physical sciences. (Sherry Turkle has appropriately called this "physics envy."[32]) They can't get past the assumption that human abilities and behavior must be analyzed in terms of lower-level processes and mechanisms. And many seem not to recognize the difference between claiming that cognitive functions are *analyzable* in terms of underlying physical processes and claiming instead that those functions are merely *mediated* (perhaps only contingently) by underlying physical processes. But there are novel explanatory options and strategies they never consider; there are alternative and profoundly different approaches to the understanding of human beings. In chapter 3 I'll pursue that topic in more detail.

REFERENCES

Almeder, R. (1992). *Death and personal survival*. Lanham, MD: Rowman & Littlefield.
Beach, F. A., Hebb, D. O., Morgan, C. T., & Nissen, H. W. (Eds.). (1960). *The neuropsychology of Lashley: Selected papers of K. S. Lashley*. New York, NY: McGraw-Hill.
Bennett, M. R., & Hacker, P. M. S. (2003). *Philosophical foundations of neuroscience*. Oxford: Blackwell.
Braude, S. E. (1997). *The limits of influence: Psychokinesis and the philosophy of science* (Rev. ed.). Lanham, MD: University Press of America.
Braude, S. E. (2002). *ESP and psychokinesis: A philosophical examination* (Rev. ed.). Parkland, FL: Brown Walker.
Bursen, H. A. (1978). *Dismantling the memory machine : A philosophical investigation of machine theories of memory*. Dordrecht, Netherlands: D. Reidel.
Byrne, J. H. (Ed.). (2008). *Learning and memory: A comprehensive reference* (Vols. 1–4). Oxford: Academic.
Damasio, A. R. (1994). *Descartes' error: Emotion, reason, and the human brain*. New York: Putnam.
Gazzaniga, M. S., Mangun, G. R., & Ivry, R. B. (1998). *Cognitive neuroscience: The biology of the mind*. New York: Norton.
Heil, J. (1978). "Traces of things past." *Philosophy of Science*, 45: 60-72.
Kelly, M. T., Crary, J. F., & Sacktor, T. C. (2007). Regulation of protein kinase Mζ synthesis by multiple kinases in long-term potentiation. *Journal of Neuroscience, 27*, 3439–3444.
Kesner, R. P. (2007). Neurobiological view of memory. In R. P. Kesner & J. L. Martinez Jr. (Eds.), *Neurobiology of learning and memory* (2nd ed.) (pp. 271–304). Burlington, MA: Academic.
Köhler, W. (1947). *Gestalt psychology*. New York: Liveright.
Köhler, W. (1969). *The task of gestalt psychology*. Princeton, NJ: Princeton University Press.
Lashley, K. S. (1929). *Brain mechanisms and intelligence*. Chicago: University of Chicago Press.
Lashley, K. S. (1950). In search of the engram. *Symposia of the Society for Experimental Biology, 4*, 454–482.
Lee, A. M., Kanter, B. R., Wang, D., Lim, J. P., Zou, M. E., Qiu, C., . . . Messing, R. O. (2013). PKMζ null mice show normal learning and memory. *Nature, 493*(7432), 416–419. doi:10.1038/nature11803
Liu, X., Ramirez, S., Pang, P. T., Puryear, C. B., Govindarajan, K. D., & Tonegawa, S. (2012). Optogenetic stimulation of a hippocampal engram activates fear memory recall. *Nature, 484*, 381–385.

Malcolm, N. (1977). *Memory and mind*. Ithaca, NY: Cornell University Press.
Menzel, R. (2008). Introduction and overview. In J. H. Byrne (Ed.), *Learning and memory: A comprehensive reference* (Vols. 1–4) (Vol. 1, pp. 1–9). Oxford: Academic.
Moscovitch, M. (2000). Theories of memory and consciousness. In E. Tulving & F. I. M. Craik (Eds.), *The Oxford handbook of memory* (pp. 609–626). Oxford: Oxford University Press.
Nadel, L. (2008). Multiple memory systems: A new view. In J. H. Byrne (Ed.), *Learning and memory: A comprehensive reference* (Vols. 1–4) (Vol. 1, pp. 41–52). Oxford: Academic.
Nader, K. (2003). Memory traces unbound. *Trends in Neurosciences, 26*(2), 65–72.
Nader, K. (2007). A single standard for memory: The case for reconsolidation. *Debates in Neuroscience, 1*(1), 2–16.
Nader, K., & Einarsson, E. Ö. (2010). Memory reconsolidation—an update. *Annals of the New York Academy of Sciences, 1191*, 27–41.
O'Keefe, J., & Nadel, L. (1978). *The hippocampus as a cognitive map*. Oxford: Oxford University Press.
Pastalkova, E., Serrano, P., Pinkhasova, D., Wallace, E., Fenton, A. A., & Sacktor, T. C. (2006). Storage of spatial information by the maintenance mechanism of LTP. *Science, 313*, 1141–1144.
Pearsall, P., Schwartz, G. E. R., & Russek, L. G. S. (1999). Changes in heart transplant recipients that parallel the personalities of their donors. *Integrative Medicine, 2*(2/3), 65–72.
Pribram, K. H. (1971). *Languages of the brain*. Englewood Cliffs, NJ: Prentice-Hall.
Pribram, K. H. (1977). Holonomy and structure in the organization of perception. In U. M. Nicholas (Ed.), *Images, perception and knowledge*. Dordrecht, Netherlands: D. Reidel.
Pribram, K. H., Nuwer, M., & Baron, R. U. (1974). The holographic hypothesis of memory structure in brain function and perception. In D. H. Krantz, R. C. Luce, & P. Suppes (Eds.), *Contemporary developments in mathematical psychology* (Vols. 1–2) (Vol. 2, pp. 415–467). San Francisco: Freeman.
Roll, W. G. (1983). The psi structure theory of survival. In W. G. Roll, J. Beloff, & R. White (Eds.), *Research in parapsychology 1982* (pp. 117–120). Metuchen, NJ: Scarecrow.
Sacktor, T. (2012). Memory maintenance by PKMζ—an evolutionary perspective. *Molecular Brain, 5*(1), 31.
Sacktor, T. C. (2011). How does PKMζ maintain long-term memory? *Nature Reviews Neuroscience, 12* (January), 9–15. doi:10.1038%2Fnrn2949
Schacter, D. L., & Tulving, E. (1994). *Memory systems*. Cambridge, MA: MIT Press.
Shema, R., Sacktor, T. C., & Dudai, Y. (2007). Rapid erasure of long-term memory associations in the cortex by an inhibitor of PKMζ. *Science, 317*, 951–953.
Stevenson, I. (1974). *Twenty cases suggestive of reincarnation* (2nd ed. rev.). Charlottesville: University Press of Virginia.
Tulving, E., & Craik, F. I. M. (Eds.). (2000). *Oxford handbook of memory*. Oxford: Oxford University Press.
Volk, L. J., Bachman, J. L., Johnson, R., Yu, Y., & Huganir, R. L. (2013). PKMζ is not required for hippocampal synaptic plasticity, learning and memory. *Nature, 493*(7432): 420–423. doi:10.1038/nature11802

NOTES

1. For representative samples of the view, see, e.g., Damasio, 1996; Gazzaniga, Mangun, & Ivry, 1998; Moscovitch, 2000; Tulving & Craik, 2000.
2. Similar problems also undermine theorizing in areas often related to parapsychology—for example, Sheldrake's account of morphic resonance. I deal with that in more detail in chapter 2
3. For extended critiques, see Bennett & Hacker, 2003; Braude, 2002; Bursen, 1978; Heil, 1981; Malcolm, 1977.
4. Heil, 1978.
5. See, e.g., Köhler, 1947, 1969.
6. Köhler, 1969, p. 122, emphasis added.

7. Braude, 1997, 2002.
8. Nader, 2007, p. 2.
9. See also Nader, 2003; Nader & Einarsson, 2010.
10. See, e.g., Kelly, Crary, & Sacktor, 2007; Pastalkova et al., 2006; T. Sacktor, 2012; T. C. Sacktor, 2011; Shema, Sacktor, & Dudai, 2007.
11. T. C. Sacktor, 2011; emphasis added.
12. See, e.g., Lee et al., 2013; Volk, Bachman, Johnson, Yu, & Huganir, 2013).
13. Nader, 2003, 65.
14. Byrne, 2008.
15. Menzel, 2008, p. 6.
16. Ibid.
17. See, e.g., O'Keefe & Nadel, 1978; Schacter & Tulving, 1994).
18. O'Keefe & Nadel, 1978, p. 373.
19. O'Keefe & Nadel, 1978, p. 374.
20. Nadel, 2008, p. 45.
21. Kesner, 2007, p. 272.
22. Ibid.
23. Ibid.
24. Liu et al., 2012, p. 381.
25. Ibid.
26. Ibid.
27. Roll, 1983.
28. See, e.g., Almeder, 1992; Stevenson, 1974.
29. Pearsall, Schwartz, & Russek, 1999.
30. Beach, Hebb, Morgan, & Nissen, 1960; Lashley, 1929, 1950.
31. Pribram, 1971, 1977; Pribram, Nuwer, & Baron, 1974.
32. For more on that topic, see chapter 8.

Chapter Two

Radical Provincialism in the Life Sciences

A Review of Rupert Sheldrake's A New Science of Life

When Sheldrake's book *A New Science of Life: The Hypothesis of Formative Causation* first appeared in 1981, it received considerable attention from both scientists and laypersons. Some hailed the book as a radically new and viable approach to a vast range of scientific issues. Its opponents, on the other hand, denounced it strongly as (at best) a work of indefensible eccentricity. Naturally, this polarization of opinion caught my attention. Because the work excited such strong contrasting positions, I figured it was likely to be interesting, and *A New Science of Life* was certainly that. However, my own assessment was that Sheldrake's staunchest supporters and detractors were both wrong: Sheldrake's view of formative causation was neither viable nor as radical as it seemed. But it wasn't crazy either; in fact, Sheldrake's proposal revealed considerable intelligence, insight, and originality. Nevertheless, it was seriously flawed, and to my surprise I found it to be flawed for the same reasons as the theories Sheldrake was concerned with rejecting.

Shedrake's treatise on formative causation is now in its third edition. In fact, the book's cover describes its latest reincarnation as a "fully revised edition" (it appeared in the United States under the title *Morphic Resonance*).[1] However, although Sheldrake did modify the original text somewhat and add some new material, the fundamental flaws of the book remain intact. So I believe the time has come for a reappraisal. But before launching into my critique, I want to make something very clear, especially since in other chapters I frequently express my contempt for various of my academic or scientific colleagues, and also since I know that many people—outside of philosophy at least—have trouble distinguishing sharp and sustained intellectual criticism from personal attacks. I know Rupert Sheldrake. I like him personally—in fact, I consider him a friend—and I hold him in very high esteem. I think he's exceptionally smart, intellectually serious and probing, and unusually creative and innovative as an experimentalist. I just think he's dead wrong about the view he propounds in his book.

Contrary to what some readers might think, there's a good reason for discussing the topic of formative causation in the context of the present volume. That's because the errors I believe Sheldrake commits are standard mechanistic errors, crucially similar to those undermining more familiar theoretical programs, particularly in the behavioral sciences. These errors are often very seductive (and by no means foolish), and some of them I discuss in other chapters and in other publications. My hope is that by seeing how classic mechanistic confusions manifest in and sabotage Sheldrake's theorizing about formative causation, readers will be better able to appreciate both the nature and scope of those errors, and hopefully they'll be better able to detect inevitable new versions of them when they appear.

BACKGROUND

Sheldrake argues that the life sciences have been strikingly unable to account satisfactorily for some fascinating and obviously important organic phenomena. The reason, he claims, is that those sciences have simply adopted the mechanistic assumptions common to other areas of the physical sciences. In particular, Sheldrake wants to resolve certain outstanding problems of *biological morphogenesis*, which he defines (following Needham) as "the coming-into-being of characteristic and specific form in living organisms."[2] From Sheldrake's viewpoint, the main puzzles of biological morphogenesis are as follows: (a) How do biological forms develop from the relatively simple structures present in the egg at the start of development? (b) How are systems able to *regulate*? That is, what explains the fact that "if a part of a developing system is removed (or if an additional part is added), the system continued to develop in such a way that a more or less normal structure is produced"?[3] (c) How are organisms able to *regenerate*—that is, replace or restore damaged structures? (d) How are we able to explain *reproduction*, in which "a detached part of the parent becomes a new organism; a part becomes a whole"?[4]

Sheldrake argues that a mechanistic science, which attempts to explain all the phenomena of life (including human behavior) in terms of physics, is impotent to solve the above puzzles. But he also thinks that a *vitalistic* alternative to mechanism is likewise inadequate. The fatal flaw of vitalism, Sheldrake claims, is that it posits an unbridgeable causal gap between two radically different kinds of thing—namely, a nonphysical entelechy (or vital force) and the physical world. According to Sheldrake, the only remaining alternative to mechanism and vitalism—and the approach he endorses—is a form of *organicism*. Rather than attempting to explain the physical facts of morphogenesis in terms of a nonphysical entelechy, the organicist posits evolutionary biological principles as primitive (rather than emergent) features of nature, extending even to the domains carved out by physics and chemistry. Sheldrake cashes out his version of organicism by describing the relevant biological regularities in terms of *morphogenetic fields*.

But before considering the details of Sheldrake's theory, I must say that I find his rejection of vitalism unconvincing. Whether or not vitalism is tenable, it won't fail for the reason Sheldrake suggests.

I've argued elsewhere that causal links are essentially explanatory links.[5] Relating two states of affairs as cause and effect is, like giving directions, a way of systematically leading a person—in this case, conceptually—from one place to another. But nothing prohibits cause and effect from being of different ontological types. As I'll illustrate in more detail below, in some contexts it's perfectly appropriate and illuminating to posit causal connections between different *kinds* of states of affairs, in much the same way as context determines what sorts of directions are appropriate to a request for directions.

Sheldrake's criticism of vitalism seems merely to be a variant of a familiar criticism of Cartesian interactionistic dualism. In both cases, critics attack the view in perhaps its least plausible form. According to Descartes's version of dualism, mind and body are two distinct kinds of *stuff* or *substance*—the latter extended in space and the former unextended. But Descartes's model of causality was that of billiard-ball collisions—that is, causation by contact. Accordingly, he took causes to be spatiotemporally contiguous with and immediately prior to their effects. So critics correctly noted that something extended could neither push nor be pushed by something unextended.

However, this objection to Cartesian interactionism applies only to a *substance*-dualism, according to which causal interactions are supposed to occur between two distinct kinds of *thing*. Moreover, it relies on a model of causality suitable only for extended things, and then only for billiard-ball-type interactions between them. But other—and usually more sophisticated—forms of dualism are immune to this criticism. For example, one could adopt a *property* (rather than substance) dualism and also admit the legitimacy of causal explanations not fitting the billiard-ball model. That is, one could argue that psychological (or mentalistic) and physicalistic *descriptive categories* don't reduce one to the other, and then one can posit causal (explanatory) links between the two domains without having to explain how two different kinds of stuff can impinge on each other.

For instance, we could say that "the mind" is merely a general term for the class of mental events (or a certain *aspect* of what a person does), just as "the weather" is a general term for the class of meteorological events (or a certain aspect of planetary phenomena) and "the economy" is a general term for a class of financial transactions and institutions. Neither the mind, the weather, nor the economy need be construed as a *substance*. And clearly, nothing prohibits causal links between different kinds of events, identifiable on different levels of description. In fact, not only do we draw such causal connections all the time with a philosophically clear conscience, but we often find them extremely illuminating as ways of drawing conceptual links between different domains of phenomena. For example, we can find causal links between meteorological and sociological or economic phenomena, as when a hurricane leads to looting and a severely damaged local economy. To draw this kind of connection, we don't need to maintain that the three classes of phenomena are all expressible on some single level of description. Similarly, we're free to draw causal links between mental and physical events, even if statements about one don't reduce to statements about the other (or even if the two types of statements fail to reduce to some other common level of description).

Now as I see it, vitalism may have been articulated in a confused way, analogous to Descartes's version of dualism. Neither entelechy nor the mind need to be reified—that is, construed as a kind of (nonphysical) stuff. Vitalism, in its classic formulations, may be no more than a confused form of the view that, on the level at which we describe organic phenomena, there are facts and regularities unique to that level—that is, not reducible to (or translatable without residue into) another level of description. These *vital* facts and regularities would simply have no analysis in the terms appropriate to mechanical or impersonal forces or processes. But in that case, vitalists wouldn't need to explain how a nonphysical force can impinge on a physical organism (especially considering that not all causality is billiard-ball causality).

FORMATIVE CAUSATION: THE BASICS

In any case, Sheldrake proposes an organicist alternative to vitalism. Its main features are the following.

1. In addition to the familiar forms of energetic causation posited in physics, a further type of causation, *formative causation*, "imposes a spatial order on changes brought about by energetic causation."[6] In other words, this type of causation helps determine the internal and external structure of things in nature. Moreover, although formative causation is a kind of physical pro-

cess, it "is not itself energetic, nor is it reducible to the causation brought about by known physical fields."[7]

This last point, I should add, seems especially peculiar in light of Sheldrake's rejection of vitalism. He seems to be arguing for the kind of "action of unlike on unlike"[8] he considers fatal to that approach.

2. Each kind of *morphic unit* (or identifiable *thing* of a particular kind) in nature has its own characteristic *morphogenetic field*. These fields affect material systems when a characteristic part of a morphic unit—a *morphogenetic germ*—"becomes surrounded by, or embedded within, the morphogenetic field of the entire morphic unit. This field contains the morphic unit's virtual form, which is actualized as appropriate component parts come within its range of influence and fit into their appropriate relative positions."[9]

3. Morphogenetic fields affect morphic units by a process called *morphic resonance*. "This influence takes place through the morphogenetic field and depends on the systems' three-dimensional structures and patterns of vibration."[10] Morphic resonance can act on a morphic unit across space and time, as when the form of a morphic unit is determined by the forms of previous similar systems.

Sheldrake ingeniously applies these ideas to a vast range of organic phenomena, and he develops his theory in considerable detail. But the three proposals just mentioned are the heart of the theory, and their weaknesses are enough to sabotage it beyond salvation. Once these are brought into the open, the poverty of the hypothesis of formative causation becomes clear. It also becomes clear that Sheldrake's approach is fundamentally that of the mechanistic theories he wants to repudiate.

FORMATIVE CAUSATION: THE PROBLEMS

We can get a first glimmer of the problems with Sheldrake's theory by asking: Are there morphogenetic fields for every possible parsing of nature? In principle, of course, there are endless ways of dividing nature into object-kinds and event-kinds. Is each resulting type correlated with its own characteristic morphogenetic field? Sheldrake seems to think so. First, he claims that morphic units will be found in "biological and physical systems at all levels of complexity,"[11] and then he says explicitly, "Each kind of morphic unit has its own characteristic morphogenetic field."[12]

But the problem with a claim like this—as I've pointed out elsewhere[13] and in chapters 1 and 3 of the present volume—is that forms, objects, events, and kinds are not intrinsic to nature. There's no absolute inventory of things in nature. *We* decide, relative to some guiding purpose or set of interests, how to parse nature or history into objects, events, and kinds (including form-kinds—morphic units, if you will). Apart from some guiding set of interests and their associated standards of relevance and importance, there's no reason to parse nature one way rather than another. In that respect, nature is intrinsically undifferentiated; no method of parsing enjoys inherent (or context-independent) priority over any other. But if objects, events, and so on aren't items from a prefabricated ontological storehouse and are instead merely elements of constantly evolving and shifting conceptual grids that we place over nature, then morphogenetic fields don't exist inherently *in* nature either.

To avoid misunderstanding, I should emphasize that none of this shows that nature has no structure or that we're not entitled to impute a structure or structures to nature. But nature doesn't have *a* structure, some *one* parsing into and arrangement of elements that enjoys inherent priority over all others. Rather, it has an infinite number of parsings and orderings, some better than others—and then only in relation to some goal or set of interests and needs. For example, what justifies our table of elements and their associated structures is that the list and analysis of elements fits into a successful scientific theory. And it's only against a background of inquiry or discussion that this scientific theory is our guide in determining the relevant inventory of things. As with any conceptual grid through which we view the world, our choice of descriptive categories (and the resulting structuring of nature) is justified by its utility, as a tool for systematizing our experience. (I'll return to this point shortly.)

But Sheldrake's view seems considerably less sophisticated than a pragmatic defense of kind terms and structural descriptions. Sheldrake seems to take the hard-line Platonist (i.e., essentialist) view that morphic units and their associated morphogenetic fields are *natural kinds*—that is, items in an interest-, purpose-, or context-independent set of natural furniture. He seems to think there is a final or preferred inventory of things or kinds (one including morphogenetic fields), not merely different inventories justified relative to their utility as intellectual tools. In fact, as we'll see shortly, that's the only way Sheldrake can make sense of his claim that morphogenetic fields can select other systems in order to act on them. If what counts as a thing, or system, or structure, is not built into nature but is instead determined only against a background of shifting organic concerns and goals, then there's no context-independent, privileged, or inherent basis for something even to be a morphogenetic field (or one rather than another) or for some morphogenetic fields (rather than others) to be causally active in nature. Another sign of this essentialism emerges in Sheldrake's remarks about similarity (which I discuss below). His views on that topic are really just another aspect of the same deep, Platonist error.

To see this more clearly, we should ask: How is it that "all past systems act upon a subsequent similar system by morphic resonance"?[14] Actually, we can ignore the temporal complexities of this claim and ask simply: How does a system's morphogenetic field *select* similar systems on which to exert its influence? Sheldrake wants to say: by morphic resonance, which he conceives according to a *vibratory* or *tuning* model. But the answer to the question can't be given in purely structural (or topological) terms. *Similarity* is a concept that is neither formally definable nor analyzable independently of a context.

The appeal to morphic resonance involves a not-too-subtle retreat back to mechanistic thinking. Yet Sheldrake's theory can't work without it. Apparently, Sheldrake fails to see that similarity is no more inherent in nature than are our divisions or inventories of things. In fact, he makes the classic mistake that undermines (among other things) memory-trace theory (see chapter 1). I'm especially surprised to see the error occupy such a prominent place in Sheldrake's thinking, given his apparent grasp (at least when he wrote the first edition of his book) of H. A. Bursen's attack on trace theory.[15]

Anyway, Sheldrake explains morphic resonance by means of a tuning model, according to which objects resonate with each other when they vibrate at the same or similar frequencies. But this maneuver is doomed from the start. Not only is similarity not built into things, but the analogy between similarity and closeness of frequency is deceptively straightforward and greatly oversimplified. Actually, not even closeness of frequency can be as straightforward as Sheldrake suggests. The context-relative nature of closeness of frequency is illustrated clearly in cases of musical performance. Contemporary practice usually dictates tuning to A440, but so-called period instrument or "historically informed"[16] groups often tune instead to some frequency below that—for example, A438, A436, or an even lower pitch (e.g., A415). Nevertheless, they see themselves as playing the same piece *and in the same key* as ensembles tuning to A440. So here's a context in which A436 (say) could count as close to A440. But if some renegade member of an A436-tuned period instrument ensemble defiantly tuned instead to A440, in that context A440 and A436 would not count as similar or close. Differences in frequency can matter greatly on an even finer-grained scale—for example, whether one is tuning according to a tempered scale or a just-toned scale. I'll return to this issue below in connection with geometric congruence.

Sheldrake concedes that similar systems may differ in their specific features.[17] But he claims that a process of *automatic averaging* will bring their common features into alignment. This process, Sheldrake maintains, is analogous to that of producing composite photographs. Now first of all, Sheldrake fails to see that the *common features* that are brought into alignment may not be exactly the same from one system to the next. So what would explain how *these* differences get adjusted for? Another appeal to automatic averaging would start Sheldrake on just the sort of vicious regress that's fatal to memory-trace theory (as Sheldrake at one time seemed to realize). Second, the process of producing composite photographs is clearly not one of automatic averaging. Composite photos are produced by a *person*, by someone who first must *decide* which features are relevant and similar and who then determines a method by which to align them. The process doesn't simply happen by itself; criteria or standards of relevance exist only against both local and global backgrounds of organic needs and practices.

At one point, Sheldrake remarks that absolute size is irrelevant to what a thing's form is. But the fact that he must point this out is a tacit concession that, under certain conditions, differences in size *might* lead us to classify two things as different in form. And here the poverty of the concept of morphic resonance stands out starkly. We must ask: What in nature (i.e., independent of human needs and interests) determines size limits on forms? The answer, of course, is *nothing*: *we* determine those limits, in different ways for different purposes. But then morphic resonance isn't a phenomenon built into nature, operating according to internal, inherent, structural principles or criteria.

My favorite example from geometry (elaborated more fully in chapter 1) should help clarify this point. Mathematicians often speak of *congruence* of different figures. But congruence—merely another name for "similarity of geometric form"—is widely recognized to be relativized to some rule of projection, to some mapping function we *choose* to adopt. Different standards of congruence are suitable for different purposes, and no one of them is inherently preferable to the others. For example, we might map a triangle only onto other triangles with the same horizontal orientation and the same internal angles, or we might allow triangles to be mapped onto triangles with a different horizontal orientation or with different angles. We might map isosceles triangles only onto isosceles triangles. But we could also regard isosceles and right triangles as congruent. We could regard all triangles as congruent and decline to map any triangle onto rectangles or circles; but we could also map a triangle onto these other types of figures and even onto lines. What sanctions any of our rules of projection is always something about the context of inquiry; it's never determined simply by the objects themselves. A question like "What other figures are congruent with an isosceles triangle?" has no answer whatsoever apart from an actual context of inquiry. But then, if we can only give a context-relative or *positional* account of similarity for geometric figures (and, by the way, for frequencies), things certainly look bleak for the concept of morphic resonance, especially when we move on to the more complex domains (e.g., human behavior) in which Sheldrake tries to deploy it.

I'll return shortly to the topic of behavior, since Sheldrake commits additional crucial errors in discussing that. First, however, let's look at another reason why Sheldrake's proposal fails to account for the phenomena he thinks are in urgent need of explanation. One genuinely interesting case he considers is how a certain region r of a developing organism could develop more than one way—say, into either an eye or a limb. Sheldrake's explanation is that *r* comes under the influence either of the morphogenetic field associated with eyes or of the one associated with limbs. But how could this be, by Sheldrake's own account? Why should a given morphogenetic field pick out the right part, or *any* part, of the developing organism? We can't just say (as Sheldrake does) that *r* comes under the eye (or limb) field and that's why *r* develops into an eye (or limb). The reason is that the morphogenetic field is supposed to apply *mechanically* (by morphic resonance) to things of the appropriate structure. But *r*, *by hypothesis*, doesn't yet *have* that structure; rather, it's supposed to be *given* that structure by the morphogenetic field that selects it. So Sheldrake has offered no reason why the eye field, say, should influence a part of the developing organism that's not yet distinguished structurally from the region that develops into a limb (or not yet distinguished so much that it can develop in only one way). That part of the organism is not yet structured so that it can resonate only with the eye field; by hypothesis, it's still morphically flexible or labile. Before region *r* comes under the influence of the eye field, it *could* also come under the influence of, and resonate with, some quite different morphogenetic field. But if *r*'s structure is developmentally indeterminate—that is, if it's compatible with (and presumably equally similar to, resonance-wise) the structure of different sorts of morphogenetic fields, then Sheldrake's appeal to resonance between similar structures doesn't explain why *r*'s development should follow one course rather than another.

Sheldrake seems to propose one possible solution to this problem.[18] He appeals to *morphogenetic germs*, the characteristic parts of morphic units, and he says that *primary* morphogenetic fields determine characteristic germs on which different *secondary* morphogenetic fields can then act in different regions of the organism. But this simply won't do. Why should a primary field pick out—presumably by morphic resonance—a part of the organism not yet distinguished enough structurally to be a characteristic morphogenetic germ? Clearly, the selectivity problem mentioned in the previous paragraph has just been pushed back a stage. There's no reason, on Sheldrake's own principles, for an undeveloped and structurally indeterminate part of the organism to resonate with *any* more specific or highly structured morphogenetic field. So long as morphogenetic fields resonate with, and thereby affect, only those items having a similar structure, this problem is insuperable. Yet without the process of morphic resonance, Sheldrake's theory can say nothing. It can only point to the phenomena or regularities to which morphogenetic fields are supposed to correspond.[19]

MORPHOGENETIC FIELDS AND BEHAVIOR

When Sheldrake finally turns to the topic of behavior, the errors mount and become more striking. Here, interestingly, Sheldrake's views are anything but novel; behavioral scientists frequently commit the same errors in one form or another. In fact, Sheldrake's comments on behavior are often as disappointingly elementary as those of your average behaviorist (see chapter 3 for more on that topic). Nevertheless, Sheldrake's discussion has the virtue of bringing his underlying explanatory principles close to the surface, where their flaws stand out clearly.

First of all, Sheldrake repeatedly blurs the critical distinction between *action* and *movement*. Briefly stated, all actions involve movement, but not every movement is an action. Moreover, actions can be described only in mentalistic or intentional terms, whereas movements are describable without reference to intent, in purely physical or mechanical terms. You might say that actions are movements intended a certain way. For example, the raising of one's eyebrow is a movement (or series of movements); but as an action, it may be a sign of astonishment, a sexual invitation, or a way of yielding to an opthamologist's examination. Movements, then, are functionally and intentionally indeterminate; the same movement may be (or be a part of) different actions. If any part of organic activities is describable in purely physical terms, movements are the most promising candidates. But which action results from a movement can only be described both intentionally and relative to the movement's *position* in a context. And even then, nothing intrinsic to a situation determines which action (rather than another) occurs. Likewise, a given structure may be associated with an indefinite number of different functions.

But Sheldrake seems not to appreciate these points, although subtle changes between the original and latest edition of the book have obscured this somewhat. Nevertheless, the changes from the first edition are merely cosmetic. Originally, Sheldrake classified both heart-beating and mating behavior as movements; in the new edition, he says searching for a mate is a form of behavior. But in his new edition, Sheldrake still maintains that action (or behavior) is explicable and analyzable as a series of movements, something to which a resonating field corresponds and whose characteristic resonance mechanically captures the distinctive pattern of the behavior.

Now even if similarity of movement could be analyzed formally, so that the concept of morphic resonance could apply to movements, similarity of action certainly can't be analyzed that way (I'll develop this point below). However, not even similarity of movement can be analyzed formally. As my earlier geometric example shows, no kind of similarity exists intrinsically between two things—that is, merely in virtue of their inherent properties. But it's easy to generate additional and more germane examples focusing on movements specifically. Consider: What natural law or rule of projection could determine, say, whether a flea and an elephant display a similar movement or whether a young beginner's golf swing contains the same movements as that of Tiger Woods? Obviously, whether those items count as similar or not depends on prevailing, but ephemeral and not even remotely universal, standards of relevance and importance. For example, the golf swings of Tiger Woods and the novice might count as similar in a context where we're comparing golf swings to tennis swings, but not when the focus is on fine differences between the techniques of different golfers. The flea and the elephant example is equally obvious; sometimes size matters, and sometimes it doesn't. And it's really that simple, no matter how scientists and philosophers pretentiously hide their confusion beneath imposing technical terms. It's also important to realize that Sheldrake's error on this issue isn't even remotely scientific. He's once again making a deep philosophical mistake about the nature of similarity—namely, assuming that similarity or dissimilarity is an inherent, rather than positional and context-relative, relation between two things.

But Sheldrake goes further. He actually proposes that there could be morphogenetic fields for behavioral types, including searching for a mate and courtship, as well as for habits generally. Apparently, he fails to grasp (a) that nothing done by an organism is inherently of a given behavioral type, and (b) that behavior, described topologically or structurally (say, in terms of movements), is functionally indeterminate. This means, among other things, that there's no limit to the range of activities that can exemplify a given behavioral type; virtually any activity, given the right surrounding history, can exemplify any behavioral type. Moreover, any activity that does exemplify a type does so because of the way *we* construe its position in a bit of history or against a background of human activity, needs, and traditions. The exemplification of a behavioral type isn't inherent in nature. It's inexorably relativized to shifting standards of relevance imposed by conscious agents in a living context. But that means there can be no purely structural or formally specifiable *essence* to that type—certainly nothing like a specifiable frequency with which some things but not others may resonate.

The procrustean and impoverished nature of Sheldrake's conception of behavior emerges especially clearly in his chapters 9 and 11. He claims that while human behavior is more flexible than that of other organisms, "this flexibility is confined to the early stages of a behavioural sequence, and especially to the initial appetitive phase; the later stages, and in particular the final stage, the consummatory act, are performed in a stereotyped manner as fixed action patterns."[20] So, for example, with regard to feeding, "people obtain their food by all sorts of different methods. . . . Then the food is prepared and cooked in many different ways, and placed in the mouth by a variety of means. . . . But there is little difference in the way the food is chewed, and the consummatory act of the whole motor field of feeding, swallowing, is similar in all people."[21]

Although feeding is a more uniform and ritualized behavior than many (giving the example of feeding behavior at least superficial plausibility here), it's still very easy to demonstrate the inadequacies of Sheldrake's position. Sheldrake suggests that feeding culminates in stereotyped processes. What makes a given sequence of movements a case of feeding is that, like behavioral fields generally, it terminates in one of the "limited number of [characteristic] goals given by [inherited] motor fields."[22] In the case of feeding, these goals are apparently chewing and swallowing (the latter being the "consummatory act of the whole motor field of feeding"). I doubt that Sheldrake realizes how he commits himself to a very unscientific thesis: that there exists a defining set of goals for feeding, a Platonic essence that can be formally described in topological terms and that permits resonance only between things of the appropriate type (or essence). Had Sheldrake described this in more archaic Platonic terms (e.g., a thing's feeding-ness), his book might have attracted even more derision than it has already received. However, by couching the view in more obscurantist technical terms, appealing to fields and resonance and morphic units, it sounds far more sophisticated. However, just as appeals to memory traces are no more intelligible or plausible than Plato's suggestion that memories are like impressions in wax (see chapter 1), Sheldrake's view is only a cosmetically altered twist on a deservedly disreputable and deeply nonsensical position.

This is easy to see even in the case of feeding. First, there's no antecedently specifiable and physically describable set of goals that distinctively defines the feeding process. And second, there's no such goal that is inherently a feeding goal. To demonstrate the first point, it's enough to consider the ways *all* organisms feed. For one thing, not all organic feeding processes terminate in chewing and swallowing. The range of organic methods of feeding is enormous, and in principle it's unlimited. Yet they're all ways of feeding. And it *is* fair, incidentally, to discuss the entire range of feeding activities rather than just human feeding behavior. If the behaviors are all ways of feeding, then according to Sheldrake's own principles there's an organic morphic unit of feeding behavior that falls under a grand morphogenetic field for feeding. But of course the varieties of human feeding alone assume many forms, even in the final stages. People may be fed intravenously or may eat nothing but liquids; so neither chewing nor swallowing is necessary for human feeding. Moreover, if some human were to feed in a currently unprecedented fashion (say, by absorbing nutrients through the skin in a food "bath," by inhaling nutritional smoke, or by using food suppositories), these acts would still be acts of feeding, despite their failing to conform to whatever limited set of goals we happen—by what amounts to nothing more than a historical accident—to specify for that behavior. So human feeding isn't defined relative to empirically necessary or fixed—much less inherited—goals.

With regard to the second point above, no human activity like chewing followed by swallowing inherently terminates a feeding event. Other sorts of events may also end with chewing and swallowing—for example, ingesting hallucinogenic mushrooms (hardly a case of feeding: it's engaged in for reasons other than organic sustenance or satisfaction of hunger), taking an appetite-suppressant candy (something intended to *frustrate* the eating process), chewing and swallowing an emetic, or chewing and swallowing a cyanide capsule in an act of patriotic suicide.

Furthermore, it's preposterous to think that there could be a nonpositional formal or structural correlate to the chewing or swallowing processes, something that—independently of a context—determines whether two such events are similar. But that's precisely what's presupposed by Sheldrake's claim that there are morphogenetic fields for those activities. Again, Sheldrake relies on the unacceptable view that similarity is built into nature. But just as geometric congruence isn't a static or inherent relation obtaining between two figures, whether or not chewing or swallowing events are similar likewise depends on context-relative standards of relevance. Even if Sheldrake is correct in claiming that "there is little difference in the way . . . food is chewed," that claim is true only relative to a certain detached and global perspective appropriate to Sheldrake's theoretical inquiry. In other familiar situations, Sheldrake's claim would be considered obviously false. More generally, whether the differences *make* a difference, and *which* differences matter, is always something we decide relative to a background of needs and interests. It's never a formally or inherently specifiable property of the activities themselves.

For example, a mother may reprimand her child for chewing on just one side of the mouth, for chewing too quickly, or for gulping down food in a boorish fashion. Implicit in the reprimand is the assertion of a *dissimilarity* between the child's activity and the mother's allegedly more correct procedures. Dentists, too, might make analogous observations for patients who (say) need to correct their methods of chewing for the sake of oral welfare. And of course, nonhuman organisms exhibit a further variety in ways of chewing whose differences would be precisely the point of a PhD thesis on chewing styles across species. Now if geometric congruence isn't an inherent, static relation between geometric figures, why should similarity of chewing activities be a relation we can specify independently of shifting background standards of relevance? The ease with which Sheldrake supposes all chewing events to be inherently similar shows either (a) that he's unaware of the context-relative standards of relevance and similarity on which he relies (those appropriate to his wide-ranging scientific inquiry but not to the perspective of the disapproving mother, dentist, or PhD candidate) or (b) that he thinks his criteria are somehow privileged or inherently fundamental. The former would be an example of methodological myopia; the latter, an example of metaphysical chauvinism.

I've learned over the years that my position on the nature of similarity is often, and somewhat reliably, misconstrued as an attack on the *concept* of similarity. Sheldrake himself did this (though, of course, in a characteristically sophisticated way) in correspondence over my criticisms,[23] and perhaps readers will be better able to avoid this misunderstanding if we examine that correspondence briefly. Sheldrake wrote to me: "You argued that similarity was a *slippery concept with no basis in nature*, rather something created in an *arbitrary* way by our own minds" (italics added). First, I never said that similarity had no basis in nature. I claim merely that whether two things count as similar is not something *intrinsic* to nature—that is, forced on us by nature itself. In other words, I've claimed only that similarity isn't a static or inherent two-term relationship between the similar things. Furthermore, I never said that determinations of similarity are arbitrary. On the contrary, determinations of similarity can have all sorts of reasonable pragmatic justifications. It's clearly a non sequitur to conclude that because similarity relations aren't intrinsic and static that determinations of similarity are arbitrary.

Sheldrake also wrote:

> Your attack on the idea of similarity is not specific to my own work, but to all of science as we know it. It is a fundamental tenet of physics that all hydrogen atoms are similar, and behave in a similar way. That is why the spectral lines of distant galaxies can be interpreted by astronomers to give information about parts of the universe that are billions of light years away. Chemists assume that all acetone molecules are similar, and hence exhibit similar properties. Biologists assume that all cell membranes are similar in their general structure involving lipids and proteins, that all genes of a given kind are similar, that all protein molecules of a given kind are similar, and that all members of species are similar. Species are defined in terms of similarity. Genera depend on similarity too, but literally less of a specific kind. Families depend on remoter forms of similarity, but one sufficiently strong to suggest a common ancestor.

I'm grateful to Sheldrake for having presented this objection so clearly and persuasively. But again, I'm not attacking or criticizing the concept of similarity. I'm trying to clarify it. I'm not saying that similarity claims are never correct, or that they're never appropriate or justified relative to a background of assumptions and theoretical interests. To repeat, I'm saying only that similarity is not merely a static two-term relation between the things said to be similar. For example, I grant that two things can each have seven grams of mass, and if so, they might count as similar in virtue of the fact that the predicate "seven grams of mass" can appropriately apply to both. But those two things may also count as dissimilar in virtue of one of their many other properties—say, if one is red and the other green, or if only one is organic, metallic, brittle, poisonous, or an appendage, or rectangular, manufactured, or valuable. The two things aren't intrinsically similar or dissimilar, and nature doesn't decide for us which kind of property trumps the other and therefore which things (according to Sheldrake) should resonate with which other things.

To return once again to my geometric example, whether or not two things count as similar depends on matters of relevance, and that's settled only against a background of organic intentions and activity, both local and global—never simply by or between the objects themselves. To put this in Sheldrake-like terms, nothing in nature, by itself, can select which other kinds of objects a given triangle should resonate with. Any triangle? Or only those with the same angles, or the same orientation, or sides of similar length? Or any geometric figure? *We* can plausibly posit similarity (or rules of projection) in any of those situations, but independently of some background there's no reason to assert that any object is similar to any other. In fact, the only background that would allow positing relations of similarity independently of some human or other organic needs etc., would be a divine background. God's perspective would, I suppose, trump that of any of his creatures. But my guess is that this deistic move is not one Sheldrake is prepared to make. In any case, it's not what the hypothesis of formative causation asserts.

Moreover, when trying to get a handle on the nature of similarity, in some ways it's potentially misleading to focus on a property like having seven grams of mass or on examples like the one from geometry. Those examples can be deceptively simple. In certain instances it's more helpful (or to the point) to consider (as Sheldrake eventually does) behavioral similarities. Because we can't characterize so neatly the relevant properties in virtue of which two behaviors count as similar, these cases may be more instructive exemplars of what similarity amounts to.

It should take only a moment's reflection to see why behavioral similarities are difficult to capture crisply in some set of necessary and sufficient topological features (as Sheldrake attempts by appealing to resonance). Consider, for example, the behavioral category of courtship (one of Sheldrake's own examples), and consider the enormous variety of things that can count as instances of courting behavior—for example, a caveman clubbing a cavewoman, a woman playing dumb so as not to threaten her chauvinistic and insecure date, erotic conversation over dinner, placing an ad in a newspaper's "Personal" column or through an online dating service, bragging to a date about one's possessions, flaunting one's exceptional physical endowments, lying to a date to conceal one's sordid past, writing poems to one's sweetheart, serenading one's beloved, purchasing an expensive gift, fighting a duel, clowning around at a fraternity party, merely combing one's hair, wearing clean clothes, or cutting back on one's conversational reliance on expletives, and on and on. Moreover, each of these subsets of courting behavior (and only human courting behavior at that) can be exemplified in endless ways. And in the present context, what also matters is that there are endless numbers of backgrounds against which any two of these courting behaviors would count as *dis*similar.

PREDICTION AND EXPLANATION

Some might protest that Sheldrake's theory predicts occurrences different from those predicted by rival theories—for example, concerning the rapidity of learning a task or the maintenance and proliferation of new forms (including learned behaviors). For instance, Sheldrake predicts that if a large number of rats are trained to learn a new behavior, then any subsequent training of similar rats will be easier as a result. That is, similar rats—no matter how remote geographically from the original—will learn the new ability faster than the original group of rats. Unlike Lamarckism, Sheldrake's theory predicts this result for *all* similar rats—not just progeny of the original trainees. So wouldn't a successful test of these predictions vindicate Sheldrake's theory?

The answer, of course, is that even if the predictions turn out to be correct, that wouldn't be sufficient to warrant accepting the hypothesis of formative causation. It takes more than predictive utility to justify a theory; false (and even incoherent) theories can make true predictions. Besides (and surprisingly), Sheldrake makes no effort to rule out the rival hypothesis of experimenter expectancy effects in such cases, some of which offer striking parallels to the experiments Sheldrake discusses and which also have the virtue of connecting to a large and varied body of replicated results (see chapter 7 for more on expectancy effects).[24] Equally curiously, Sheldrake refrains from making conjectures about possible paranormal interactions between experimenters and nonhumans or between members of nonhuman species. I can understand why Sheldrake might have wanted to avoid that option, considering the already apparently radical nature of his proposals. But in the years since he first published *A New Science of Life*, Sheldrake has done a great deal of innovative and interesting experimental work in parapsychology. So his interest in the topic is hardly a secret (he even discreetly mentions some of his recent work in a few places—mostly footnotes). And appeals to ESP or PK would be obvious alternative explanations to that of formative causation—not simply (as Sheldrake entertains briefly) phenomena that might be explained in terms of morphic resonance.

Nevertheless, Sheldrake may have performed a service to science in drawing attention (for whatever reason) to phenomena or regularities that merit our attention and which other theories have ignored or missed. But the fact remains that the conceptual underpinning of Sheldrake's theory is deeply defective, no matter how serendipitous some of its predictions may be. So Sheldrake's theory may have the virtue of pointing science in new and important directions. But it remains a false start nevertheless.

There's simply no reason to posit morphogenetic fields if we're forced to accept false or absurd presuppositions in order to explain how they work. But then there's no reason to posit morphogenetic fields at all. Unbuttressed by a plausible (or even coherent) mechanism of operation, the positing of morphogenetic fields adds nothing to the regularities they were designed to explain. Morphogenetic fields would merely be a new and technically imposing name for old or hitherto unappreciated phenomena.

So keep in mind that my objections to Sheldrake are compatible with the facts he alleges and predicts. That is, even if his theoretical explanations don't work, it may well be that there's some causal connection between, say, the widespread learning of a given ability and the greater ease with which subsequent populations learn it. All I'm arguing is that *if* Sheldrake's alleged facts *are* facts, and *if* they have an analytical explanation in terms of lower-level processes, then Sheldrake's proposed explanation is unsatisfactory. It could also be that the alleged facts are genuine facts but have no explanation (or analysis). I've already considered such a possibility in connection with Sheldrake's criticism of vitalism, but I'll say more below about the kinds of facts we can take to be primitive—that is, at scientific ground level.

EXPLANATORY LIMITS

In light of Sheldrake's avowed opposition to mechanistic theories in the life sciences, it's very interesting that his own view should turn out to be so classically mechanistic. Perhaps one reason is that Sheldrake doesn't understand what a mechanistic theory is. At this point, I need to review several issues considered repeatedly throughout this book. The overlap with other chapters is unavoidable, because the mechanistic thinking I want to attack appears in many different guises and in different theoretical arenas.

First of all, a mechanistic explanation is not simply one that explains a phenomenon in the language of physics. In fact, mechanistic theories can be dualistic or idealistic; the differences in these variants are merely differences in "hardware." What makes an explanation mechanistic is that it explains a system's or structure's function entirely in terms of the operations, interactions, and organization of its component parts. Moreover, this feature of a mechanism is something that can be captured in a *generalization*. That is, mechanisms exhibit regularities in their behavior or operation, and we can express those regularities by stating in a general way which initial conditions or properties of the system lead to which results. For example, that's the way we explain how a machine's inner workings produce a certain output. In addition to specifying the underlying processes leading to that output, one requirement of this approach is to be able to state or define in a general way what the output is. But to do that in a manner that scientists find acceptable and useful, a loose characterization of the output or function of the mechanism isn't enough. Something more specific and precise is needed; in fact, what's needed are characterizations that specify *necessary and sufficient conditions* for something's being an instance of the mechanism or an instance of its function (or output).

To this extent, Sheldrake's theory is disappointingly conventional. By appealing to morphic resonance and to the alleged existence of essences or defining structures for *kinds* (including behavioral kinds), he commits the same errors that undermine memory-trace theory—in fact, all theories (including cognitive or computational psychological theories) positing physical correlates or mechanisms for kinds of organic or psychological phenomena. In fact, Sheldrake's theory attempts the reduction of *types* of behavioral states which even hard-core philosophical physicalists recognized long ago to be untenable. It's why sophisticated physicalists many years ago abandoned comparatively naive type-identity reductions of the mental to the physical in favor of token-identity theories—not that that actually helped.[25]

What else might account for Sheldrake's lapse into traditional mechanistic thinking? One likely possibility is that (in addition to erroneously equating mechanism with physicalism) Sheldrake failed to recognize a fundamental presupposition of most mechanistic theories—what I've called the *small-is-beautiful assumption*. According to this assumption, there can't be unanalyzable phenomena or facts at the observable level. Scientists agree, reasonably, that explanation by analysis (i.e., into constitutive lower-level processes) can't continue indefinitely. In other words, they admit that some regularities in nature are primitive in the sense that we can't go behind them and profitably ask *how* they occur. *That* they occur is simply a basic fact about the way the universe works, and there are no deeper corresponding regularities that explain why. In this way we arrive at one kind of scientific ground level. Now so far, this is fine; there's no problem in holding that some facts or regularities in nature should be considered as ultimate or primitive. However, most scientists go further and assume that these fundamental regularities can exist only at the level of the very small—say, the atomic, microscopic, biochemical, or neurological level, and never at the level of observable behavior. But that's simply an assumption, not an empirically established fact, and I believe antimechanists have marshaled powerful arguments against it, similar in many ways to the arguments I deployed against memory-trace theory in chapter 1.

In any case, had Sheldrake been willing to abandon this small-is-beautiful assumption, he would never have had to look *beneath* the surface of the phenomena of morphogenesis for an account of how they work or occur. He could have let the phenomena stand as primitive and unanalyzable biological or organic regularities, and then he wouldn't have needed to postulate morphogenetic fields and the literally unintelligible mechanism of morphic resonance by which they work. Moreover, stopping the search for vertical explanation at this point is neither unscientific nor a failure in understanding. In fact, it's a *victory* of understanding to figure out where analysis comes to an end and where regularities can't be analyzed further in terms of more primitive constitutive processes. Besides, not all explanation stops once we identify ground-level phenomena; only vertical explanation (explanation by analysis) grinds to a halt. Scientific explanations take many forms; explanation in terms of lower-level processes is only one of them. And in the realm of behavior (as I consider in more detail in chapter 3), explanation by analysis is especially wrongheaded. The discussion in that chapter helps illustrate the crucial point that some patterns emerge first at the observable level (including the level of behavior).

It's interesting, then—and I suppose ironic—that many view Sheldrake's theory as radical. In most important ways it's thoroughly traditional. Sheldrake has adopted wholesale the standard assumption that observable phenomena should be analyzed in terms of unobservable lower-level processes and mechanisms. He's accepted the parochial and received view that only by offering such analyses can a discipline be scientific or provide an understanding or explanation of the phenomena. And that's precisely the mistaken view which has failed so conspicuously in the behavioral sciences.

Granted, at times it seems as if Sheldrake wants to move in a different theoretical direction. He often seems eager to oppose the common view that nature operates according to immutable laws (presumably, those uncovered by an adequate physical theory). At least at these points in his book, Sheldrake embraces the nonstandard view that the physical sciences should be modeled to some extent on evolutionary (if not teleological) principles fundamental to the life sciences, of which formative causation is arguably the most important. But what Sheldrake seems not to appreciate is that his analysis of formative causation is merely the old mechanical view of nature in new garb.

Nevertheless, despite all my reservations concerning the tenability of Sheldrake's theory, I still consider *A New Science of Life* to be a serious, interesting, and thought-provoking work. For one thing, Sheldrake deserves to be commended for his care and ingenuity in working out the details of his hypothesis and for extending its scope to many domains. And even more important, his book has the virtue of pointing out the possible existence of hitherto unrecognized or underappreciated phenomena and regularities.

But (as I've insisted repeatedly throughout this book) no scientific theory is thoroughly empirical, and like many theories in science, Sheldrake's looks more empirical than it is. First of all, like all scientific theories, it rests on philosophical presuppositions. Every scientific theory starts from some assumptions or other about what nature is like, what observation is, and what properties are, as well as methodological assumptions about which investigative and explanatory procedures are appropriate to which domains. And no matter how carefully the superstructure of a theory is worked out, the theory can only be as strong as its foundations. Regrettably, Sheldrake's theory is fatally vulnerable to the criticisms noted earlier, and those errors are thoroughly philosophical, not empirical. They concern very abstract (and apparently unrecognized) presuppositions about what *must* be the case (what nature *must* be like) for the theory to work as well as assumptions concerning the nature of science itself. Nevertheless, Sheldrake has done a first-rate job of presenting and describing a range of phenomena and problems which the life sciences must confront, but which they haven't yet dealt with adequately.

My own view is that no *science* in the traditional sense of the term can do the job. We need something much more radical than a new but methodologically and conceptually conventional scientific theory. We must be prepared to describe and explain many organic phenomena in ways currently regarded as nonscientific or prescientific. We must radically reconstrue the goals of science and aim for a more robust, balanced, and enlightened view of what *understanding* and *explanation* are. I sympathize with Sheldrake's rejection of many theories in the life sciences; but as I see it, Sheldrake hasn't carried his rejection far enough. The failures of the current life sciences and behavioral sciences are due less to problems specific to particular theories and more to their underlying shared presuppositions about what a science is and what a life science can be.

As I argue throughout this book, different domains demand different methodologies and modes of explanation. Because of Sheldrake's failure to appreciate this point, his theory must ultimately be consigned to the ash heap along with many others hailed as revolutionary but which at their core are merely crude mechanistic views in fancy new clothing—for example, sociobiology, Pribram's holographic analysis of memory, and (more generally) information-theoretic and computational analyses in the so-called cognitive sciences. As I've tried to show to some extent here and also in chapters 1 and 3, the assumptions underlying these approaches to the behavioral and life sciences are fundamentally incoherent at worst and transparently false at best. Despite their provocative (and only superficial) novelty, the theories really have nothing to stand on.

Only when the life sciences stop trying to mimic the methods of physics, only when they recognize that there's more than one way to be scientific, will we begin to see theories adequate to the domains of organic phenomena. Of course, that insight alone would force a profound change in the life sciences as we know them. It would lead to an awareness that the life sciences may never be scientific in the ways theories of physics have traditionally been. But unless science experiences a change of that magnitude, it will never competently address the problems and phenomena Sheldrake discusses—or for that matter, organic phenomena generally.

REFERENCES

Beloff, J., Emmet, D., Morgan, M., Sheldrake, R., & Thompson, I. (1981). Discussion: Memory. *Theoria to Theory, 14*, 187–203.
Braude, S. E. (1997). *The limits of influence: Psychokinesis and the philosophy of science* (Rev. ed.). Lanham, MD: University Press of America.
Braude, S. E. (2002). *ESP and psychokinesis: A philosophical examination* (Rev. ed.). Parkland, FL: Brown Walker.
Braude, S. E. (2007). *The gold leaf lady and other parapsychological investigations*. Chicago: University of Chicago Press.
Goldberg, B. (1977). A problem with anomalous monism. *Philosophical Studies, 32*, 175–180.
McDaniel, S. V. (2010). Review of Rupert Sheldrake, *A new science of life* (revised edition). *Journal of Scientific Exploration, 24*(1), 138–148.
Rosenthal, R. (1976). *Experimenter effects in behavioral research* (Enlarged ed.). New York: Irvington.
Rosenthal, R. (1977). Biasing effects of experimenters. *et cetera, 34*, 253–264.
Rosenthal, R., & Rubin, D. B. (1978). Interpersonal expectancy effects: The first 345 studies. *Behavioral and Brain Sciences, 1*(3), 377–415.
Scriven, M. (1975). Causation as explanation. *Noûs, 9*, 3–16.
Sheldrake, R. (1981). *A new science of life: The hypothesis of formative causation*. London: Blond & Briggs.
Sheldrake, R. (2009a). *Morphic resonance: The nature of formative causation*. Rochester, VT: Park Street.
Sheldrake, R. (2009b). *A new science of life: The hypothesis of formative causation*. London: Icon.
Yalowitz, S. (2011). Anomalous monism. *Stanford Encyclopedia of Philosophy*. Retrieved from http://plato.stanford.edu/archives/fall2011/entries/anomalous-monism/

NOTES

1. Sheldrake, 1981, 2009a, 2009b. Since no two editions have the same pagination for the passages they have in common, for simplicity I'll limit my references to Sheldrake, 2009b.
2. Sheldrake, 2009b, p. 34.
3. Ibid.
4. Ibid., p. 36.
5. Braude, 1997. See also Scriven, 1975.
6. Sheldrake, 2009b, p. 143.
7. Ibid.
8. Ibid., p. 65.
9. Ibid., p. 143.
10. Ibid, p. 144.
11. Ibid., p. 95.
12. Ibid., p. 143.
13. For example, Braude, 1997, 2002, 2007.
14. Sheldrake, 2009b, p. 144.

15. Sheldrake, 2009b, pp. 31–32; Beloff, Emmet, Morgan, Sheldrake, & Thompson, 1981.
16. A self-serving term if ever there was one.
17. Sheldrake, 2009b, p. 122.
18. Ibid., pp. 135ff.
19. Recently, Stan McDaniel has also called attention to this flaw in Sheldrake's account, but from a slightly different angle. See McDaniel, 2010.
20. Sheldrake, 2009b, p. 232.
21. Ibid., p. 233.
22. Ibid.
23. Personal communication, Nov. 22, 2007.
24. See also Rosenthal, 1976, 1977 and Rosenthal & Rubin, 1978, and compare the results with the experiments Sheldrake describes in chapter 11.2.
25. See, e.g., Braude, 2002; Goldberg, 1977; Yalowitz, 2011.

Chapter Three

In Defense of Folk Psychology

Inner Causes versus Action Spaces

To explain why a man slipped on a banana peel, we do not need a general theory of slipping.
—Sidney Morgenbesser

Over the centuries, philosophers and psychologists have explained behavior in terms of causes of one sort or another. Some appeal to the will, others to the self, the soul, reasons, intentions, decisions, or states of the brain. But behind this apparent diversity of opinion is a significant point of agreement—namely, that *the proper way to explain behavior (or render it intelligible) is to trace it back to an initiating cause (a state or set of states) inside the agent*. Let's call this class of theories *inner-cause theories* (ICTs).

The lure of this position is undeniable. However, its appeal is only superficial, and in what follows I'll explain why that is. Of course, ICTs have all along had their detractors, and I, too, believe that these theories face ineliminable and very serious problems. But although I'll mention some of those problems briefly, I can't deal thoroughly with the issues in the space of a chapter. Besides, there's already a substantial literature dealing with problems afflicting ICTs. So the focus of this chapter will be elsewhere. I've often wondered why so many cling tenaciously to internal-cause theories even in the face of apparently formidable objections. One reason, I suspect, is the lack of a viable alternative proposal or strategy for explaining human behavior, along with a failure to articulate clearly how inner-cause explanations fall far short of the power and subtlety of explanations couched in the everyday language of what's often called "folk" or commonsense psychology. Accordingly, I want to take a closer look at what it really means to explain a person's behavior and understand action, and in the process I'll sketch an alternative approach to that of the ICTs. Tantalizing hints as to what's required are sprinkled through the later writings of Wittgenstein, and Bruce Goldberg clarified many of the relevant issues in an outstanding paper titled "Are Human Beings Mechanisms?"[1] This chapter, I hope, will take matters a step further.

THE LURE AND FAILURE OF ICTS

As far as I can tell, relatively few cognitive scientists have a reasoned and sophisticated grasp of the nature of scientific explanation generally and psychological explanation in particular. Those who do recognize that if psychology hopes to explain behavior in both a useful and scientifically respectable way, it must satisfy two crucial goals: (a) to explain why an agent acted one way rather than another and (b) to predict how the agent will act in the future or how the agent would act in various hypothetical circumstances. From the perspective of a contemporary IC theorist, the trick is to locate the right kind of inner cause for behavior—one that provides the needed degree of explanatory systematicity and predictive fecundity. Moreover, the prevailing cognitive science assumption is that this systematicity is attained only when the relation between inner cause and outer behavior can be subsumed under general laws. As I hope will become clear, the ICT position is wrong on both counts. Behavior is not explained by locating a putative internal cause, and genuinely informative psychological explanations needn't be (and are probably never) lawlike.

As readers probably know, most current theoretical work in cognitive science takes brain states to be the initial inner causes of behavior. However, it doesn't matter what the "hardware" description of the initiating state is, and in fact it needn't even be physical. The relevant defect with ICTs is not that they're physicalistic; it's that they're *mechanistic*. That is, they try to explain a system or structure's function (in this case, a person's behavior) entirely in terms of the operations, interactions, and organization of its component parts. The mechanist mistake, then, is to think we can explain behavior in terms of a causal chain leading from *any* kind of internal initiating state to the final emitting of the behavior. But in that case, the defective theories in question could even be dualistic or idealistic, and the triggering or initiating states could just as well be mental as physical. Nevertheless, since the received wisdom is that we explain a particular behavior by locating its cause in the brain, I'll proceed as though ICTs frame their explanations in physical or physiological terms.

We saw in chapter 1 that memory-trace theories suffer from tempting but very deep mistakes, and the ICTs likewise are initially—but ultimately only very superficially—attractive. To see why, consider two different actions, A and B (say, shaking hands and giving a kiss), and consider how IC theorists would explain these two items of behavior. According to the standard view, since actions A and B differ in many ways, their internal causes—respectively, a and b, must differ in corresponding ways. The underlying intuition is that for cognitive science to have any explanatory utility at all, it must posit intimate structural similarities—a kind of matching—between psychological or behavioral states and their internal causes. That's what many IC theorists have in mind when they say that the latter somehow *represent* the former. Predictably, IC theorists have various ways of cashing out what it means to speak of representation in these contexts. Sometimes we're given equally unhelpful expressions, such as "mirroring," and frequently we're told that the relation between inner cause and outer behavior is *computational*. But behind these variations is the underlying view that the structural differences between actions A and B will be analogous to—that they will somehow match—the respective underlying differences between their internal causes a and b. And that's why many regard the tenability of cognitive science as resting on the tenability of a representational theory of mind.

But as I and others have pointed out,[2] the notion of representation required by these theories is problematical (in fact, incoherent). The major problems arise in the following way. To say that one structure represents another is to say that the two structures or their elements match or connect (and, presumably, that we can specify how this matching works). Many express this point by saying that one structure represents another when a function maps the former onto the latter. But the problem is that, given any two structures x and y, there will always be *some* function that maps x onto y.[3] But in that case, presumably *any* internal state can be mapped onto—or can represent, or (in the case at hand) be considered the cause of—action A. And if so, there seems to be no reason to single out internal state a in particular as the cause. In fact, since internal state a can just as well be mapped onto action B, we could take it to be the cause of B.

The only way IC theorists can avoid this awkward situation is to say that even though the structure of an internal cause can, *in principle*, be mapped onto that of any action, the *way* internal state a maps onto A is different from the way it maps onto another action—say B. According to the IC theorist, the reason internal cause a represents action A rather than B is that a's structure is such that we can only *arbitrarily* correlate it with that of B. By contrast, the similarity between the structures of a and A is supposed to be intimate and intrinsic—that is, to be built in somehow, so that any mapping of a's structure onto that of B will be transparently artificial or contrived.

Naturally, IC theorists believe that the occurrence of A isn't fortuitous. They claim that A occurs because the right kind of internal cause occurred—namely, one whose structure inherently represents (or uniquely or nonarbitrarily matches) its effect. That's why they believe we can explain *A* by reference to *a* rather than to *b*; and allegedly that would allow one (in principle at least) to design programs for human behavior or correctly infer a person's behavior from an adequate description of the relevant state of the person's brain. Most cognitive scientists acknowledge that we're nowhere close to being able to do that now. But they hold fast to the belief that this will be possible somewhere down the road.

The mistakes underlying this approach to ICTs are very serious, and perhaps the most glaring error is something I discussed at length in chapter 1—namely, the assumption that similarity—or the relation of representation or matching—can be an *inherent* relation between two things. Forgetting for the moment about whether we can take inner or outer states to have a fundamental or privileged *structure* (the things between which these relations of similarity or representation obtain), it's preposterous to suggest that two things are similar (or that one represents, mirrors, matches, or stands in a computational relationship to the other) in virtue of a set of intrinsic or inherent features of those two things. In fact, as I noted in chapter 1, *anything can represent or mean anything*. That's because a thing's representational options are limited only by the situations into which it can be inserted, and that set of situations is as indefinite and vast as the set of possible twists and turns human life can take. But in that case, what something represents can't simply be a function of how it's configured. Things must be *made* to represent or mean something, and so representation or meaning is irreducibly situation specific.

So representation (like meaning) can't be built into ICT's hypothetical inner objects any more than it can be built into familiar objects such as words or images. It's no more defensible to suggest that internal objects have their representation or meaning inherently than it is to suggest that a picture or word can represent or mean one and only one thing, or that it means or represents what it does independently of a context, or (as noted in chapter 1) that a geometrical figure can be mapped properly or nonarbitrarily only onto certain kinds of objects. Partisans of ICTs often lose sight of this point—perhaps even guard themselves against it—with the use of obscurantist engineering terms. But whether we use the term "inherent" or (say) "hardwired," it's still just bad philosophy to suppose that meaning, representation, matching, copying, or computational relations are things that could *ever* exist inherently in or between objects, whether they be familiar observable objects, or hypothetical neurophysiological objects, or still more hypothetical elements in the language of thought.

No doubt many will protest. They'll say that if we stop explaining human action in terms of inner representations of some kind, the science of psychology will have nothing to fall back on, and in that case human action can only be regarded as mysterious from the scientific point of view. They'll say that if a person's behavior is explicable and not mysterious, it has a cause. And presumably a fundamental part of the cause of that behavior is something *in* the person. Moreover, the only kind of thing within the person that could explain the behavior is an entity having an appropriate structure. This entity must be some sort of representation of the action.

Obviously, the appeal of this viewpoint is very strong, enough so that its adherents seem unmoved by the underlying absurdity of the notion of an inner representation—a structure that determines its own application. That's one reason it's important to develop an adequate alternative account of the explanation of human behavior. But that's also why it's important to note additional serious problems with the ICTs. For one thing, they rest on further questionable presuppositions. And for another, they have fatal and unavoidable explanatory limitations. For the purposes of this chapter (and because there's a substantial literature dealing with the former), I'll focus mostly on the latter.

EXPLANATORY INADEQUACY

One of the most revealing failures of ICTs is their inability to handle dispositions, traits, abilities, or more fundamentally still, a person's *character* or *personality*. It's not enough, as many seem to think, to focus initially (much less only) on the expression of simple or uninteresting beliefs, such as the belief that the Red Sox beat the Yankees, or low-level abilities, such as the ability to tie one's shoes[4] or the ability to practice swimming.[5] We often explain a person's behavior by noting such facts as that the person is shy, funny, tactless, insightful, compassionate, considerate, practical, bitter, vain, etc. Indeed, these character traits and regularities have great explanatory and predictive utility in everyday life. Our understanding of them in general, as well as our grasp of their idiosyncratic manifestations in different people, guides most of our actions in life, from the mundane to the critical. Without this understanding, we couldn't reliably determine, say, how to speak to certain people or when not to raise certain subjects with them, who would make a pleasant dinner companion, which group of people together would be compatible as party guests, whom we should trust with an intimacy or secret, who can help us in times of stress, and so on. And I'd say that a putative psychological theory is simply a failure if it omits these familiar character traits and other dispositions from its arsenal of explanatory weapons—or alternatively, if it's unable to explain at least as much as everyday psychology can explain by means of the appeal to these regularities.

But how would an ICT accommodate such regularities? Astonishingly, hardly any IC theorists even try. Jerry Fodor, one of the most sophisticated and influential figures in cognitive science, at least concedes that it would be desirable (if possible) to explain personality traits and other dispositions. But he admits that he's unable to explain such traits as wit, judiciousness, and cupidity.[6] And that failing isn't idiosyncratic to Fodor. *No* ICT can explain these abilities, not even as extensions of the very rudimentary regularities some attempt to analyze. To see why, consider philosopher D. M. Armstrong's heroic but wildly unsuccessful attempt to explain the disposition *ill-tempered behavior*.[7] Although Armstrong's suggestions are relatively unsophisticated, the flaws in his approach are instructive. They'll help illustrate why other versions of ICTs also fail; and they'll eventually help us to see what a viable alternative to the ICTs would be.

In the spirit of Armstrong, then, let's consider the disposition *friendliness*. And let's consider how to explain why Jones made the friendly remark, "That's a nice dress." Of course, a generally unfriendly person can behave in a friendly way on occasion. But since our present concern is with the dispositions and traits which we commonly identify and on which we successfully rely in our everyday personal interactions, let's restrict our attention for now to cases where a person's particular friendly behavior reflects a general disposition to be friendly.

Now first of all, it's clear why on Armstrong's view we can't be content to explain merely why Jones said, "That's a nice dress." After all, that remark isn't inherently friendly. If Jones had produced it in different circumstances, it might even have been an unfriendly action—for example, if Jones knew that the dress's owner didn't want attention called to what she considered a hideously ugly garment. So, since by hypothesis Jones's remark reflects his friendly disposition and since the disposition to be friendly differs from the disposition to be unfriendly, IC theorists must trace unfriendly and friendly productions of the sentence to different internal causes.

So let's consider how an ICT might accommodate the behavioral regularity, friendliness. We're supposing that Jones's particular friendly behavior manifests a general and (we may suppose) reliable disposition to be friendly. ICTs can make sense of this only by tracing Jones's friendliness to some internal feature that explains why Jones tends reliably to behave in friendly ways. So to explain in a particular case why an agent behaved in a friendly (rather than unfriendly) way, the IC theorist must appeal to something *in the person* that produces friendly (rather than unfriendly) intentions, or efficient causes for bits of behavior. Similarly, ICTs require a different internal basis in the agent for intentionally unfriendly behavior. If the IC theorist denied this, it would be a concession that we can't specify an internal cause for Jones's saying a friendly (rather than unfriendly) "That's a nice dress." So the IC theorist posits an internal cause in Jones that's distinctively linked to friendly behavior. And since the goal of the IC theorist is to satisfy the explanatory demands of science, this internal cause must be something that would enable one to predict with considerable accuracy—or at least as much accuracy as we display in ordinary life—whether Jones will behave in friendly ways in specific situations.

It's also why an inner-cause explanation of a bit of friendly behavior is supposed to license statements about how the agent's friendly disposition would be expressed in various hypothetical (but not actual) circumstances. These conditional statements are called "counterfactual (or subjunctive) conditionals," or just *counterfactuals*, and in this case they would concern the agent's friendly behavioral regularities. Of course, Jones's friendliness will be exhibited in many ways. Even in our hypothetical example, Jones's friendliness might have taken a different form. He might have said simply, "Nice dress," or, "I like that," or (winking), "Pretty foxy"; or, he might have said nothing and instead merely offered an approving look, perhaps accompanied by a gesture of some sort. Thus, the IC explanation of Jones's particular friendly behavior must appeal to something in Jones that has an extensive *range* of potential manifestations—not just the production of one sentence.

Conveniently, Armstrong's treatment of familiar dispositions such as ill-tempered or friendly behavior has the virtue of bringing the issues clearly to the surface. He argues, as any good mechanist must, that dispositional states must be rooted somehow in the object having the disposition. Just as salt's solubility is explicable in terms of underlying properties of salt, a person's dispositional states (say, friendliness) will be explicable in terms of underlying nondispositional, or *categorical*, states. Armstrong also recognizes that these categorical states must be *structured* somehow, and structured in a way that matches (or otherwise connects to) the differences in their associated regularities. He correctly sees that this is the only way an IC theorist can explain why the right disposition is activated in a given situation—that is, why an internal state produced one kind of predictable, regular response rather than another.

So how would this type of explanation work? We explain why a bit of salt dissolved in water by describing how water interacts with certain categorical structural states of salt. Similar strategies work for explaining how the brittleness of glass is exemplified by the glass's shattering when it hits the floor, or how the elasticity of a rubber band is exemplified in the ways the rubber band changes shape when it's pulled. In those cases, too, we frame our explanations in terms of some categorical state of the object having the disposition. Thus (in a later work), Armstrong says, "*in fact* the rubber band has some nature in virtue of which the conditionals hold of it."[8] He continues, "When we say that an object is elastic, the predicate 'elastic' applies to the object by picking out a micro-structural property of the object."[9] Analogously, the IC theorist will explain why Jones behaved in a friendly way by describing how external events triggered a certain internal state, presumably some microstructural property of the person, which produces friendly behavior. And (as in the case of salt's solubility and rubber band's elasticity) the IC theorist believes that this type of explanation will work only if the internal state has features different from those that lead to behavior of other sorts.

Here's another way to see why IC theorists posit different internal structures corresponding to different behavioral dispositions and also why they insist on some kind of intimate form of representation or matching between the internal object and the behavior it causes. Let's consider what follows from supposing that when Jones says, "That's a nice dress," his allegedly causally relevant brain state has no such internal structure. And to illustrate the point starkly, let's imagine (admittedly, implausibly) that we identify this unstructured state of Jones's brain as a red spot. Now from the point of view of an IC theorist, if the red spot is unstructured, there are no resources for explaining its alleged effect—Jones saying a friendly "That's a nice dress." That is, there's no reason why the spot produces that particular behavior rather than some other, especially behavior of some other psychological kind. That sort of IC explanation can be secured only when there's a sufficiently intimate representational, derivational, or semantic relation between the cause and the utterance of the sentence. However, an unstructured state like a red spot couldn't stand in logical relations to any other state. Thus (as Fodor notes),[10] if we treat the belief that elephants are gray as "fused" (i.e., unstructured), then that belief would be neither more nor less related to the belief that some animals are gray than to any other belief—say, that cookies are fattening. That's why Fodor argues that in order for these sorts of relations to obtain, there must be something *about* the cause, something about its structure, that determines effects of certain corresponding structures (in this case, the production of a certain bit of friendly behavior) rather than others.

Remember, we don't want to explain merely why Jones uttered a particular sentence. We want to be able to explain why Jones uttered the *friendly* (rather than unfriendly) remark, "That's a nice dress." The IC theorist must do this in terms of some internal state of Jones, responsible not only for the friendly (rather than unfriendly) intention on this occasion to say, "That's a nice dress," but also for his predictable and regular friendly behavior on other occasions. Presumably this would be the categorical state of Jones, analogous to the categorical state of brittleness in glass (or solubility in salt), causally responsible for Jones's regular friendly behavior.

But now suppose, as no doubt many would contend, that the behavioral type *friendliness* has no discernible underlying structure. In that case, as in the case of the unstructured red spot, the relationship between the friendliness in Jones and its immediate effects (the intentions to do friendly things) wouldn't satisfy the demands of computational psychology or any other form of ICT. If the behavioral type friendliness has no specifiable and distinct structure, ICTs can't specify what it is about various behaviors in virtue of which they're friendly rather than unfriendly (or of some other behavioral type). But then they can't identify what it is about Jones's friendly behavior, both on this occasion and in general, which certain of his internal states allegedly generate and which they allegedly match, represent, or mirror.

But that's precisely the situation IC theorists confront. They want to explain specific dispositions and behaviors in terms of categorical states having associated specific structures. The structure of the internal categorical state must represent, mirror, or stand in a computational relation to the structures of its effects, either its immediate effect (the intention to behave in a certain way) or its indirect effect (the behavior). Thus, the categorical state for friendliness must represent or mirror the structure of friendly intentions and ultimately that of friendly behavior. And of course, since friendliness is predictably exemplified by people in addition to Jones (just as solubility is predictably exemplified in different samples of salt), the ICT account of the categorical state of friendliness in Jones must be linked nonarbitrarily to the corresponding categorical states of friendliness in others. So to explain why friendliness is the efficient cause of friendly intentions (rather than intentions of other sorts) and therefore the indirect cause of specific friendly behaviors (rather than behaviors of other sorts), IC theorists must indulge in some very nonscientific—and very suspicious—Platonistic or essentialist philosophizing. They must assign a structure to the *type* friendliness so that it can be exemplified by, first, the categorical state of friendliness in both Jones and others and, second, by the friendly intentions or behavior produced by the categorical state so that the pairs of states can stand in the needed representational or computational relations to one another.

Armstrong is remarkably explicit about this. He writes, "Our concept of a *mental* state is the concept of a cause whose complexity mirrors the complexity of the behaviour it is apt for bringing about."[11] States of the liver, he says, might be apt for bringing about certain kinds of behavior (e.g., ill-tempered or friendly). But only brain states have "the complexity to bring about such complexities of behaviour as are involved even in ill-tempered behaviour."[12] In fact:

> *Only* when the causal chain reaches the brain can we call the series of causes "adequate," because only then does it have a complexity adequate to the complexity of the behaviour it initiates. The "adequate" cause in the series of causes is what we call the mental event.[13]

Thus, only when the chain of causes reaches the brain "do we get processes which are sufficient to produce and sustain ill-tempered behaviour,"[14] processes which are *adequate* to produce those effects, and which accordingly deserve to be considered *mental* states.

What Armstrong (and others) fail to see, but what Armstrong's discussion makes unusually clear, is that the structure of the categorical friendly (or ill-tempered) state must mirror (represent) something in the structure of the friendly (or ill-tempered) states it produces—specifically, something in those states (e.g., intentions, behaviors) that makes them friendly (or ill-tempered) rather than states of different kinds. So, for example, when Jones says, "That's a nice dress," the IC theorist is committed to the wildly implausible essentialist view that there must be something in that behavior, something about its structure, in virtue of which the remark is friendly (rather than unfriendly). And according to the IC theorist, that specific structural component of the behavior must be mirrored (represented) in the categorical state of Jones causally responsible for Jones's friendly behavior.

No doubt some will protest that we needn't look for a relevant structure *in* Jones's behavior any more than with manifestations of other sorts of dispositions. After all, they might say, although the brittleness of glass is explained in terms of the structure of an underlying categorical state of glass, that structure needn't be found in any manifestations of brittleness—for example, when glass shatters and flies apart. Curiously, Armstrong himself makes this point when he claims that mental and physical explanations have the same form. But in fact, Armstrong clearly (and apparently unwittingly) contradicts himself. By distinguishing aptness from adequacy of causes, he shows that he does *not* consider mental and physical causes to be the same. Mental causes have to satisfy a condition appropriate to no merely physical cause. Mental causes must stand in a relation of structural isomorphism to their effects, or at least something very much like that. That's why Armstrong takes a cause to be mental only when it has a structure sufficiently complex to mirror that of its effect. Indeed, every IC theorist requires a structural correspondence, isomorphism, mirroring, or computational relation—some intimate and fine-grained relation of matching or representation—between a mental cause (the categorical state within the person) and its behavioral effects.

In this way, IC accounts of psychological dispositions differ profoundly from those of mere physical dispositions. In order to explain why a piece of glass shattered (rather than melted) in certain circumstances, we needn't posit a representation of the shattering in the categorical structure of the glass. For example, the structural details of the shattering needn't stand in (say) a computational relation to the molecular or atomic structure of the glass. By contrast, friendly (rather than unfriendly) behavior, or manifestations of the belief that p (rather than the belief that q), must stand in an appropriately intimate relation to the categorical state that produces it. That's why Armstrong requires a mental state to be *adequate* for its effect and not merely *apt*. The only sort of state that could be adequate for producing behavior is one whose structure is complex enough to represent the behavior's structure (rather than the structure of some other behavior). Fodor's position is similar. He describes the computational connection between disposition and behavior in terms of logical relations between propositions, and those relations hold in virtue of their underlying syntactic and semantic structures. So the basic ICT strategy is the same, although of course the details change from one theory to the next. To explain why Jones made the friendly remark, "That's a nice dress," ICTs must specify how the structure of the categorical state associated with Jones's friendliness mirrors or represents something in Jones's behavior in virtue of which it's friendly.

But that requirement is fatal to the ICTs. It's unacceptable to suppose that Jones's remark has an inherent underlying structure in virtue of which it's of one behavioral type rather than another. What makes the remark friendly (or a manifestation of a certain belief) is the way we position it against a larger pattern of action. The very same behavior in different circumstances might have been a token of a different behavioral type, just as a smile might be friendly in one situation and menacing in another. One would think that this point no longer needed to be made in the philosophical literature. It's an obvious error to suppose that a particular behavior is the kind of behavior it is in virtue of some inherent underlying structure. But every ICT requires it. ICTs need the notion of an inner representation to secure explanatory power for the theory, because only then can they explain why a person behaved one way rather than another. But explanations in terms of inner representations require that inner causes and outer effects bear the appropriate structural (mirroring, computational) relation to each other. So ICTs are committed to the untenable view that particular behaviors have inherent structures in virtue of which they're the kinds of behavior they are.

EXPLANATORY ADEQUACY

But the flaws in the ICTs run further and deeper. To see why, we must first credit IC theorists with an important, but only partial, insight. One key and reasonable requirement of a psychological explanation is that it be able to render our actions intelligible by systematizing human behavior in an enlightening way. And to do that, presumably, it must be able to capture important regularities or generalizations about human action and allow us to predict behavior. After all (as I noted earlier), we can do that already with ordinary commonsense or so-called folk psychology. It's precisely because we can successfully generalize over and predict behavior that we know how to conduct our lives and how to behave appropriately with different individuals.

That's the key to why behaviorism failed; it couldn't even come close to our everyday, homegrown standard of psychological insight. I realize that many would say that the main problem with behaviorism was that it neglected to acknowledge the reality of inner episodes or experience. Of course that's true, but it's also thoroughly unenlightening. The whole *point* of behaviorism was to eschew ostensibly unscientific talk of inner episodes. Behaviorism's goal was to develop a psychological theory stated in a vocabulary uncorrupted by terms that were mentalistic or intentional. The more interesting (and deeper) issue is why *that* program failed. And the answer is that because behaviorism focuses only on irrelevant physical differences or similarities in behavior, it can't pick out differences where they exist, and it introduces differences where they don't exist.

Remember, behaviorism's ideal was to describe, predict, and explain behavior nonintentionally, without appeal to unobservable (inner) cognitive states. So the behaviorist wanted—again ideally—to refer only to activities described in strictly physical terms—that is, what philosophers typically call *movements* rather than *actions*. For instance, an example of a person's movements would be pressing numbers on a telephone keypad. But depending on what the person intended, that set of movements could be any number of actions—say, dialing a phone number, testing the phone's speaker, rehearsing and trying to memorize a sequence of keypad presses, entering a phone number to confirm the caller's identification, or purposely annoying the person on the other end of the phone connection. As it turned out, behaviorists were confused in the way they understood behavior and as a result they were inconsistent in their commitment to describing behavior simply in terms of movements. In many cases they (presumably unwittingly) lapsed into citing actions, movements *intended* in a certain way, as examples of behavior describable solely in physical terms.[15] In any case, because the concept of behavior was supposed to be understood nonintentionally, behaviorism couldn't even describe—much less explain—relevant and important generalizations about human actions. In fact, within a strictly behaviorist taxonomy or system of classification devoid of mentalistic terms, it's impossible to pick out crucial behavioral patterns and regularities (what we could call the relevant *equivalence class* of behaviors). It's precisely because of those patterns that we see what's coherent and systematic in human behavior, and those patterns are what we rely on to predict what people will do.

Consider, for example, the behavioral type *answering the question "How much is 1 + 2?"* Clearly, that type can be realized in a great variety of ways; that is, *tokens* (or instances) of that type can take many different forms. For instance, a person might say, "Three," write the number "3," press a key on a computer keyboard, point to a number on a chart, hold up three fingers, mimic a horse by stamping his leg three times, say condescendingly, "The same as 4 minus 1, you nitwit," or say in a mock romantic voice, "Trois, mon cheri." Actually, strictly speaking those would be instances of the type *correctly answering the question "How much is 1 + 2?"* Obviously, one can answer the question without doing so correctly and without even providing a solution to the equation. For example, tokens of the type *answering the question "How much is 1 + 2?"* could also include replying, "What do you care?" or "You mean you don't know?", writing "4" (or of course any other number), and indefinitely many other things. Moreover, none of these particular behaviors is inherently of the type *answering the question "How much is 1 + 2?"*. For example, saying, "What do you care?" or pressing "3" on a computer keyboard could be tokens of an indefinite number of different behavioral types. To know what sort of behaviors they are, we must at the very least know what the agent intended, something about which behaviorists are proudly (and foolishly) mute.

Similarly, the type *making a phone call* can be realized by (say) using a rotary or touch-tone phone, using operator assistance, using a land line or cell phone or computer, dialing the number with one's hand or with a voice command, and so on. What makes these various behaviors tokens of the same behavioral type is not something that can be captured in purely physical terms. So behaviorism's failing was that it attempted to describe behavior at a level of description where the relevant patterns for identifying and predicting behavior vanish.[16]

Moreover, relying on cognitive or intentional terms is only one major requirement for capturing the relevant patterns of action. Those patterns must also be explained in terms of counterfactuals—statements describing what agents *would* do *if* the conditions were different (say, if the mathematical question had been asked in another language, or if one had been expected to write the answer on a piece of paper and seal it in an envelope, or if—in the other case—the cell phone failed but there was a phone booth, Internet café, or another cell phone user nearby). So a satisfactory explanation of behavior will, among other things, support or license the relevant counterfactuals. And of course, because behaviorism lacked the descriptive resources for capturing the relevant equivalence classes of behavior, it couldn't support a sufficiently broad range of counterfactuals.

Naturally, IC theorists believe they avoid the pitfalls of behaviorism. But ironically, they too miss these patterns of action. Neither behaviorist nor inner-cause theories achieve the needed degree of systematicity and predictive fecundity. One way to characterize their shared failing is that both bodily movements and the posited inner causes occur at too low a level of description to adequately classify and systematize behavior. That is, at those levels of description we can't license the counterfactuals we make successfully all the time when we accurately predict how people will behave. And that's because the relevant behavioral patterns simply disappear when we attempt to analyze them in terms of bodily movements or by means of the standard candidates in ICTs: neurological or biochemical states, propositional attitudes, or inner representations. In fact, the patterns appear *first* on the level of behavior.

One reason for this failure, I suspect, is that many theorists have been seduced by their own examples. Too often they've assumed, unjustifiably, that we can reveal what's essential for the explanation of human behavior by focusing initially on apparently simple cases—for example, the ways people express their beliefs (such as the belief that elephants are gray), or low-level abilities such as the ability to remember that elephants are gray, or the ability to identify objects. These examples maximize the temptation to suppose that something *within* the person explains the relevant behavior. So I suggest instead that we examine significantly different sorts of cases, which minimize that temptation, which have great explanatory and predictive utility in everyday life, and which (as a result) make the limitations of the received ICT approach to explaining behavior seem even more glaring.

Granted, the scientifically or academically more familiar technique of theorizing from allegedly simple cases to more complex or "degenerate" cases has a distinguished history; it works very nicely in some disciplines, especially in mathematics and in certain physical sciences. But it fails conspicuously in the behavioral sciences and also in related fields such as the philosophy of language. For example, when philosophers of language tackle the topic of sentence meaning, a regrettably familiar approach is to begin with an allegedly simple and theoretically "clean" or "transparent" sentence such as "The cat is on the mat" and then to try analyzing more complex human utterances in terms of principles derived from the simple cases. This may well be another instance of the physics envy I've lamented elsewhere (see chapter 8). But in any case, the technique simply doesn't work. The relevant and important features about language use—that is, the features essential for grasping what kind of instrument of communication language is—are apparent first and foremost in the more flagrantly vague and ambiguous utterances many philosophers of language regard as theoretically opaque or degenerate. "Simple" sentences such as "The cat is on the mat" are, in fact, not theoretically transparent. *They're* the degenerate cases; their apparent simplicity is due entirely to their artificiality, attained by omitting or abstracting out the various considerations that actually fix sentence meaning for real language users in real situations. I'll return to this point below and provide some examples that are obviously more illuminating.

In order to move away from ICTs, we must embrace a richer and more realistic conception than they provide of what it is to understand behavior. Pointing to an alleged internal cause simply won't give us what we need. Instead, we must first be able to place the behavior in a pattern or set of patterns—that is, to see the same behavior in a different guise, to see it as a token of some behavioral type. And that type must lend enough systematicity to the behavior so as to enable us to know what to expect from the person. Our degree of understanding will be roughly proportional to the number and range of patterns into which we can place the behavior. In fact, since a particular behavior will often fit usefully into more than one pattern, we can see how behavior has, as it were, different "dimensions" and thus how the behavior simultaneously illuminates different aspects of the person's life.

In order to appreciate more fully the explanatory inadequacy of ICTs, we can begin by considering why it's a mistake to think that for some behavioral type *T* we can profitably answer the general question "How is one able to *T*?" (e.g., placate, tell a joke, keep a person at a distance, express sympathy or gratitude). The problem is that there's little, if anything, to be gained by looking for personality-neutral explanations of behavior. Granted, sometimes we can answer a question of this form by means of rough generalization about how people in fact *T*. But in so doing, we're merely giving a very rough personality *sketch*. And not surprisingly, this bare-bones sketch won't get us very far, much less to a point where we'll understand how actually to deal with the people whose behavior we're trying to explain. To do that, we must resort to examples and much more detail, by saying something substantive and specific—and not capturable in a behavioral schema—about the person's *character*.

To see this, we need now to look at personality- and situation-specific examples of explanations that are not neatly generalizable but are genuinely insightful. These help illustrate why formulating general laws or crisp behavior schemata in a theory of behavior leaves out too much, with no gain in return. In fact, that traditional, ostensibly scientific strategy rules out the kind of understanding that's actually at the root of human life. In order to get along day to day, our first concern is to negotiate this world and to understand those around us with whom we have no choice but to interact. And to pull that off, we need—urgently—to grasp specific behavioral regularities—for example, concerning whom we can trust with intimacies and under what conditions, whom we can rely on to moderate a dispute, turn to in a crisis, or ask for a favor, who would make a good collaborator or project leader at work, or which people are quick to anger or take offense (and under what conditions). Not surprisingly, then, the personality-specific explanations on which we rely appeal to features of a person's character—say, by noting that the person is cooperative, finicky, selfish, bossy, mature, playful, jealous, sympathetic, secretive, irascible, or vulgar. So by focusing on the underappreciated examples that follow, we should be able to see what sort of alternative approach is needed instead. And that will help illustrate why we need a pluralistic approach to scientific explanation, an approach which recognizes that psychology is most useful, illuminating, and systematically rich when it stops trying to emulate the methods of the physical sciences.

So let's begin by considering how we often explain a person's behavior as resulting not from a disposition, belief, or ability (i.e., something ostensibly *belonging to* or *contained within* the agent), but from a *lack* or *deficiency* of some sort. For example, we often—and effectively—explain a particular behavior in terms of the agent's ingratitude, immaturity, lack of concern, self-esteem, or tact, or the person's inability to cope with stress. I don't mean to minimize the well-known problem mentioned briefly above—namely, the fatal Platonic or essentialist presuppositions at the root of inner-cause theories. Contrary to what those theories require, no bit of tactless or ungrateful behavior has an underlying structure in virtue of which it's of that behavioral type rather than another. But that issue has been widely discussed, and although I'll return to the topic of Platonism briefly below, I want now to explore the problems of ICTs from another and much less familiar angle. Specifically, by focusing on an agent's inadequacies or deficiencies, it's perhaps less enticing from the start to seek an inner structure, some specific thing *within* the person (such as friendliness, or the belief that p) which—as IC theorists contend—mirrors or represents the structure of the behavior.

For example, consider a case where we explain Jones's behavior by observing that he's *ungrateful*. When we do that, we're offering something similar to (but looser than) a so-called covering law explanation. We're saying that a lack of gratitude is a characteristic feature of Jones's behavior—that is, that he's a generally ungrateful person, and so we're explaining Jones's particular behavior as an instance of a regularity in the way Jones acts. Moreover, by accurately attributing that trait to Jones, we license true counterfactual statements about his behavior (about how Jones would have behaved in different circumstances), and we're in a position to predict what Jones will do in the future.

Now there should be little temptation to think that Jones's behavior is ungrateful for the sorts of reasons favored by IC-theorists—that is, in virtue of the presence within Jones of some categorical state that emits behavior of the appropriate kind, or a structure that mirrors the structure of ungrateful behavior, or a set of propositional attitudes standing in a computational relation to the behavior. Rather, we're explaining the behavior in terms of a general regularity, one that reveals a *deficiency* in the agent. And most important, that deficiency can only be understood against the background of a vast reservoir of knowledge concerning things both the agent and others might have done instead, and also about the ways people generally behave and interact, and the sorts of values they cultivate. You can think of this as a kind of *action space* or *space of possibilities*.

That last point is the key to the alternative approach I'm recommending. A particular behavior is ungrateful *only* against a background of a space of possibilities; it's not inherently ungrateful. Even the remark "Thank you" can be ungrateful—say, in a situation where much more would be appropriate. For example, suppose someone risks his life to save you from a burning building and all you do is say "Thank you" and walk away. Or suppose a man acknowledges an expensive gift from his wife with only a curt "Thank you," and (say) neither a hug nor a kiss. Of course, what's appropriate in these cases, and therefore what's ungrateful, can only be determined relative to a broad fund of knowledge about the ways humans generally behave and what they expect and value. Equally important, we must also know how that particular individual behaves. For instance, a simple "Thank you" may be a sign of ingratitude for most people in a certain kind of situation. But for a generally unexpressive person, it might be a sign of a great effort to combat inhibitions for the sake of expressing appreciation. So the reason it's explanatory to classify a person's behavior as ungrateful (or grateful, for that matter) is that it enables us to see how to connect it to a large class of actual and possible behaviors. It licenses or supports true counterfactuals about what that person, and people generally, would do in various circumstances.

Similarly, suppose A says to B "I love you," and that B responds, "Thank you" (or "That's interesting"). And suppose we explain B's remark in terms of his inability to handle intimacy or his inability to respond appropriately and comfortably to expressions of emotion. Here again, those deficiencies can only be understood against the background of an action space. To understand B's reply, we must first know what sorts of things B and others might have said instead, and we must also possess a substantial body of knowledge about the personal and social import of declaring one's love for another, both casually and otherwise. In fact, it's only against the background of human practices generally, behavioral standards specific to B's family or community, and also specific regularities in B's behavior, that we're able to classify B's comment with respect to one of those deficiencies, rather than (say) an example of B's general insensitivity, or a rejection, or a cruel response, or B's reluctance to reveal his feelings to a specific third party observing the dialogue, or a lame (but characteristic) attempt at humor, perhaps to conceal B's discomfort. But no internal state of B can reveal those counterfactual spaces or that degree of understanding.

Here's another example, though not obviously or necessarily concerning a lack or deficiency in the agent. Suppose Jones is hemming and hawing, obviously hesitating to come to the point. A real-life and useful explanation of that behavior might be (say) that Jones finds it difficult to ask *this person* (e.g., a spouse or a new friend) for a favor, or that he finds it difficult to ask a superior for a favor, or that he finds it difficult to ask anyone for a favor. Those options pick out different ranges of possible behaviors from Jones and can convey genuinely useful information about what we can expect from him. But we can't determine, much less understand, which of those options explains Jones's behavior apart from a rich background of information about Jones's behavior in other situations, as well as a very broad body of knowledge about how people behave generally, about obligations created by asking for favors, and about power relations implicit in family, social, and employment settings. Once again, no internal state in the agent can mirror or represent the action space provided by our humble folk-psychological explanation.

In some cases, understanding behavior relative to an action space requires seeing how the behavior is part of a *pattern that develops over time*. That's what happens when we explain a person's behavior as immature. For instance, we might explain Jane's remark by saying such things as "She's young," or "She doesn't yet understand the complexity and depth of human frailties." Of course, this is both a familiar—and a genuinely illuminating—explanatory strategy. And again, what renders the behavior intelligible is something the person *doesn't have*—in this case, experience, wisdom, or perspective. But that sort of personal inadequacy can be understood only by seeing the individual's life, and human life generally, as a process of development. Immaturity isn't simply a state or property inherent in a person, something—like a muscle spasm or a twinge of excitement—with relatively well-defined and limited temporal and spatial boundaries. To see a remark as immature rather than (say) cruel or merely insensitive, we must first view it within the context of the person's evolution and see it as marking a stage of development. For example, we must see it as the sort of remark *that* person presumably won't make a few years later, after having experienced a little more of life. And second, our understanding of the agent's development presupposes an enormous and much broader fund of knowledge about the ways people generally develop emotionally. In other words, to understand a single action as immature, not only must we understand the significance of that action for the person's life in particular; we must also see how it fits into broader patterns of behavior for human beings in general.

An action's immaturity, then, can only be understood against the background of a kind of action space. We must see how the action fits into an evolving pattern of actual and possible behaviors, things the agent did, might have done instead, and might do later, as well as the kinds of changes people generally undergo over the course of their lives. That's why, when we explain someone's behavior as immature, we license true counterfactuals about aspects of the behavior of that person in particular and also about the behavior of people generally.

Remember, by the way, that when we explain an action as immature, that explanation might vie with others—for example, seeing the action as cruel or insensitive. Each of those options can only be explained relative to an action space of possibilities for the agent in particular and for people generally. And there needn't be an absolute victor in this contest. Each approach might, in fact, capture a real and illuminating pattern in the person's behavior.

Perhaps even more revealing are cases where we explain a person's behavior in terms of a *dynamic relationship* between that person and others. Suppose, for example, that Alice and Barry have been married for several years, but that in the past year their marriage has been going downhill. They're less friendly and considerate to each other than they used to be; they no longer care to offer many kindnesses they once offered freely. So suppose

Alice asks Barry, "Would you stop by the cleaners on the way to work?" and that Barry replies, "I don't have the time." How would we explain Barry's response? Not, I want to suggest, by locating an internal cause or formulating a general (personality- and context-neutral) behavioral schema.

In this case, Barry's remark is one of the many signs that the marriage is in trouble and that his relationship with Alice is less friendly than it used to be. At one time, Barry would gladly, or without question, have done Alice the favor. So Barry's behavior can be explained relative to a change within the marriage. By contrast, no internal state of Barry can by itself explain Barry's behavior. At the very least, Barry's remark needs to be placed within the context of a deteriorating relationship. And in doing that, we're implicitly comparing Barry's current behavior to his past behavior, as well as to other things that he (idiosyncratically) might have done instead and might do later. Moreover, we're also seeing Barry's actions as belonging to more general patterns of human behavior. As in the case of an agent's immaturity, Barry's behavior can't be explained in terms of a state within Barry alone. If there's any structure to which we can point in this example, it's Barry's deteriorating *relationship* with Alice, and there's not another thing, inside either Barry or Alice, that represents it. Likewise, we can't explain Barry's behavior solely in terms of static relationships between the remark and external contemporaneous states of affairs.

I must emphasize that in order to understand Barry's remark as a symptom of a marriage in decline, we must see it relative to the evolution of the relationship over time, *including the future*. That's why this explanation helps us to understand how in a year things could be even worse. At present, Barry won't go three blocks out of his way to stop at the cleaners; but he *would* still pass the salt. But in a year, let's say, he won't do even that. What's central to our understanding of this case is that what's happening now (the refusal to go to the cleaners) is part of the decline of the marriage, part of a long-term pattern. We understand the character of Barry's behavior only when we see the process of which it's a part. And equally important, to understand these specific features of Barry's relationship, we must already possess a considerable background of general knowledge about human interactions—for example, concerning the institution of marriage and widespread attitudes about it, how people compromise and moderate their selfishness in relationships, how ungiving or hostile we consider certain actions to be compared to others, and the subtle ways people retaliate against each other without overtly condemning themselves. And certainly, nothing exclusively within Barry could give us that vital and subtle understanding of his behavior. So in the same way as many reject behaviorism and others reject Donald Davidson's anomalous monism [17] for their inability to accommodate even the simplest behavioral patterns, I suggest we reject inner-cause theories for their inability, in principle, to capture illuminating behavioral patterns that can't even be *described* relative to a single agent or to static properties or relations, much less assigned to representations or inner states within the agent.

PROPOSITIONAL ATTITUDES AND MORE EXAMPLES

Nevertheless, some die-hard readers might think we can explain Barry's behavior relative to an appropriately robust propositional attitude within Barry. This would be a variant of the general inner-cause explanatory strategy I've been criticizing, according to which a mechanism first produces a representation of an action, which then emits or gets transformed into that action—some particular behavior. A propositional attitude is supposed to be a psychological state in Barry having representational content and expressible in cognitive terms (unlike conventional neurophysiological accounts). The content of the propositional attitude is supposed to represent the action which that attitude emits—in this case, Barry's remark, "I don't have the time." And some would claim also that every propositional attitude has a corresponding brain state. So Barry's remark, in this view, would be explained in terms of the brain state within Barry that represents and thereby emits the remark.[18]

But what would Barry's propositional attitude be? Perhaps it would be something like this: "When you find yourself in a marriage going downhill, refuse to grant favors requested by your spouse." But that won't work, because we can suppose that Barry doesn't refuse everything that Alice requests; after all, the marriage's decline still has a way to go. So maybe the propositional attitude will be more elaborate—for example, "One way to express your growing dissatisfaction with your marriage is to refuse your spouse's requests for favors. If your spouse asks you to do something that's not terribly inconvenient and that you used to do before, like going a few blocks out of your way to the cleaners, decline to do so using a fabricated excuse (such as not having the time)."

Of course, the problem with this explanatory gambit is that it doesn't yield any insight into Barry's behavior, and ironically enough, it fails for the same reason behaviorist explanations fail. No matter how accurately the IC theorist's proposed propositional attitude captures Barry's behavior *on this occasion*, it still fails to capture the relevant equivalence class of behaviors. It doesn't account for what we've learned about Barry by explaining his behavior dynamically, relative to a marriage in decline. But then it doesn't support the relevant counterfactuals, and it doesn't help us predict how Barry will behave later on when things get even worse. To do that, we also need a much more fertile and general vocabulary—specifically, one that allows us to refer to character traits. And the broad fund of knowledge on which that relies is something we can't capture by appealing to propositional attitudes.

It should be clear, in any case, that very little can be gathered about people from a listing of the propositions they believe. For example, even if we were told that Jones believes proposition *P*, we don't thereby know how Jones interprets or understands it. That's why we can't decide, simply on the basis of knowing what propositions two people believe, whether we should rely on one of them rather than another. Suppose we know that both Jones and Smith believe it's right to keep promises. That doesn't mean that they'll apply that belief in the same way or that their range of "defeating conditions" is the same. In fact, even if their defeating conditions are the same, they might still behave quite differently because (say) Jones is quick while Smith is slow to allow new conditions to defeat the promise (e.g., that Jones is more *decisive*), or because Jones is more courageous (or reckless) than Smith, or because Smith is more easily intimidated, or less secure in his convictions and more easily convinced that he's mistaken, and so on. Again, what's at the root of our understanding are the patterns themselves and the general character or personality they reveal.

Another sort of example might further reduce the lure of explaining behavior by appealing to propositional attitudes. Sometimes we explain what a person says or does, not as the expression of a belief that can be captured neatly in a propositional attitude, but as the expression of a general orientation in life or way of seeing the world. Even a single remark can convey or reveal this, but not because of its determinate propositional content. If someone said to you, "The trouble with kids today is they got no respect," or "He's just another bleeding-heart liberal," you could learn a great deal about that person's attitudes and perspective and how they permeate his or her behavior in many contexts. Similarly, it can be genuinely illuminating and useful to note that a person's behavior shows that he regards himself as better than other people, or more entitled to things than others. We can come to see that this person won't apply the same standards to himself as to others. That's how we learn about a person's character and understand how to interact with him. But, I submit, no entity within the person (a structure or a propositional attitude) can contain, capture, or generate this understanding by itself. We get the understanding only when we see the pattern. And the pattern encompasses things that both the agent and other people do.

Consider, next, cases in which we find regular and reliable *unintentional* characteristics of someone's intentional actions. Often, these unintentional characteristics make the person the kind of person she or he is. But we can't make those regularities intelligible by tracing them back to an initiating state within the agent or to a specification of the agent's beliefs or propositional attitudes. For example, suppose we ask, "Why did Jones respond to her in that way?" and suppose our answer is that Jones is an *abrasive* person. That might very usefully systematize a broad range of Jones's actions, even though no state within Jones is an intention to be abrasive—that is, even in the absence of a corresponding belief or propositional attitude about behaving abrasively. Furthermore, the category of abrasiveness can only be understood against a background of knowledge concerning norms of behavior (locally and more globally) and an action space about what the agent might have done instead and what others might do. Similarly, we can learn a great deal about people from noting that they're (unintentionally) cowardly, naive, conceited, snobbish, thoughtless, insipid, or trusting.

But enough about propositional attitudes. A different sort of example illustrates another way in which behavior (in this case, linguistic behavior) must be understood against the background of an action space. Consider Oscar Wilde's remark, "I'm dying beyond my means." This comment means what it does only because another particular sentence is widely used in a certain way. We understand the point and humor of the remark only because we understand its relationship to a certain background of linguistic conventions—in particular, talk of living beyond one's means. There's no state within Oscar Wilde that could have explained the humorous import of his remark. Even if there were (implausibly) a Fodorian *language of thought*, an inner atemporal mental language assigning meaning to our linguistic productions, the parallel sentences in it wouldn't stand in this kind of relation to each other. Sentences in the language of thought can never become cliches or commonplaces from overuse. But then other sentences in the language of thought can't have meaning that depends essentially on such features of actual language use. The correct view, I submit, is that *every* sentence is intelligible (or can be understood) only against a linguistic action space or background of linguistic behavior. That's why this case is more theoretically revealing or transparent than the artificially simple cases considered theoretically ideal and illuminating by many philosophers of language. And if that's correct, then sentence meaning (linguistic behavior), like other forms of action, can't be explained mechanistically in terms of inner states, structures, or representations.

Analogous observations can be made about Oscar Levant's remark, "I knew Doris Day before she was a virgin." To grasp the meaning, and thus the humor, of the remark, we again must place it against a rich background of facts, both about human life generally and the entertainment industry in particular. Consider also the extensive background required to fix the meaning of another remark from Oscar Wilde—his description of a foxhunt as "the unspeakable in pursuit of the inedible."[19]

Die-hard eliminativists might protest that the examples I've offered needn't be accounted for by a successfully explanatory theory of behavior, on the grounds that character traits and vague categories such as ingratitude, immaturity, and so on needn't be embraced by a scientific psychology.[20] But that position is simply bizarre. Those descriptive categories are no more dispensable than *making a phone call*, *being humorous*, and *speaking a lan-*

guage. However, if eliminative materialism were to be taken seriously, all these categories might go the way of phlogiston. And in that case, we'd have to conclude that people never spoke a language, made phone calls, or were humorous. But *that* is clearly ridiculous. All these familiar descriptive categories capture real regularities, regularities which enable us to successfully predict behavior and which license true counterfactuals.

We know, for example, that some people have the ability to make phone calls, and that if they didn't manifest the ability by using a land line on a particular occasion, they'd have used a cell phone or Internet-based service instead. We know that some people are humorous, and that their conversations, letters, or e-mails are more likely than those of others to evoke laughter, and that in a tense conversational situation they're likely (or more likely than others) to successfully dispel the tension with a witty remark. We even know that some people are humorous in very specific ways and that in certain situations they're especially likely to produce a remark (say) more in the style of a nightclub comedian than to resort to Shavian sarcasm, or to tell a raunchy (or off-color) joke rather than a joke more appropriate to a church social gathering. Similarly, ingratitude, immaturity, marriages in decline, and so on are genuine regularities in the world (as are character traits generally, such as being cowardly, callous, generous, or unselfish). And as I noted earlier, these regularities have great explanatory and predictive fertility as well as great subtlety.

Moreover, the examples I've just given aren't different in kind from the simple ones addressed by inner-cause theorists. Even the simplest beliefs, dispositions, and abilities must be understood against a background of actual and possible behaviors, of the agent in particular and of human beings in general. It's just that the importance of a background emerges more vividly in the sorts of examples I've chosen to emphasize. That's why I warned earlier of the danger of building models of explanation from the sorts of cases favored by IC theorists (or cognitive scientists generally). Contrary to what those theorists think, the apparent simplicity of cases like tying one's shoes or even making a phone call is not a sign that they're closer to a theoretical ideal than the more complex cases considered so far. Rather, it shows that in the simple cases, the theoretically crucial features are merely more obscure.

I considered earlier and very briefly why it's a mistake to think that for some behavioral type *T* we can profitably pose the general question "How is one able to *T*?" Now I'd like to pursue the matter a bit further. Fodor asks just this sort of general question in "The Appeal to Tacit Knowledge in Psychological Explanation,"[21] when he considers what explains a person's ability to tie his shoelaces. The general question "How does one tie one's shoelaces?" is tailor-made to lend superficial plausibility to some kind of

ICT, and predictably it leads Fodor to propose that a specification of the action must be contained within the person.

To see the problem, suppose we ask: "How was Jones able to say something amusing?" Taken generally or in the abstract, that question is quite unlike what we'd be asking in everyday contexts in which we're trying seriously to understand a person's action. If the question were posed in real-life contexts, it would be tied specifically to both the agent and the context. For example, we might be asking: How was Jones able to say something amusing in such a tense atmosphere? How was he able to say something amusing when he'd just been told to stop joking? How was he able to say something amusing five minutes after his mother died (or to someone about to die, or in response to the information that he had just lost two million dollars)? And so on. However, Fodor asks a very different sort of question when he considers what makes shoelace tying possible—namely, "How is *one* (a human being) able to T (e.g., say something amusing, exaggerate, act courageously)?" But I submit that it's futile to ask what, *in general*, makes courage, friendliness, exaggeration, cruelty, and so on possible. Nothing *makes* these things possible. They simply *are* possible.

Moreover, looking for something deeper (i.e., an internal structure) to ground that possibility only pushes the problem back a stage. For we can then ask what makes those structures possible. To suppose that we must always go deeper (to some microlevel) to explain why things are the way they are is merely another example of blind adherence to the small-is-beautiful assumption (discussed already in chapter 2 and later on in chapter 8). Like it or not, at some point we must accept that some facts of nature are ultimate and have no underlying analytical explanation or cause, and there's no compelling reason at all to suppose that such ultimate facts can't be at the observable level.

Let me put the point another way. Consider the real-life question "How was Jones able to T?" asked by one person about another. For example, suppose someone asks, "How was Jones able to sell her that car even though she was broke?" Or "How was he able to go to work the day after his wife died?" These questions aren't answered by specifying something from which the behavior *follows*. Suppose the answer to the question about the salesman is "He appealed to her sense of pity. He made it seem as though he needed the sale very badly." Someone unpolluted by cognitive science wouldn't object by responding, for example, "No, that couldn't be true. Other salesmen have appealed to her sense of pity and she didn't make the purchase." That's because when we explain behavior in real life and convey genuinely useful information about the agent, we're not searching for the behavior's sufficient conditions, much less something that stands in a deductive or computational relation to the action. Rather (and in the case at hand), we're conveying information about Jones's character—for example, his persuasiveness or manipulativeness, and perhaps also his dishonesty.

It's easy enough to see why Fodor is interested in articulating personality-neutral explanations of behavior. Like many others, he believes that a scientific psychology must be lawlike. In fact, he says, "If there are no intentional laws, then there are no psychological explanations."[22] And not surprisingly, he buttresses this position by looking at the ostensibly "simple" cases that (as I've mentioned) so frequently lead theorists down blind alleys in the behavioral sciences. His paradigm example in this context of a (lawlike) psychological explanation is "The Moon looks largest when it's on the horizon." But I hope that two lessons of this chapter are that genuinely illuminating real-life explanations of complex and much richer cases can't be subsumed under general laws and that attempts to fit them within conventionally nomological theoretical frameworks modeled on simple cases fail spectacularly. It would be futile (and in Fodor's case, disingenuous) to object that these everyday attempts to explain behavior aren't real psychological explanations. First, as we've noted, we rely on them, successfully, all the time, and far better than we do with anything proposed by cognitive scientists. And second, Fodor concedes as much, writing, "The *successes* of commonsense psychology . . . are ubiquitous and—for that very reason—practically invisible."[23]

Interestingly, by asking the impersonal and general question of the form "How is one able to *T*?" Fodor shows his true Platonistic colors. Remember that the core of Platonism is the claim that if some particular thing *a* has the property *F*, there must be a something (*F-ness*) which is (or is the essence of, or the representation of) the property *F*. So that something is what makes it possible for *a* to have the property *F*. That is, without the form (or abstract essence) *F*, action *a* couldn't be of that kind. Similarly for Fodor and other IC theorists, it seems that an action can't even exist without there being an internal structural representation of it—that is, a representation of its kind. So for example, the action can't be friendly or courageous unless its *type* (friendliness or courage) is mirrored or represented internally. Thus, the inner object, the representation, is the Platonic form of the action, and that form is what makes it possible for the action to be the kind of action it is.

But that's preposterous. The reason physically distinct behaviors belong to the same behavioral type is not that they share a similar underlying cause or structure. In fact, behaviors of the same type needn't be linked by any common underlying cause at all. I suggest that the classification of behavioral types rests *ultimately* on regularities alone, on the categorizations living agents determine in the course of their lives. And those vastly useful and subtle classifications, which are at the heart of ordinary or folk psychology, reflect the evolving interests, purposes, and perspectives of real agents, not a Platonic realm of abstract or timeless inner structures.

THE ROLE OF REASONS

However, that doesn't mean that reasons, intentions, decisions, and the like are irrelevant to the understanding of behavior. Rather, the point is that it's a mistake to conceive of reasons, intentions, etc., simply as internal states that cause behavior—that is, as behavior-emitting mechanisms (or components of such mechanisms). We can agree to say that Jones φd *because* he intended, decided, etc., to φ. But the reason that *explains* why Jones φd can't be that there is, in Jones, a state that emits behavior of the kind φ. Instead, the explanatory force of the appeal to reasons, decisions, etc., is analogous to what we considered before, in connection with regularities such as immaturity and ingratitude. That is, the observations made already about explaining behavior relative to an action space of possibilities apply equally to our understanding of reasons, decisions, intentions, etc.

Consider: when we explain someone's behavior by appeal to reasons etc., we're again talking about a certain *range* of behavior—not only for that person, but for humans generally. We commit ourselves to counterfactuals about the sorts of things the agent might have done instead or would do on other occasions and also about what people generally might do. That's the sense in which talk of reasons, intentions, etc., is genuinely and robustly explanatory. It gives us a broad grasp of what the person did by helping us to classify the behavior or link it up with other actual and possible behaviors.

A final example should make this clearer. Suppose we want to explain why Jones said "That's a nice dress" to his friend. And suppose our explanation is that Jones decided that a compliment in this situation would help ease the bad feelings caused by an argument the two had been having and that Jones wanted (intended) to improve the conversational atmosphere. That explanation succeeds because it helps us identify Jones's behavior as part of a larger and illuminating pattern of behaviors. We then see it as part of an action space of things Jones might have done instead (e.g., things he wouldn't have said to *this* person but could have said to someone he knew more intimately, or things he might have said in private rather than in public). We also see it as part of a larger action space of things people generally do to be complimentary or to improve a conversational atmosphere. With appropriate changes, the same would be true if our explanation of Jones's remark had been different—for example, if he said "That's a nice dress" because he wanted to impress the dress's owner and show what good taste he had or if he wanted to extract a display of affection from her. And clearly, no state within Jones can yield that kind of explanatory systematicity or capture that broad understanding of human behavior and customs generally, and Jones's idiosyncratic patterns specifically.

Notice that even if Jones isn't a generally friendly (or manipulative) person—that is, even if we don't explain his behavior in terms of a regularity to behave in that way—the appeal to intentions, decisions, etc., works in much the same way as the appeal to other behavioral regularities. In both cases, we're employing categories of behavior that can only be understood against the background of an action space. And in both cases, the explanatory power of these categories is due entirely to their providing us with the appropriate conceptual linkages to physically distinct behaviors of the same sort, both for the agent and for people generally.

So although I agree with many others on the need to systematize behavior, the position sketched here is profoundly different from that of the ICT. To understand what someone said, did, meant, intended, decided, and so on, we must know what else the person (and others) might have done instead and how the person (and others) might have altered the behavior if the circumstances had changed. For example, to understand that Jones is trying to be complimentary (or to improve the conversational atmosphere), we must know what else he might have done in trying to accomplish the same thing or how he might have acted differently with a different person or with the same person in different circumstances. By contrast, the IC theorist argues (quite ludicrously) that if we understand or identify the source of the behavior (e.g., a particular state of the brain), we see the behavior's nature because the source is a representation of (or stands in a computational relation to) the behavior's nature.

THE ROLE OF THE BRAIN

But to avoid misunderstanding, I should emphasize that I'm not denying the brain a role in the production of behavior. I'm simply challenging the received view of what that role is. I'm denying that there is a *system* of causal connections leading from inner states to outer behavior—that is, a *behavior-emitting system* or governor within the person. I'm not denying the existence of causal connections between the brain and behavior. I'm denying only that those connections can be systematic in the way the ICTs require.

No doubt some will protest that there clearly *are* rather specific and systematic causal connections leading from the brain to behavior. And probably they'd cite data concerning the effects of alcohol, drugs, or brain lesions on behavior. Now even if it were true that specific brain impairments or damage resulted in specific kinds of behavioral limitations or impairments (a point worth examining in detail some other time), it's a serious mistake to think that these facts would count in favor of the ICTs. The sort of systematicity of causal connections posited between brain lesions and behavior is profoundly different from that required by the ICTs. And since the arguments in this chapter are directed against features of the ICTs that are peculiar to those theories, the appeal to brain lesions and so on is simply irrelevant.

My criticism of the ICTs has centered on its need for items in the person that are supposed to explain bits (indeed, entire classes) of behavior in virtue of their underlying structure. IC theorists demand that the structure of these inner items represent or mirror that of the behavior they cause (or explain). But notice that to assert that there are causal connections between the brain and behavior (as in the case of behavioral impairments) is not the same as asserting that states of the brain *represent* the structure of the behaviors they produce. Only the latter relies on a significant and fatally abused philosophical component—namely, the notion of a representation. That notion vitiates the ICTs, and we can posit a great variety of causal connections between the brain and behavior without having to invoke it. In fact, even IC theorists recognize that not every causal regularity leading from the brain to behavior requires a representationalist explanation. They merely posit that kind of causal connection to explain a certain limited range of phenomena. That's why the appeal to brain lesions is irrelevant. We might justifiably claim, for example, that the use of alcohol or drugs produces depression or giddiness or that a brain lesion resulted in the inability to remember names. But that neither presupposes nor implies the *philosophical* claim that relations of representation obtain between brain states and those behavioral states. There's neither the need nor even the temptation to explain the behavioral effects of brain damage (say) in terms of a representation within the person of the new behavioral limitations. Analogously, we can assert a causal connection between stomach aches and irritability or between a fractured toe and walking with a limp without having to posit a relation of representation between cause and effect. So the evidence from brain lesions, such as it is, concerns the wrong kind of systematic causal connections between inner states and outer behavior. It's not the kind required by the ICTs and in virtue of which the ICTs are fatally defective.

Of course, some IC theorists recognize the importance of systematizing behavior. That is, they realize that our understanding of a particular behavior requires linking it up with other behaviors of its kind. As philosopher and cognitive scientist Zenon Pylyshyn (for example) observed, understanding behavior requires that we be able to organize behavior into the appropriate equivalence classes.[24] And that's why anomalous monism is doomed to be nonexplanatory. It's unable, say, to link the act of rotating a telephone dial to physically quite distinct actions in the class *making a telephone call*. Ironically, however, IC theorists have also failed, though for different reasons, to find a way of organizing behaviors into the appropriate equivalence classes. They tend to assume, incorrectly, that this systematicity will be achieved only by positing internal states that represent behavioral patterns in virtue of having the same structure—in fact, internal states that make the behaviors possible. Now, quite apart from the various reasons we've already considered for rejecting the IC theorists' notion of an inner representation, this procedure is deeply misguided. In order to achieve explanatory systematicity, it's not necessary to locate an analogous or duplicate system at some level other than the level of behavior.

Interestingly, IC theorists are already committed to the view that patterns are the basic tools in the explanation of behavior. But they look in the wrong place for the patterns; they claim that the fundamental patterns are the patterns inside (in the brain)—for example, mental representations. But why continue the search for patterns until we come to an internal pattern? The interior patterns aren't inherently more fundamental than those in the domain of behavior, and they're certainly not more fundamental simply in virtue of being interior.

Of course, IC theorists attribute a special status to the internal patterns. For the ICTs to work, the internal patterns have to be of a different kind than the patterns they duplicate in the realm of behavior. But as we've seen, the ICTs give the internal patterns that special status by paying a steep price: they make them impossible objects—abstract (Platonic) types. In fact, the problem is precisely that inner representations are *objects*, not patterns; no sort of object can do what representations are required to do.

When we examined memory-trace theory in chapter 1, we saw that representation is not an inherent (or static) property of a thing. That's why objects can't intrinsically mean or represent anything; they do so only against a shifting and contingent background of interests, purposes, and so on. Similarly, behavioral patterns and types exist only relative to a background. The background provides the grid, as it were, against which the patterns and types emerge. For example, a particular behavior may be seen or taken to be of a certain type or related in certain ways to physically distinct behaviors. But it's not of that type inherently; nor does it stand in those relations (e.g., the relation of similarity) inherently. It's only against a background of interests, purposes, etc., that a particular behavior counts as one type rather than another. Otherwise, it's completely indeterminate what type of behavior it is or which pattern it fits into.

But the ICTs ignore these obvious and related general points. They take inner states (representations) to mean or function the way they do intrinsically; they require that representations stand in relations of context-independent structural isomorphism or similarity to other things (behaviors). And even more outlandishly, they suppose that behaviors are of a certain type in virtue of their causal linkage to objects existing in the brain, never mind the background of action against which the behaviors occur. Hence, the ICTs make the Platonic blunder of taking an object (a representation) to be a type and to be that type inherently. Representations are, impossibly, supposed to be *framework-independent* types. Representations are of the kind they are simply in virtue of their structure, no matter what the background is against which they're viewed. And, in a move every bit as suspect—and certainly every bit as nonempirical—as its analogue in Plato's original Theory of Forms, bits of behavior come to be of a certain type in virtue of their causal ancestry, which gets traced back to an abstract essence of that type in the brain. Of course, the ICTs would lose most of their luster if they were explicitly to require the One-Over-Many principle or insist that behaviors are of the type they are because they participate in certain forms. But the only relevant difference between the ICTs and the Theory of Forms is that for the former, essences reside in the brain rather than in an abstract realm accessible only through the use of reason. But once we cut through the obfuscating technical jargon of the ICTs, we find a view just as confused and unscientific as that of Plato. This, almost comically, is what much of the widely heralded field of cognitive "science" comes to.

REFERENCES

Armstrong, D. M. (1968). *A materialist theory of the mind*. London: Routledge & Kegan Paul.
Armstrong, D. M., Martin, C. B., & Place, U. T. (1996). *Dispositions: A debate*. London: Routledge.
Bennett, M. R., & Hacker, P. M. S. (2003). *Philosophical foundations of neuroscience*. Oxford: Blackwell.
Braude, S. E. (1997). *The limits of influence: Psychokinesis and the philosophy of science* (Rev. ed.). Lanham, MD: University Press of America.
Bursen, H. A. (1978). *Dismantling the memory machine: A philosophical investigation of machine theories of memory*. Dordrecht, Netherlands: D. Reidel.
Churchland, P. M. (1981). Eliminative materialism and the propositional attitudes. *Journal of Philosophy, 78*(2), 67–90.
Churchland, P. M. (1988). *Matter and consciousness* (Rev. ed.). Cambridge, MA: MIT Press.
Churchland, P. S. (1986). *Neurophilosophy: Toward a unified science of the mind/brain*. Cambridge, MA: MIT Press.
Fodor, J. A. (1968). *Psychological explanation*. New York: Random House.
Fodor, J. A. (1981). *Representations*. Cambridge, MA: MIT Press.
Fodor, J. A. (1987). *Psychosemantics: The problem of meaning in the philosophy of mind*. Cambridge, MA: MIT Press.
Fodor, J. A. (1994). *The elm and the expert: Mentalese and its semantics*. Cambridge, MA: MIT Press.
Goldberg, B. (1982). Mechanism and meaning. In C. Ginet & S. Shoemaker (Eds.), *Knowledge and mind* (pp. 191–210). Oxford: Oxford University Press.
Goldberg, B. (1999). Are human beings mechanisms? *Idealistic Studies, 29*, 139–152.
Heil, J. (1981). Does cognitive psychology rest on a mistake? *Mind, 90*, 321–342.
Heil, J. (1983). *Perception and cognition*. Berkeley: University of California Press.
McDonough, R. (1986). *The argument of the "Tractatus."* Albany: State University of New York Press.
McLendon, H. J. (1955). The uses of similarity of structure in contemporary psychology. *Mind, 64*, 79–95.
Pylyshyn, Z. W. (1984). *Computation and cognition*. Cambridge, MA: MIT Press.
Stitch, S. (1983). *From folk psychology to cognitive science*. Cambridge, MA: MIT Press.
Yalowitz, S. (2011). Anomalous monism. In *Stanford Encyclopedia of Philosophy online*. Retrieved from http://plato.stanford.edu/archives/fall2011/entries/anomalous-monism/

NOTES

1. Goldberg, 1999.
2. Bennett & Hacker, 2003; Braude, 1997; Bursen, 1978; Goldberg, 1982; Heil, 1981, 1983; McDonough, 1986; McLendon, 1955.
3. Cf. my geometric example in chapter 1.
4. Fodor, 1981, pp. 63ff.
5. Fodor, 1968, pp. 31–32.
6. Fodor, 1981, p. 72.
7. Armstrong, 1968.
8. Armstrong, Martin, & Place, 1996, p. 138 (emphasis in original).
9. Armstrong, Martin, & Place, 1996, p. 140.
10. Fodor, 1981, chapter 6.
11. Armstrong, 1968, p. 119.
12. Ibid.
13. Ibid.
14. Ibid.
15. For a compact and clear account of this problem, see Goldberg, 1999.
16. For more on this, see Goldberg, 1999.
17. For a state-of-the-debate presentation of the issues concerning anomalous monism, see Yalowitz, 2011.
18. This, somewhat surprisingly, is Pylyshyn's view, surprising because he seemed to understand so well the same underlying problem afflicting behaviorist and traditional neurophysiological attempts to explain behavior. See Pylyshyn, 1984.
19. Thanks to Ed Kelly for reminding me of this.
20. See, e.g., P. M. Churchland, 1981, 1988; P. S. Churchland, 1986; and Stitch, 1983.
21. Fodor, 1981.
22. Fodor, 1994, p. 3.
23. Fodor, 1987, p. 3 (emphasis in original).
24. Pylyshyn, 1984, pp. 8–9.

Chapter Four

The Creativity of Dissociation

The study of dissociation can be approached from many angles and from three broad perspectives: clinical, experimental, and theoretical. Of course, these three perspectives overlap, and the topic of this chapter is relevant to each. I'm concerned here with some intriguing and surprisingly underappreciated features of the dissociative process. In particular, I want to consider how dissociation can be a profoundly—and in fact, *continually*—creative activity, and I want to examine that creativity in detail.

The dissociative creativity I have in mind here differs from what I've examined in previous works.[1] There, I consider how hypnotized or dissociated subjects sometimes display gifts or facilities they never exhibit in normal waking states. But in this chapter my focus is on the creative maneuvering or adaptation required both to become and to remain dissociated. I discuss this topic briefly (almost in passing) in my book *First Person Plural*,[2] but I've come to believe that it deserves a closer look. I now believe that this topic can shed light on long-standing and hotly debated questions about the nature of the self and cognition, not to mention our clinical understanding of dissociative disorders.

CREATIVITY AND HYPNOSIS

Let's begin with relatively simple illustrations of the processes I have in mind. These examples highlight crucial features of the more complex, clinically substantive cases I'll examine next. So let's consider the creative side of two closely allied states: dissociative anesthesia (or as clinicians are more likely to call it, conversion disorder with sensory deficit) and hypnotically-induced negative hallucinations. Surprisingly few people are familiar with the fascinating and colorful history of studying these phenomena experimentally,[3] and I believe a great deal can be learned by reviewing that research. One thing the experiments show is that highly hypnotizable subjects can respond successfully to some curious *negative* suggestions—in particular, the suggestion *not* to have certain otherwise unavoidable bodily sensations, and also the suggestion *not* to perceive selected objects (e.g., a wooden match marked with an "x," a chair, or a person on a chair). Moreover, these studies show that although subjects are consciously oblivious to the selected sensations or objects, they nevertheless "remain sufficiently aware at some level of the excluded sensory data to act upon them for any important purpose."[4]

These curious phenomena are more impressive than most realize. Century-old studies of hypnotic and so-called hysterical (conversion) anesthesia occasionally noted how subjects made themselves anesthetic in areas that don't correspond to natural anatomical regions, "such as would be affected by the actual lesion of any given nerve."[5] Instead, they experienced insensibility in parts of the body corresponding to apparently popular or highly idiosyncratic conceptions of bodily operations. For example, some subjects have experienced anesthesia in a belt or band around the arm. And Pierre Janet noted,

> In hysterical blindness the anesthesia is not confined to the retina, but extends to the conjunctiva and even to the eyelids; the amaurotic hysterical patient has a pair of anesthetic spectacles across her face. That is to say, she has lost the use of the eye, taking the *eye* not in the physiological but in the popular sense, as including all that is contained in the orbit.[6]

Similar observations continue to this day. For example, David A. Oakley observed that "conversion symptoms defy the normal rules of neuroanatomy and neurophysiology" and that "hypnotically suggested anaesthesia of a hand . . . will typically show a glove pattern with sharply defined boundaries in apparent correspondence to a naïve understanding of sensory innervation patterns."[7]

Negative hallucinations are even more curious. The first thing worth noting about them is that they often pose a special kind of challenge to the hypnotic subject—namely, to fill in the gap left by the now unperceived object. This is especially urgent in cases where the missing object had previously occupied a prominent place in the subjects' perceptual field. In those situations, subjects often take imaginative measures to avoid intolerable perceptual gaps or anomalies. What they do is fill in the gap with a *pseudoperception*. So in those cases at least, negatively hallucinating is not a passive process, as (for example) when external obstacles merely block our perceptions. In order to reduce cognitive dissonance while complying with the suggestion to negatively hallucinate, these subjects produce a positive hallucination.

I should note in passing that the literature on negative hallucination is sometimes unclear or confused about the need in these cases for positive hallucinations to fill in the gaps. For example, some make the strong claim that *all* negative hallucinations require positive hallucinations.[8] However, that seems to be false, even when hypnotic suggestion leads to the disappearance of prominent objects. Martin Orne reported that most subjects negatively hallucinating a chair saw, in its place, "an empty space that was 'somewhat more empty than the rest of the empty space in front of them.'"[9]

Moreover, both Ernest Hilgard and Alan Gauld claim that the reverse is also true, that positive hallucinations must be supplemented by negative ones. But that's questionable as well. Granted, a negative hallucination is a kind of failure to perceive something when no external physical obstacle prevents that perception. And granted, if I positively hallucinate a hippo in the corner, I don't see the corner (despite the absence of external corner-blocking obstacles). But I don't think we should describe this as negatively hallucinating the corner. There aren't two distinct hallucinations here: the positive hallucination of the hippo and the negative hallucination of the corner. There's just the positive hallucination of the hippo. In fact, we should perhaps adopt a similar view for cases properly classified as negative hallucinations but in which there are no resulting gaps in the subject's perceptual field. There, too, we have only one cognitive act, the positive hallucination of something in place of the object no longer perceived.

At any rate, the forms of creativity exhibited in these hypnotic responses are certainly part of what I want to discuss. They illustrate our capacity for generating novel mental contents and also (as I'll discuss shortly) our capacity for choosing a plan of action from a wider set of options. But I want to focus primarily on another aspect of dissociative creativity, something that has received surprisingly little attention, despite its obvious importance. And for now we may safely ignore the conspicuous dynamic differences between experimental hypnotic phenomena and the profound experiences of DID patients. In experimental (rather than clinical) contexts this creativity takes the following form: during both dissociative anesthesia and hypnotically induced hallucinations, ongoing events may conflict with the hallucination and thereby threaten to interfere with and undermine the novel effect. And when that happens, subjects may need to deal spontaneously and resourcefully with those forces to find some way of countering their potentially disruptive influence.

As I mentioned earlier, the reason for this seems to be that subjects are aware, at some level, of what they fail to experience consciously, and the literature on hypnosis contains many interesting illustrations of the phenomenon. Curiously, however, the kind of hypnosis research that interests me here just isn't being done anymore. Current work typically focuses instead on neurophysiological correlates to hypnotic hallucinations or the connection between degrees of hypnotizability and capacity to hallucinate. And many somewhat related studies concern only the Stroop effect, which has to do with reaction time of a task (sometimes called the "name-that-color" task) or similar tasks, such as trying to experience known words as gibberish or as words in a different language. But here, too, the work focuses on underlying neurophysiological processes or simply whether suggestion can modulate the Stroop effect.[10] One particularly interesting study found that subjects hallucinating a cardboard box could totally or partially block the normal response to an outside stimulus.[11] But this likewise did not track the kind of creative responding that interests me here.

Another ingenious study employed the use of a hypnotically induced "virtual" mirror to combat phantom limb pain.[12] This study comes quite close to what concerns me here, because in response to his spontaneous needs, the subject of the study went beyond what was strictly suggested to him. At one point he was feeling hot and thirsty, and so he imagined his phantom left hand picking up and holding a full cup of water. The authors write, "Once the constraints of synchronous movement by the right hand had been removed the experience of the phantom limb was free to be shaped by environmental influences and [the subject's] own motivational state."

At any rate, despite the paucity of relevant recent work, there are enough previous studies, including those conducted by the pioneering investigators from the late nineteenth and early twentieth centuries, to provide ample food for thought. These offer fascinating insights into what subjects are experiencing and sensing during hypnotically induced hallucinations and dissociative anesthesia, and in particular, how those subjects apparently adopt conscious or unconscious strategies to handle difficulties in completing suggested tasks.

For example, F.W.H. Myers noted a peculiar and revealing feature of dissociative anesthesia. He wrote,

> Hysterical anaesthesia rarely leads to any accident to the limb;—differing in this respect, for instance, from the true anaesthesia of syringomyelitus, in which burns and bruises frequently result from the patient's forgetfulness of the part affected. There is usually, in fact, a supervision—a *subliminal* supervision—exercised over the hysteric's limbs. Part of her personality is still alive to the danger, and modifies her movements, unknown to her supraliminal self.[13]

Analogous forms of subliminal awareness have been noted more recently in related hypnotic contexts. For example, Oakley reported,

Hysterically deaf individuals . . . raise their voices when their speech is masked by white noise and hysterically blind individuals show nystagmus when faced with a vertically striped rotating drum. Similarly, subjects made hypnotically blind in one eye are subject to perceptual illusions which could only be effective if they have good vision in both eyes, and hypnotically deaf subjects not only respond to the verbal command "now you can hear again" but their speech is disrupted by delayed auditory feedback just as it is in nonhypnotized subjects.[14]

Furthermore, in some well-known mid-twentieth-century studies, subjects were hypnotized to *not* see the chair in front of them. Although there were good reasons for thinking that the hypnotic induction had been successful and that subjects no longer consciously perceived the chair, aspects of the subjects' behavior suggested otherwise. When asked to move around the room, they avoided contact with the chair by walking or stumbling awkwardly around it. In some cases the protocol was changed slightly; subjects were told they were directly testing negative hallucination, and they were requested to walk straight ahead. Under those conditions, some walked into the chair and appeared surprised that something had touched them. But even in that situation, some subjects still walked around the chair.[15] Similar behavior has also been reported in recent studies of hypnotic blindness and visual conversion disorder (a.k.a. hysterical blindness), in which subjects seem to be influenced by objects or information of which they're apparently unaware.[16]

Moreover, in experiments with both negative and positive hallucinations, genuinely hypnotized subjects tend to behave differently from simulating subjects asked to fake being hypnotized. As Hilgard observed, "Simulators tend to overplay their parts."[17] This conclusion is supported by several successfully replicated experiments that compared the behavior of so-called reals (i.e., genuinely hypnotized subjects) with simulators (control subjects feigning hypnosis). For example, in experiments with a *doubled person hallucination*, subjects were induced to hallucinate a co-experimenter in a chair across the room, while that experimenter was still present in the room but in a different location. After subjects apparently began hallucinating and interacting with the hallucination, the investigator pointed to the real co-experimenter, who had been standing outside the subject's field of vision. The investigator then asked, "Who is this?" The interesting and replicated result of this protocol is that only genuinely hypnotized subjects tended to report the co-experimenter as being in two places. Simulators uninformed about hypnosis tended to believe they shouldn't recognize the real co-experimenter. So they tended to respond to the question "Who is this?" by saying, for example, "I don't know," or "There's no one there," or by identifying the experimenter as someone else. By contrast, hypnotized subjects often seemed startled and confused—for example, by doing a "double take" and offering lame explanations for their experience (e.g., that the co-experimenter must have a twin, or that it's a trick with mirrors).[18]

Of course, why subjects accept these explanations remains something of a mystery. Orne concluded that during both positive and negative hallucinations, the responses of deeply hypnotized subjects are "always characterized by a remarkable incongruity that does not appear to unduly trouble" them.[19] He called that tolerance of incongruity "trance logic," but of course that does little to resolve the mystery. For one thing, it doesn't explain why subjects seem perplexed. In fact, their cognitive discomfort seems to *presuppose* their understanding that something has gone wrong. Moreover, subjects demonstrate their ability to reason even when they invent implausible explanations of their experiences.[20] For example, Orne noted that an occasional subject

> who is usually both highly intelligent and experienced in hypnosis . . . will look at both the hallucination and the real person and finally identify the real person. When asked the process by which this decision was reached, he will say that he thought Dr. X [the co-experimenter] should carry out an action, perhaps raise his right hand, and one did and the other did not; he therefore decided that the one that raised his hand must be the hallucination.[21]

At any rate, no matter how we understand their cognitive tussle, it seems clear that the hypnotized subjects are coping actively with conflicting impulses or experiences. Those having negative hallucinations are trying both to follow and to ignore a hypnotic suggestion, and all seem to be trying to make sense of an experience that somehow mystifies them. Whether or not their efforts succeed (or succeed fully), the subjects are clearly dealing with their dilemma in an active and creative way. Their responses are certainly not passive, much less those of mindless automata (Richard Bryant and Kevin McConkey reach a similar conclusion in their experiments with hypnotic blindness[22]). On the contrary, the hypnotized subjects need both imagination and reasoning to make (even poor) sense to themselves of what's happening and to figure out how to proceed during their hallucinatory episode.

Now these internal dilemmas and responses were of only peripheral interest to Orne. Instead, he was concerned primarily with the important and very interesting methodological issue of what a control group should be for hypnosis experiments. However, during an earlier period in the history of psychology, beginning toward the end of the nineteenth century, several studies focused squarely on the phenomena themselves, especially the intriguing phenomenon of negative hallucination (or, as it was sometimes called, *systematized anesthesia*). Actually, inducing negative hallucinations was something of a fad in late nineteenth- and early twentieth-century psychology. And all along, subjects coped creatively with situations tending to counter their suggested hallucinations. For example, Hippolyte Bernheim induced negative hallucinations in an eighteen-year-old servant girl, Elise B.[23] While

Elise was in trance, Bernheim said to her, "When you wake, you will no longer see me. I shall have gone." Then, with the cavalier (and ethically suspect) attitude toward human subjects characteristic of many experiments in that era, he subjected poor Elise to various indignities and ordinarily painful procedures. Bernheim reports as follows:

> When she awoke she looked about for me and did not seem to see me. I talked to her in vain, shouted in her ear, stuck a pin in her skin, her nostrils, under the nails, and thrust the point of the pin in the mucous membrane of the eye. She did not move a muscle. As far as she was concerned, I had ceased to exist, and all the acoustic, visual, tactile, and other impressions emanating from myself made not the slightest impression upon her; she ignored them all. As soon, however, as another person touched her with the pin unknown to her, she perceived it quickly, and drew back the member that had been pricked.[24]

Bernheim next tried verbal assaults, insisting that Elise was faking. But she remained peaceful, as if she heard nothing. Then, Bernheim writes,

> Wishing to see, on account of its medico-legal bearing, whether a serious offence might be committed under cover of a negative hallucination, I roughly raised her dress and skirt. Although naturally very modest, she allowed this without a blush. I pinched the calf of her leg and her thigh. She made absolutely no sign whatever. I am convinced that she might have been assaulted in this state without opposing the slightest resistance.[25]

Very similar results were obtained by Liégeois.[26]

These experiments are interesting for several reasons. But in this context, one feature is especially noteworthy: how the subject dealt with assaults that would ordinarily be linked inextricably to perceptions of the assailant. Consider the situation from Elise's point of view. Given Bernheim's suggestion, she could have responded appropriately in any number of ways, some more obvious than others. For example, she might have consciously perceived Bernheim despite his suggestion to the contrary. She might have perceived the pins as floating in the air, as if carried by unseen hands (some subjects have responded in this way). She might have positively hallucinated another assailant or attributed the assaults to one of the other experimenters present in the room. And I suppose she might have consciously perceived the needle pricks, touches, etc., but not experienced them as either painful or embarrassing. In fact, she might have experienced them as intrasomatic sensations, or as self-inflicted effects. But Elise did none of these things. Instead, she experienced *no* sensations from having her body or clothing touched by Bernheim. Yet when other experimenters subjected her to the same procedures, with the very same objects she had previously not perceived consciously, she was aware of what transpired.

Now strictly speaking, what Elise experienced was not what Bernheim had suggested. Bernheim had said merely, "When you wake, you will no longer *see* me. I shall have gone" (italics added). So what we need to appreciate is that *it was up to Elise to figure out what to do with that suggestion*. Bernheim's instruction didn't even make clear in what sense he would be gone (e.g., out of the room or simply invisible), and he didn't specify how Elise was to experience either the objects Bernheim carried or the procedures inflicted on her. So Elise wasn't compelled to implement Bernheim's suggestion in one and only one way. She chose one, and arguably not the most obvious, of many options. Her creative way of making the suggestion work was to dissociate not simply her visual perceptions of Bernheim but also the perception of *any* direct effect he had on her.

CREATIVITY AND DISSOCIATION

Many would agree that dissociating traumatic memories and developing alter personalities or identities in cases of DID are likewise ways of coping with exceptional (usually, intolerable) situations. For example, Colin Ross describes alter formation as "a strategy for surviving a traumatic childhood,"[27] and Richard Kluft describes alters "as rather desperate efforts to disavow and mitigate the impact of overwhelming life events."[28] Many would also agree that alter formation requires ingenuity and creativity. Ross calls it "an adaptive use of the human imagination" and "a specialized development of the normal ability to become intensely involved in childhood play."[29] Similarly, Walter Young claims that "the production of any personality with its own name and history implies the use of fantasy."[30]

But few authors seem to appreciate how much creativity it takes to *maintain* an alter once it's created or to keep a traumatic memory dissociated after it's been shielded initially from conscious awareness. It's not that clinicians fail altogether to recognize this. They often mention creative coping strategies as they focus on clinically relevant aspects of a patient's history or the patient-therapist relationship. For example, Kluft notes that alters "express the wish, the fantasy, of supplanting an intolerable reality with a more tolerable one."[31] However, this familiar type of comment concerns only the initial, and fairly obvious, adaptational nature of alter formation. More remarkable to me is how much monitoring, vigilance, and creative maneuvering is required to keep the wish or fantasy alive. And curiously, clinicians seem not to have noticed (or been impressed by) vital details and subtleties of the process.

To explain what I have in mind, I need first to consider some important points about the nature of memory. Moreover, to simplify discussion, let's focus on one type of memory: memory-*that* or *propositional* memory. To put it roughly, this is memory of facts or of pieces of information. Another type of memory is memory-*how*, or skill memory (e.g., how to write, drive a car, open an envelope, etc.). Memories of both sorts can be dissociated, but to make the points necessary for this discussion, we can concentrate on just propositional memory. In fact, to simplify matters further, let's restrict our attention to autobiographical instances of memory-that, having to do with one's own experiences (e.g., the memory that I did such-and-such or that a certain event happened to me).

With this in mind, the first thing to note is that remembering is the sort of thing philosophers describe as *dispositional*. That is, we can remember something even when we're not expressing our memory in conscious episodes of active remembering—what philosophers would call *occurrent* states. Consider, for example, my memory of high-school graduation. It's true of me that I remember that event even when I'm sleeping or (more generally) at times when I have no specific occurrent thoughts about it. It's true that I remember it because I *can* have such thoughts or give other signs of remembering my graduation under appropriate circumstances. So I remember the event in the sense that I'm disposed to act in relevant ways or experience relevant things under certain circumstances. Moreover, we can say that a person *presently* remembers an event even when no occurrent conscious episode seems to "refer" or point specifically to it. For example, I'm remembering where my house key is when I reach automatically for it in my pocket. Similarly, I'm remembering that I cancelled a lunch date as I'm rescheduling another with my friend. That's because even though I'm having no overt thoughts about the house key or cancelled lunch, my memory is *presupposed* by what I'm doing.

In fact, we risk underestimating the complexity of memory even when we say, correctly, that remembering is dispositional. Perhaps we should say instead that remembering is *multiply dispositional*, because a memory can be expressed in a great variety of ways, both in inner experience and in outer behavior. For example, I can remember my high-school graduation by having thoughts, images, or sensations of various kinds (e.g., visual, auditory, olfactory, kinesthetic). But remembering that event is more than a disposition to have conscious inner episodes of one kind or another. It's also a disposition to act—for example, to speak about different aspects of the occasion, to gaze wistfully at graduation photos, to reenact the defiant gesture I made when I received my diploma, or to hum a little Elgar. Similarly, remembering the location of my house key is something that can manifest in different remarks, different physical actions, different mental images, and so on.

These observations apply equally to cases having greater clinical significance. To see this, let's now consider what might be involved in remembering an episode of parental sexual abuse. Just as remembering an ordinary, nontraumatic event can manifest in many different ways, an abuse victim's memory likewise can take a great many forms. She might express that memory by means of certain bodily sensations associated with the abuse or through images of herself having those sensations. She might reexperience or recall the fears or other thoughts she had at the time. Or she might think about the patterns on the ceiling that had helped distract her from the abuse she was suffering. Of course, in this case, too, the abuse memory needn't be an occurrent conscious episode. It could be expressed in automatic aversive responses to touch, or to certain smells, or in new sets of dispositions to dislike certain things—for example, certain types of fondling, or men of a certain bodily type, or a song that played on the radio while the abuse occurred.

These are, arguably, creative ways in which traumatic memories can be expressed. But there's another, and in some ways more interesting, level of creative adaptation. It concerns the requirements for dissociating a traumatic memory and then *maintaining* that dissociated state, and it parallels what we noted earlier in connection with negative hallucinations. The crucial point is this. Once a memory of a traumatic event has been dissociated, a wide variety of situations can unearth it or make it available again to conscious awareness. So to prevent that from happening, appropriate countermeasures will be required when those situations arise (I'll give examples shortly). It might also be necessary to remain vigilant for situations that threaten to expose the hidden memory. And perhaps most important, since remembering is multiply dispositional, dissociating the memory requires not simply isolating a complex disposition or rendering it functionally inaccessible but *replacing* it with a new complex disposition.

To appreciate these points, we need to consider, first, why dissociating a belief or memory requires replacing one complex disposition with another. When someone dissociates a memory of abuse, that memory is no longer available for *voluntary* recall. That, you might say, is the fundamental adaptational point behind dissociation, and it's why we're justified in saying that this person does *not* believe or remember (or no longer believes or remembers) that the abuse occurred. However, that doesn't mean that the old dispositions disappear entirely when they're dissociated. Although dissociation legitimately counts as a kind of forgetting, it's not one in which information is lost irretrievably. As I've explained elsewhere in detail,[32] a dissociated state is always potentially recoverable (e.g., through hypnosis), even if in everyday circumstances it's effectively isolated from thoughts, feelings, and behavior. We could describe this by saying there's a level of consciousness at which the previous belief or memory persists, despite its unavailability to waking consciousness. So in these cases, the dissociated state tends not to emerge, or else it emerges indirectly, much in the way hypnotized subjects demonstrate subconscious awareness of objects they don't perceive consciously. And just as the hypnotized subject's perceptions are dominated by a negative hallucination, the abuse victim's dissociated belief or memory gets supplanted by others that fill in the gap and that now govern behavior and register in waking consciousness. For most of the time at least, the person now thinks, feels, and acts in a way consistent with *not* believing or remembering that abuse occurred. That's why, when the memory of abuse has been dissociated, we can say that the person doesn't believe or remember that abuse occurred. A new complex dispositional state has supplanted the old dispositions, affecting behavior, thought, and feeling.

I should mention, at least in passing, that there's an ambiguity in saying that a person doesn't believe or remember that abuse occurred. The statements

(1a) S doesn't believe that p
(1b) S doesn't remember that p

can mean either

(2a) S believes that not-p
(2b) S remembers that not-p

or

(3a) It's not the case that S believes that p
(3b) It's not the case that S remembers that p

Clearly, the truth conditions for (2) and (3) differ. For example, (3a) will be true and (2a) false when S is agnostic about p—that is, when S believes neither p nor not-p. So an abuse victim might have no belief (memory) one way or the other about whether abuse occurred. In that sense it would be true that she doesn't believe that she was abused. But it would be false that she believes that she was not abused. From a clinical point of view, the difference between these two epistemic states might be important. In fact, in clinically interesting cases beliefs might conflict with memories. That is, some patients might believe they were abused but not remember it, and some might remember being abused but not believe it. But the point here is merely a modest one concerning the disambiguation of two closely related claims about dispositional states. And having taken note of it, we can note further that for present purposes it doesn't matter whether (2) or (3) most accurately characterizes the scenario in which dissociation occurs. In either case, the abuse victim replaces one complex dispositional state with another.

Now it's easy to see why all this is important. Mental states, such as believing or remembering, are not isolated or conceptually isolable elements of a person's psychology. They have an indefinitely large array of what I like to call *autobiographical tentacles*. That is, they connect intimately and extensively with other beliefs, feelings, or memories, and also with our habits and personality traits. Consider, for instance, my memory that I had a pet pig named Hamlet (this is a genuine memory). What makes it *my* memory and what gives it its distinctive texture (so to speak) are the many ways it connects to an enormous web of additional memories, both general and specific. This memory network includes, for example, memories of my home (where Hamlet lived) and my neighborhood (where I took Hamlet for walks, where we invariably stopped traffic, and where I watched him enjoy eating acorns and anything else he could find). It also includes memories of attempts to take Hamlet's temperature, bathe him, and clean his litter box, and the time Hamlet tried to eat his inflatable wading pool and flooded the backyard. And of course, those are just a few of my associated Hamlet memories. Moreover, all those memories connect in many intimate ways with other mental states—for example, my feelings of love for Hamlet, my feelings of annoyance and frustration over spending inordinate amounts of time chopping vegetables for him, my love for animals generally, my newfound love and respect for pigs in particular, my reinforced inclination to be a vegetarian, and my enhanced abhorrence of the idea of eating pork products, among many other dispositions. And in turn, these various feelings and other dispositions connect with many other feelings, with my values, and with my self-image.

And that's just the beginning. This period in my life was also the time of an earlier marriage, and owning Hamlet was very much a family affair. So my memory of having Hamlet as a pet is intimately bound up with memories of my ex-wife and stepson—for example, collaborative efforts in caring for him, preparing the house for his arrival, picking him up from the breeder, and (even before getting Hamlet) long discussions about the viability of having a pet generally and a pig in particular. In fact, my memory of having Hamlet connects with what I learned at the time (and since) about pet allergies and the virtues of pig ownership in a household whose occupants suffer from such allergies and also asthma. And of course, it also connects to an enormous network of feelings and additional memories having to do with details of my ultimately unsuccessful marriage.

So if I were to dissociate my memory of Hamlet, I would probably have to adjust many and remote parts of my overall psychology. Likewise, dissociating a painful abuse memory will also be a complex process. It will have repercussions for the vast web of dispositions linked to that painful memory. For abuse victims to avoid believing or remembering consciously that abuse occurred, they must be disposed to act, feel, and think differently than they would have otherwise. They must establish new dispositions appropriate to not believing or remembering that abuse occurred. And those new dispositions might infiltrate their waking lives in many and far-reaching ways.

Consider: even if abuse victims dissociate their memory of the actual abuse, they might still recall other aspects of the occasion or related events. So they might need to reinterpret a broad range of past events (perhaps by constructing screen memories), and they might need to do this frequently.

For instance, if victims still remember being in the same room as the abuser (or being in physical contact with the abuser), those memories will need to be purged somehow of their abusive features or associations, perhaps by concocting a benign story to which they apparently connect. And if victims dissociate memory of the entire occasion on which abuse occurred, they will likely need to sever, reinterpret, and creatively reconstruct the many links between that memory and other memories, feelings, etc. in their overall psychological economy—in particular, the connections which make the memory specific to *them*. At the very least they might need to compose a new personal history linking the period immediately before the traumatic and dissociated episode to the period afterward—say, one that makes sense of the still consciously recalled physiological damage resulting from the abuse. Moreover, they will need to deal quickly and resourcefully with later events that point to the earlier abuse. So, like subjects experiencing negative hallucinations, victims might also need to improvise contrived reinterpretations of *present* events in order to obscure the nature of the earlier (painful) episode.

But for these coping strategies to work, patients may need to reconstruct their past and creatively interpret their present in order to bring various other memories and experiences into harmony with the life history they now try to accept. And that process might be ongoing or at least recurrent, and it might demand continued vigilance, because everyday events can raise new issues or threaten to dredge up genuine memories that are incompatible with the screen memories or stories patients create about themselves.

For example, suppose the abusive parent continues to make sexual advances or sexual innuendos. That poses a clear challenge to patients dissociating memories of the parent's earlier abuse. So to prevent those memories from being triggered, patients can interpret the parent's actions in some way that preserves the desired illusion that abuse never occurred. For example, they might interpret the parent's actions as nonsexual (i.e., as only appearing to be sexual) or as only very recent occurrences of inappropriate sexual behavior (resulting, say, from years of heavy drinking). Similarly, patients might need to deflect inquiries from others who suspect that sexual abuse had occurred, and they might need to explain away, both to others and to themselves, various lingering signs of the former abuse—for example, bruises or torn clothing. And, of course, they will have to ignore, reinterpret, or otherwise cope actively and often with dreaded associations or memories linked to the dissociated memory but connected with sounds, smells, objects, persons, or locations they can't avoid.

Presumably, DID only complicates the process further, as patients implement these strategies by creating different types of alter identities to dissociate memories of abuse.[33] For example, patients might erect and maintain a type of *a*sexual identity (or self-image), designed to distance themselves from their sexuality. Or they might erect and maintain a sexually promiscuous identity (or set of dispositions), designed to minimize their horror of sexual encounters generally. Similarly, they might create a controlling or powerful identity to reduce their feelings of vulnerability or helplessness or a guilt-ridden identity to maintain the illusion that the abuse was deserved.

In the clinical and theoretical literature, it's common to describe dissociation, or alter identities, as mere "boundaries" or "barriers" for maintaining disconnections to the past. Those descriptions aren't false, but perhaps we can now see that they don't go far enough. For example, in posttraumatic stress disorder (PTSD) no mere boundary (like a fence), no passive structure has the requisite degree of flexibility and adaptability. It can only repel the kinds of trespassers for which it was designed, and it can't be alert for or modify its structure in the face of novel challenges. Similarly for cases of DID, it isn't enough to say (as many do) that a specific alter is "holding" the dissociated memory. Dissociative barriers can be breached; secrets can be exposed. Even if it's correct to say that alters can hold dissociated memories, presumably we want to understand how, in the face of an enormous variety of real-life pressures and triggering surprises, those alters are kept from surfacing, or what shields other alters from their memories, or what shields sufferers of posttraumatic stress from remembering the dissociated trauma. To understand these people, we need, at some point, to specify scenarios that indicate the plasticity of response and the active strategizing this requires.

In certain respects it seems likely that those scenarios will resemble the moment-by-moment vigilance often required to ensure that our lies don't get exposed. Of course, some forms of lying are clearly conscious efforts to deceive others. But my point here is not that dissociation generally (or DID in particular) is conscious deception or any kind intentional effort to deceive others. Perhaps dissociation should be considered a form of self-deception, at least when it concerns experiences the person wishes not to believe or recall. But all that matters here is simply that both dissociation and lying may require regular or frequent vigilance, and sometimes split-second adaptation, to keep them going, to keep the falsehood from being revealed.

For example, in the case of dissociation the falsehood may be the belief that no abuse occurred. In the case of lying, the falsehood could be (say) telling my wife that I missed her mother's party because I was working late (when in fact I was drinking with friends). Clearly, the lie, like the dissociation of abuse, can be exposed in various ways. That's why I need to guard against my friends alluding to our night on the town in the presence of my wife. And when they do make such remarks, I need to find ways of neutralizing or deflecting attention from them. And of course, there are many other possible threats to my alibi—for example, my being inexplicably inebriated after allegedly working late, or the mysterious puncture wounds sustained when my drunken game of darts got out of hand. I might suddenly find myself in a situation where, as Desi would say to Lucy, I have some "'splaining to do." Here, too, it's not enough simply to adopt a position or attitude of innocence with respect to my night's activities. The initial fib forces me to construct a larger web of lies or at least to attempt other sorts of defensive maneuvers (e.g., attacking the challenges to my credibility, making light of those challenges, changing the subject). That's why it's easier to tell the truth than to lie. When we lie, there's much we may need to remember and be alert for, sometimes continually, to keep the lie going. And dissociating memories of abuse apparently requires a similar sort of monitoring and evasion.

So, just as our lies can trap us into telling more lies, there may be similar consequences to keeping a belief or memory dissociated. For example, if the abuse victim interprets the parent's current sexual advances as nonsexual, that has continuing repercussions for her view of the parent generally, and it might require interpreting as nonsexual an unjustifiably wide range of parental behavior (not merely behavior directed toward her). And if she made up a story to deflect questions from those who suspect prior abuse, she'll need to remember the story, and she may need to elaborate on it later.

Moreover, when current events threaten my alibi and I don't want to reveal the truth, I must make a selection from an indefinitely large range of options. I could explain the alcohol on my breath and my obvious inebriation in many ways, constrained primarily by my imagination and resourcefulness. For example, I could tell a tale about the vodka I discovered in the copy room, or the beer I borrowed from the conference room because I was thirsty and the building's water was turned off, or how my boss insisted I join him for a celebration of second-quarter earnings, or the visit I paid to a bar only *after* working late, and so on. (The matter of the puncture wounds poses a greater creative challenge, but even so, I have explanatory alternatives.) Clearly, this parallels Elise's options for implementing Bernheim's suggestion, or the options faced by Orne's subjects as they confront the negatively hallucinated chair and then try to explain their subsequent behavior. And of course, it also parallels the way abuse victims may choose, from a broad set of options, a method of deflecting or neutralizing forces threatening to revive a dissociated mental state.

To avoid misunderstanding, I should also emphasize that lying is not a simple or unitary phenomenon. Not all lies (whether to oneself or to others) demand vigilance in order to be maintained. In fact, some lies may be smoothly incorporated into the liar's belief system and never face a serious challenge. In contrast, other lies will be more empirically problematical. But here, too, we see a parallel with dissociation. Presumably, some mental states can be dissociated with little or no subsequent subliminal wariness and maneuvering, whereas others will require much greater attention. For example, although I couldn't dissociate my memory of having a pet pig without massive autobiographical reconstruction, I could presumably dissociate a specific but inconsequential Hamlet memory (say, a particular episode of walking, feeding, or bathing Hamlet) and experience little if any impact on my sense of self. Similarly, some dissociated memories might just be put "out of mind" with no or relatively few consequences for day-to-day coping. They might be isolable (and potentially retrievable) without seriously impacting a person's self-understanding and memory links. For example, they might simply leave a kind of hole or blank spot in one's self-narrative. And in such a case, it seems that one could dissociate the memory without having to creatively establish new dispositions (or at least any dispositions worth mentioning).

Clearly, then, we can't rule out the existence (and subsequent dissociation) of impactless memories. Obviously, not all mental states are as pregnant with significance or as rich in connections as (say) my memory of my pig or one's memory of parental sexual abuse. In fact, that should remind us of one important respect in which the dissociation of traumatic memories differs from hypnotic hallucinations. The former is self-generated; the latter is not. And the two typically differ in the strength and nature of the underlying motivations to isolate mental states. But when a memory (or remembered event) is meaningful, and perhaps especially if it's psychologically painful or traumatic, it will resonate with our history, our present relationships, self-image, and so on. It's that network of relationships close to the heart that we're driven to protect and which seems, inevitably, to need tweaking and some continued vigilance. So even if some mental states can be dissociated without further complications or adjustments, they will presumably be of a kind that have few, if any, repercussions for the agent, and they're unlikely to be clinically interesting.

So I should not be understood as claiming that *all* dissociation *requires* continued and creative adaptation. Just as mental states vary in their meaningfulness or personal significance, dissociations will vary in the amount of creative coping they demand. However, I think it's easy to see why clinically interesting cases, and no doubt many less rich or significant cases, are likely to require the sorts of adjustments I've been describing.

DISSOCIATION AND THE NATURE OF ABILITIES

There's another respect in which creativity and resourcefulness help keep a dissociated belief or memory isolated from everyday conscious awareness. This is probably most pronounced in cases of DID, where we find alter identities with complex and distinctive sets of traits and abilities. Just as beliefs and memories are not strictly isolable elements of a person's psychology, the same is true of abilities, traits, and skills. They are all complex, indefinite, and overlapping webs of dispositions. A particular ability or trait will rely on many other abilities and traits, and those subsidiary abilities and so on may also be components of still other abilities and traits. Moreover, abilities, traits, and skills are as multifaceted as the virtually unlimited range of situations in which they can be expressed. In fact, there are no clear boundaries separating an ability (trait, etc.) from nearly everything else a person may do. And in that case, when DID patients form a new alter identity to dissociate a traumatic experience, they will draw on an entire repertoire of related capacities, many of which will now be put to novel uses.

Consider, first, how even seemingly modest or simple abilities or traits extend both deeply and pervasively into a person's behavioral repertoire. An example I've used before illustrates the point nicely. Suppose an alter identity has the personality trait of being gregarious and friendly. Clearly, that trait isn't separable from a person's other abilities and traits. It involves (among many other things) the ability and desire to initiate conversation, perpetuate conversation, and talk to strangers (or mingle at parties). In some people, it might also involve the ability and desire to host parties, go on blind dates, frequent singles' bars, actively participate in clubs or other organizations, and go to festivals or other venues with large crowds.

All these abilities likewise involve a complex network of dispositions common to an enormous number of other traits and abilities. For example, the ability to make conversation is multifaceted and is exhibited in varying degrees and styles. It involves the ability to use language, the ability to pay attention to what others are saying, discuss unfamiliar subjects, and respond relevantly and appropriately. And once again, those abilities draw on a wide range of subsidiary capacities that extend throughout a broad spectrum of human activities. For example, in order to respond relevantly and appropriately in a conversation, one must be able to avoid cutting people off or in some other way dominating the conversation, determine when it's acceptable to change the subject or when it's important to suppress one's own opinion, show interest in what others are saying, draw people out by asking pertinent questions, and so on. Moreover, the ability to respond relevantly and appropriately strongly overlaps one of its subsidiary abilities—namely, the ability to show interest in what others are saying. Both require (among many other things) the ability to *understand* what others are saying (e.g., detect hidden messages or meanings behind people's words) and the ability to ascertain when a person is joking, teasing, insecure in one's opinions, revealing intimate secrets, fishing for compliments, being defensive, etc., so that one can determine whether to laugh, praise, express sympathy, seek additional information, or feign horror in an appropriately jocular way.

Furthermore, manifesting an ability draws on, and is shaped and modified by, a person's *character traits*, not just the person's other abilities. Consider again the general ability to make conversation and the more specific ability to converse with strangers. As shy people will readily attest, it requires a certain amount of courage, or self-confidence, or perhaps recklessness, or the trait of being carefree to be able to speak to strangers. Even in the case of speaking to people one knows, it's only in virtue of having certain appropriate character traits that one can risk rejection or ridicule for one's opinions, manner of speaking, or personal appearance. Some people, of course, might be good at making conversation because they're simply too naive to recognize those potential risks in the first place.

These various abilities and traits can also be enlisted in the service of other personality traits, and in that case they might be deployed in novel and original ways. Suppose, for example, that a DID patient creates a new alter that is asexual, or sexually promiscuous, or guilt ridden. Although those character types are very general and can appear in highly stereotypical form, they might also be created in forms that are distinctive and idiosyncratic. But in either case, the patient will probably express friendliness, the ability to make conversation, or the ability to make people feel comfortable or important in new ways. Patients will place themselves in what for them are novel situations, and they will exhibit new behaviors in formerly familiar situations. Their behavior will have different nuances and emphases than before. They will be especially attentive to a new range of people, places, and objects and responsive in different ways to old influences.

Similar observations apply to cases less extreme than DID. Consider the case of Jane, who neither cries nor experiences grief at a relative's funeral and who's surprised at not feeling any grief. Suppose, further, that two days later Jane finally begins to grieve and is able to cry. We could interpret this case plausibly in different ways—for example, as an instance of dissociation or as an instance of repression.[34] So let's suppose we decide that dissociation is the correct interpretation. What do we then say Jane is dissociating? Presumably, it's not a case of dissociating memories, at least not primarily. In fact, we can suppose that Jane remembers her relative and at least some of their times together. That seems to leave at least two major options. On the one hand, we might say that Jane dissociated *feelings of grief* at the time of the funeral (or before). That is, we could say that those feelings existed at the time of the funeral but were cut off from conscious awareness. On the other hand, we could say that Jane dissociated the *ability* to grieve and that at the time of the funeral she experienced no feelings of grief (even subconsciously).

But no matter which option we choose, we can see how dissociation in this case demands creative adjustments. If Jane dissociates feelings of grief, she will presumably need to make sense of, both to herself and to others, her lack of grief. She might do that by reinterpreting her relationship to the deceased, minimizing its significance, and perhaps ignoring or dissociating particularly fond memories. And she will have to cope with many situations that threaten to dredge up additional fond memories—for example, when the other mourners share their reminiscences, or when she returns home and encounters old gifts, letters, or other objects associated with her relative, or the first time she fails to receive her eagerly awaited weekly phone call from this relative.

If Jane instead dissociates the ability to grieve, that, too, will require creative adjustments. It will presumably impact her ability to respond predictably or appropriately to other situations that would ordinarily elicit emotions of grief or sadness. In fact, it might affect her ability to empathize generally. Granted, Jane needn't compensate for these deficits; she might simply become unresponsive in situations where she had previously been able to respond. However, she might also develop new dispositions, such as various obsessions or compulsions, or what Reich called *character armor*, as a defense against experiencing grief. For example, she might become a workaholic or be continuously (and often inappropriately) happy-go-lucky.

Some might be tempted to minimize the creativity required in all these cases. They might argue that subjects' responses are more automatic or brutely instinctual than creative. But I think that would be a mistake. For one thing, it's far from clear how we should understand what instincts are and to what extent we must interpret them as noncreative. And for another, it's obvious that the responses needed to maintain a state of dissociation are not involuntary or reflexive (like recoiling from ammonia). Rather, they're responses that we can describe appropriately as (say) cunning, perceptive, devious, inventive, misguided, poorly judged, and so on. But that's a tacit concession that the responses are, at bottom, intelligent (if not rule governed) and creative.

Consider the following episode from my own life. It's not one of my proudest moments, and it's not an example of maintaining a dissociation. But it illustrates the demanding and creative nature of even elementary adaptations (or evasions) of the sort we've been considering. Some time around the age of three, I was angry at my mother for something she'd done. And in my anger I called her "stupid." My mother was astonished at my audacity and said to me (no doubt imperiously), "Did you call me *stupid*?" Recognizing that I'd gone too far, I replied, "I didn't say 'stupid.' I said 'mupid.'"

To her credit, Mother was unconvinced by this. But however ineffective my gambit might have been, it was still naively crafty. First, a good deal of conceptualization was required merely to *understand* that my behavior had gotten me into trouble. Then, in order to respond to that recognized peril, I was forced to draw on my limited arsenal of possible responses. But my behavior was no less intelligent or creative for being constrained by a young child's vocabulary and behavioral repertoire. Of course, I'd like to think that today I'd be able to handle my mother's challenge more effectively and with more élan. But that wouldn't make my response more creative than what I did as a child. It would only make it more sophisticated or mature.

CONCLUSION

I must leave it to mental health professionals to decide whether (or to what extent) these matters are of clinical importance. I do believe they're of considerable theoretical interest. They help focus needed attention on the complexity and inventiveness of a process that's all too easy to oversimplify and view as a mere severing of associative connections or erecting of psychic barriers. Moreover, when we consider the complex web of relations between our mental states (including dispositions) and other elements of our psychology, we can perhaps better appreciate how human coping and adaptation resist mechanistic analyses. (But see chapters 2 and 3 for more on the limits of mechanistic analyses of human behavior.) Finally (and this requires a separate and lengthy defense), I believe we find ammunition here against attempts to explain dissociation generally, or DID in particular, in terms of literally distinct modules or ego states comprising a self. As I've argued in detail elsewhere,[35] the sorts of coping strategies discussed above make best sense in terms of a single underlying subject for whom conflicts exist and for whom the strategies are appropriate.

REFERENCES

Barber, T. X., & Calverley, D. S. (1964). Experimental studies on "hypnotic" behaviour: Suggested deafness evaluated by delayed auditory feedback. *British Journal of Psychology, 55*, 439–446.
Binet, A. (1896). *Alterations of personality.* New York: D. Appleton.
Braude, S. E. (1995). *First person plural: Multiple personality and the philosophy of mind* (Rev. ed.). Lanham, MD: Rowman & Littlefield.
Braude, S. E. (2000). Dissociation and latent abilities: The strange case of Patience Worth. *Journal of Trauma and Dissociation, 1*(2), 13–48.
Braude, S. E. (2003). *Immortal remains: The evidence for life after death.* Lanham, MD: Rowman & Littlefield.
Braude, S. E. (2009). The concept of dissociation from a philosophical point of view. In P. F. Dell & J. A. O'Neil (Eds.), *Dissociation and the dissociative disorders: DSM-V and beyond* (pp. 27–36). New York: Routledge.
Bryant, R. A., & McConkey, K. M. (1989a). Hypnotic blindness: A behavioral and experiential analysis. *Journal of Abnormal Psychology, 98*, 71–77.
Bryant, R. A., & McConkey, K. M. (1989b). Hypnotic blindness: Awareness and attribution. *Journal of Abnormal Psychology, 98*, 443–447.
Bryant, R. A., & McConkey, K. M. (1989c). Visual conversion disorder: A case analysis of the influence of visual information. *Journal of Abnormal Psychology, 98*, 326–329.
Gauld, A. (1982). *Mediumship and survival.* London: Heinemann.
Gauld, A. (1992). *A history of hypnotism.* Cambridge: Cambridge University Press.
Hilgard, E. R. (1986). *Divided consciousness: Multiple controls in human thought and action* (Expanded ed.). New York: Wiley-Interscience.
Hilgard, E. R. (1987). Research advances in hypnosis: Issues and methods. *International Journal of Clinical and Experimental Hypnosis, 35*, 248–264.
Janet, P. (1901). *The mental state of hystericals: A study of mental stigmata and mental accidents* (C. R. Corson, Trans. & Ed.). New York: Putnam.

Kirsch, I. (2011). Suggestibility and suggestive modulation of the Stroop effect. *Consciousness and Cognition, 20*, 335–336.

Kluft, R. P. (2000). The psychoanalytic psychotherapy of dissociative identity disorder in the context of trauma therapy. *Psychoanalytic Inquiry, 20*, 259–286.

Kosslyn, S. M., Thompson, W. L., Costantini-Ferrando, M. F., Alpert, N. M., & Spiegel, D. (2000). Hypnotic visual illusion alters color processing in the brain. *American Journal of Psychiatry, 157*, 1279–1284.

Lamas, J. R., & Valle-Inclán, F. (1998). Effects of a negative visual hypnotic hallucination on ERPs and reaction times. *International Journal of Psychophysiology, 29*, 77–82.

Marks, D. F., Baird, J. M., & McKellar, P. (1989). Replication of trance logic using a modified experimental design: Highly hypnotizable subjects in both real and simulator groups. *International Journal of Clinical and Experimental Hypnosis, 37*, 232–248.

Myers, F. W. H. (1903). *Human personality and its survival of bodily death.* London: Longmans, Green.

Oakley, D. (1999). Hypnosis and conversion hysteria: A unifying model. *Cognitive Neuropsychiatry, 4*, 243–265.

Oakley, D., & Halligan, P. W. (2002). Hypnotic mirrors and phantom pain: A single case study. *Contemporary Hypnosis, 19*(2), 75–84.

Oakley, D., & Halligan, P. W. (2010). Using hypnosis to gain insights into healthy and pathological cognitive functioning. *Consciousness and Cognition, 20*, 328–331.

Orne, M. T. (1959). The nature of hypnosis: Artifact and essence. *Journal of Abnormal and Social Psychology, 58*, 277–299.

Orne, M. T. (1962). Hypnotically induced hallucinations. In L. J. West (Ed.), *Hallucinations* (pp. 211–219). New York: Grune & Stratton.

Orne, M. T. (1971). The simulation of hypnosis: Why, how, and what it means. *International Journal of Clinical and Experimental Hypnosis, 19*, 277–296.

Orne, M. T. (1972). On the simulating subject as a quasi-control group in hypnosis research: What, why, and how. In E. Fromm & R. E. Shor (Eds.), *Hypnosis: Developments in research and new perspectives* (pp. 399–443). Chicago: Aldine-Atherton.

Pincus, J. H., & Tucker, G. J. (2003). *Behavioral neurology* (4th ed.). New York: Oxford University Press.

Raz, A., & Campbell, N. K. J. (2011). Can suggestion obviate reading? Supplementing primary Stroop evidence with exploratory negative priming analyses. *Consciousness and Cognition, 20*, 312–320.

Raz, A., Fan, J., & Posner, M. I. (2005). Hypnotic suggestion reduces conflict in the human brain. *Proceedings of the National Academy of Sciences USA, 102*, 9978–9982.

Raz, A., Kirsch, I., Pollard, J., & Nitkin-Kaner, Y. (2006). Suggestion reduces the Stroop effect. *Psychological Science, 17*(2), 91–95.

Raz, A., Moreno-Íñiguez, M., Martin, L., & Zhu, H. (2007). Suggestion overrides the Stroop effect in highly hypnotizable individuals. *Consciousness and Cognition, 16*, 331–338.

Raz, A., Shapiro, T., Fan, J., & Posner, M. I. (2002). Hypnotic suggestion and the modulation of Stroop interference. *Archives of General Psychiatry, 59*, 1155–1161.

Ross, C. A. (1997). *Dissociative identity disorder: Diagnosis, clinical features, and treatment of multiple personality.* New York: Wiley.

Spiegel, D. (2003). Negative and positive visual hypnotic hallucinations: Attending inside and out. *International Journal of Clinical and Experimental Hypnosis, 51*(2): 130–146.

Spiegel, D., Cutcomb, S., Ren, C., & Pribram, K. (1985). Hypnotic hallucination alters evoked potentials. *Journal of Abnormal Psychology, 94*(3), 249–255.

Terhune, D. B., Cardeña, E., & Lindgren, M. (2011). Dissociative tendencies and individual differences in high hypnotic suggestibility. *Cognitive Neuropsychiatry, 16*(2), 113–135.

Underwood, H. W. (1960). The validity of hypnotically induced visual hallucinations. *Journal of Abnormal and Social Psychology, 61*, 39–46.

Wagstaff, G. F., Toner, S., & Cole, J. (2002). Is response expectancy sufficient to account for hypnotic negative hallucinations? *Contemporary Hypnosis, 19*(3), 133–158.

Young, W. C. (1988). Dissociation and psychodynamics: All that switches is not split. *Dissociation, 1*(1), 33–38.

NOTES

1. Braude, 2000, 2003. I cover some of the same ground more briefly in this book, in chapter 6.
2. Braude, 1995.
3. Braude, 1995; Gauld, 1982.
4. Gauld, 1992, p. 447.
5. Janet, 1901, pp. 9–10; Myers, 1903, vol. 1, p. 45.
6. Janet, 1901; Myers, 1903, p. 10. The translation is from Myers, 1903, vol. 1, p. 45. It's more idiomatic than Corson's 1901 translation.
7. Oakley, 1999, p. 244.
8. Gauld, 1992, p. 446; Hilgard, 1986, p. 97.
9. Orne, 1962, pp. 218–219.
10. See, e.g., Lamas & Valle-Inclán, 1998; Spiegel, 2003; Spiegel, Cutcomb, Ren, & Pribram, 1985; Terhune, Cardeña, & Lindgren, 2011; Wagstaff, Toner, & Cole, 2002. For some interesting recent, but not really relevant, studies of the Stroop effect, see Kirsch, 2011; Kosslyn, Thompson, Costantini-Ferrando, Alpert, & Spiegel, 2000; Oakley & Halligan, 2010; Raz & Campbell, 2011; Raz, Fan, & Posner, 2005; Raz, Kirsch, Pollard, & Nitkin-Kaner, 2006; Raz, Moreno-Íñiguez, Martin, & Zhu, 2007; Raz, Shapiro, Fan, & Posner, 2002.
11. Spiegel, 2003.
12. Oakley & Halligan, 2002.
13. Myers, 1903, pp. 44–45.
14. Oakley, 1999, p. 246. See also Barber & Calverley, 1964; Pincus & Tucker, 2003; Underwood, 1960.
15. Orne, 1962, p. 218.
16. Bryant & McConkey, 1989a, 1989b, 1989c; Oakley, 1999.
17. Hilgard, 1987, p. 255.
18. See Orne, 1959, 1962, 1971, 1972; Marks, Baird, & McKellar, 1989. For analogous results in the case of hypnotic blindness, see Bryant & McConkey, 1989a, 1989b.
19. Orne, 1972, p. 427.
20. Similar reservations about the clarity and importance of the concept of trance logic have been expressed by Hilgard, 1987, pp. 254–256.
21. Orne, 1972, p. 428.
22. They write,
Many of the reals [i.e., genuinely hypnotized subjects, as opposed to simulators] who experienced hypnotic blindness seemed to approach the overall situation as a problem-solving task, in which they had to use whatever strategies were personally appropriate to achieve the desired effect of experiencing blindness in addition to performing as well as they could on the decision task with which the hypnotist confronted them. (Bryant & McConkey, 1989a, p. 76)
23. Bernheim's account is quoted verbatim in Binet, 1896, pp. 305–308.
24. Binet, 1896, p. 305.
25. Binet, 1896, p. 307.
26. Also quoted in Binet, 1896, pp. 312ff.
27. Ross, 1997, p. 93.
28. Kluft, 2000, p. 267.
29. Ross, 1997, p. 80.
30. Young, 1988, p. 35.
31. Kluft, 2000, p. 267.
32. Braude, 1995, 2009.
33. Kluft offers a very helpful list of possibilities in Kluft, 2000, pp. 267–268.
34. See Braude, 1995 for a comparison of dissociation with repression in connection with this case.
35. Braude, 1995.

Chapter Five

Multiple Personality and Moral Responsibility

THE CHALLENGE OF ASSIGNING RESPONSIBILITY

By now, the philosophical literature on multiple personality/dissociative identity disorder (DID) is substantial enough to include several book-length treatments of the topic.[1] And for the most part, that literature has focused on traditional problems concerning the nature of persons, personal identity, and psychological explanation. It's easy enough to see why that is. On the surface at least, multiples appear to be more than one person or more than one intentional agent. That is, in some sense obviously requiring explanation, multiples seem to be a community of distinct individuals, each (or at least many) of which can act intentionally and whose actions we can—and often do—evaluate in the same way we assess the actions of nonmultiples. Of course, the intriguing conceptual challenge is to figure out what exactly is going on, and so the philosophical focus on the metaphysics of multiplicity is completely understandable. But I find it equally intriguing that philosophers have paid relatively little attention to problems of responsibility in these cases.[2] Probably, that's because they believe that ethical questions about multiplicity can be settled only after first resolving the metaphysical issues surrounding personal identity.[3] And if so, then I believe these writers are mistaken, and one of the primary objectives of this chapter is to explain why that is.

We can begin by noting that questions about responsibility in DID cases can be every bit as challenging as questions about identity and personhood. And arguably the most vexing and peculiar of those questions is: In what respect(s) and to what extent should a multiple be held responsible for the actions of his or her alternate personalities/identities (or *alters*)? Unlike questions about personhood and identity (or metaphysical questions generally), this isn't simply an abstract matter we can ponder at our leisure. On the contrary: clinicians treating multiples *must* decide whether it's appropriate— or even just therapeutically beneficial—to hold their patients (or specific alters) responsible for behaviors they apparently can't control or remember. Similarly, our courts must occasionally decide whether to hold a defendant claiming to be a multiple guilty for actions committed by one or more alters. And in these cases the legal issues can be dramatic, if not bizarre. Consider: When a multiple faces criminal prosecution, what sort of individual is standing trial? An alter or the multiple as a whole? Should courts consider the subject being questioned on the stand to be different from the subject who is accused of committing the crime? If so, other questions come immediately to mind. For example, would it be appropriate for each alter of a criminal defendant to have separate legal counsel?

Contrary to what some might think, these are not frivolous questions. And they're merely the tip of the iceberg. Moreover, their solutions have implications extending beyond the courtroom. Consider the following passage from Ralph Slovenko, who asks:

> Should a search or arrest warrant be issued for each personality? Must a *Miranda* warning be given to each personality of a suspect with MPD? May the other personalities exclude evidence on the ground that they were not properly read their rights at the time of the arrest? Would each one of the personalities have to waive his or her rights, or would one waiver be sufficient? Does the doctrine of double jeopardy bar the trial of a personality when another has been put to trial? Must each personality testifying at trial be sworn in and administered the oath?[4]

Jennifer Radden describes the legal questions arising over DID and responsibility as "pragmatic and consequential, as compared to those arising in a therapeutic context."[5] But that's not quite right. The legal questions have obvious parallels both in clinical situations and also in personal contexts— say, between friends or members of a family, one of whom is a multiple. These seem equally pragmatic and consequential; it's simply that our answers to the legal questions tend to be more far-reaching. Nevertheless, it matters greatly whether (or to what extent) a DID patient should be held responsible for the problematic (e.g., counter-therapeutic) behavior of a single alter. Similarly, moral considerations about sexual consent arise not only in connection with the alleged date rape of a multiple but also in the context of a marriage to a multiple. For example, what if—during intercourse—the multiple switches to an underage alter or simply to an alter who's an unwilling sexual partner? And just as the legal community must consider the propriety of punishing multiples in criminal cases, analogous questions arise when a multiple's friend (or spouse) wonders how to deal with the hostile (or insensitive) behavior of a single alter. Is anger appropriate, and if so, toward whom should the anger be directed? Here, too, we may be unsure how to assign responsibility for an alter's behavior and to what extent we should treat different alters as if they're distinct moral or prudential agents.

As I noted, some think that we should settle questions concerning responsibility for an alter's actions by appealing to the identity (or lack of it) between the alters themselves or between the alters and the multiple as a whole. Presumably, the underlying intuition is this. In general, we don't hold a person responsible for the actions of another. So if alters are really significantly distinct—both as subjects and agents—from each other and also from the multiple as a whole, then the same standard should apply. That is, barring certain kinds of exceptions, alters shouldn't be held responsible for things done by *another individual*.

But that strategy doesn't seem very promising. To see why, let's begin by considering how problems of responsibility arise in relevantly similar cases less dramatic than DID. In particular, let's consider if we should hold an individual responsible for what he or she thinks, feels, or does while dreaming. An alternate strategy might be to consider responsibility for behavior that occurred prior to a major change in attitude or character—for example, of the sort that tends to occur in the transition from youth to adulthood or by means of an ideological or religious conversion. However, unlike cases of dissociation (and certainly cases of DID), those transitions are relatively permanent once they've occurred. So since this chapter is focusing on a condition in which apparent identity shifts can occur frequently, the case of dreaming should provide a richer and more relevant basis for comparison.

RESPONSIBILITY AND DREAMING: AUGUSTINE'S DILEMMA

Suppose I dream about wanting to kill my wife or that I have a dream in which I perform the action of killing my wife. Am I responsible for the murderous thoughts or actions in the dream? Or (in a truly grim scenario) suppose that while dreaming about killing my wife, my body moves so violently in my sleep that I inadvertently injure her or beat her to death. Can I be held responsible for those actions?

In his *Confessions* (X, 30), Saint Augustine worried about such matters (although he focused more on carnal than on homicidal impulses). As far as his sexual urges and rational capacities were concerned, he noted that he thought and acted quite differently during his dreams than he did when awake. So Augustine wondered if there was some crucial respect in which he was a different self while dreaming. As it happens, he didn't resolve that question clearly one way or the other. Nevertheless, he concluded that the difference between sleeping and waking is so great that "because of this difference, I was not responsible for the act [dreamed during sleep]." But then he added, "although I am sorry that by some means or other it happened to me."[6]

Augustine's concern about whether he's the same person while asleep falls within a venerable philosophical tradition regarding the concept of identity. Since antiquity, philosophers have wondered whether (or at what point) the inevitable changes to a thing over time influence its identity—that is, whether in virtue of those changes it becomes a different thing. That's why Heraclitus said one can't step into the same river twice. As I noted, it's unclear whether Augustine believed that his identity actually changed as he moved from waking to sleeping (and vice versa). Nevertheless, he clearly took that possibility seriously, and he certainly regarded the changes to be profound enough to justify disavowing responsibility for what occurred during sleep. So (to see where it leads) let's suppose that Augustine decided he was *not* the same individual when he slept and that it's because of that shift in identity that he's entitled to disavow responsibility for what happened during his dreams. This will help us bring important issues into focus.

Notice, first of all, that if we read Augustine this way, then his expression of regret seems not just peculiar but difficult to interpret. We're understanding Augustine to say that Waking-A is a different individual from Sleeping-A and, therefore, that the former isn't responsible for the feelings or actions of the latter. But then Augustine (i.e., Waking-A) says that he regrets the experiences and deeds of Sleeping-A. Granted, we often say that we regret things done by others. But Augustine's regret isn't the externalized regret of a mere spectator. After all, Waking-A concedes that the experiences and deeds of Sleeping-A "happened to me" (i.e., Waking-A). So Augustine seems to be expressing what Bernard Williams called "'agent-regret,' which a person can feel only toward his own past actions (or, at most, actions in which he regards himself as a participant),"[7] and which can be directed not only to voluntary but also to involuntary or accidental forms of agency. But then it seems that Augustine's position is inconsistent. On the one hand, he disavows responsibility for dreams of fornication and ensuing erections or orgasms on the grounds that it wasn't he who did those things. But on the other hand, he regrets the dreams and their physical or physiological by-products because they were *his* dreams, *his* erection, etc.

Probably many readers sympathize with certain features of Augustine's dilemma. They might agree that we're not responsible for thoughts or actions during sleep, even when we're justified in feeling regretful, remorseful, or guilty over them. In fact, apart from the concerns over possible changes in identity, Augustine's case seems analogous to Williams's example of the truck driver who, through no fault of his own, runs over a pedestrian. Even if we don't hold the driver responsible for the pedestrian's death, we'd expect the driver to regret his involvement in the tragedy. In fact, we'd probably consider him to be morally defective, or at least we'd regard him with suspicion, if he felt nothing but the sort of external or detached regret that a spectator would feel over the incident. But then how should we resolve Augustine's dilemma? How can we disavow responsibility for the things *we* did and which *we* regret without counterintuitively claiming at the same time that *someone else* was the agent?

One strategy would be to say that moral judgments or reactions are appropriate or inappropriate only relative to a context or background and that different sorts of moral assessments rest on different presuppositions. For example, perhaps we justify feelings of remorse, guilt, and so on along different lines than assignments of responsibility. So perhaps the different identity assumptions in the two cases aren't really incompatible, provided they're made relative to different backgrounds of needs and interests. In other words, perhaps from one perspective it's appropriate to claim that two individuals are identical, while from a different perspective we can plausibly and appropriately deny that identity. If so, then Augustine's position would be no more logically or conceptually suspect than the position people often adopt toward multiples they know well—namely, acknowledging that alters count as different in some situations but not in others. For example, people in established relationships with a multiple might consider two alters to be different within the contexts of gift giving and establishing friendships but the same as far as social security numbers and voter registration is concerned. In fact, it's almost impossible to have a functioning relationship with a multiple without shifting between identity assumptions in this way. Besides, as I've noted in other chapters in this book, it's commonplace and unproblematical to regard two things as the same for certain purposes but not for others. Sameness and similarity aren't static or inherent relations obtaining between two things.

Unfortunately, this gambit probably won't help us understand Augustine because it's questionable whether he ever considered affirming and denying his identity to Sleeping-A relative to different (and apparently incommensurate) contexts. After all, it's within a single context of evaluating what he admits is *his own* dream that Augustine simultaneously disavows responsibility and feels regret. So perhaps the lesson to be learned here is that issues of sameness or identity over time simply don't play as pivotal a role in the determination of responsibility as Augustine makes it appear. So long as Augustine (Waking-A) concedes that Sleeping-A's thoughts (or erection) happened to him (i.e., Waking-A), then perhaps he needn't (and shouldn't) disavow responsibility for Sleeping-A's thoughts or deeds on the grounds that Waking-A and Sleeping-A are profoundly distinct. Perhaps there's some other reasonable justification for disavowing responsibility in such cases, one that would eliminate the need to adopt separate and at least superficially incompatible positions regarding our identity over time.

That's not to say that concerns over problems of identity have no place in moral deliberations. Indeed, some philosophers have argued that these concerns arise even in relatively humdrum cases.[8] It's just that, in this context at least, worries about identity may be less appropriate or fruitful than some have thought. In fact, so long as agent regret of the sort experienced by Augustine is understandable and even *commendable*, it may not even be coherent to disavow responsibility for one's earlier offenses by disavowing one's identity to the offender.

In that case, an obvious alternative strategy is simply to avoid notoriously tricky issues of identity altogether and to see whether more widely recognized requirements for responsibility will do the job instead. Not surprisingly, however, writers on responsibility disagree over which (if any) of these more familiar conditions is most important, and they differ over how, precisely, those conditions should be formulated. But ignoring those debates and subtleties for the moment, it's fair to say that philosophers generally agree that requirements for assigning responsibility fall into two broad classes.[9] To be responsible for one's actions, one must satisfy both a metaphysical (or causal) requirement and a cognitive requirement. According to the first, an agent is responsible only for actions that are voluntary or for states of affairs whose occurrence the agent could have controlled and prevented. And according to the second, agents are responsible only if they possess certain reflective or rational capacities—for example, the capacity to evaluate the relevant moral and nonmoral features of actions and to act *on the basis of* moral reasons.

Therefore, one way to avoid Augustine's dilemma would be to say that dissociative agents can be held responsible only for thoughts and actions they can control or evaluate rationally. That's why we routinely disavow responsibility for mental states or behaviors that were produced coercively or surreptitiously—say, by overwhelming physical force, drugs, or brainwashing. And it's why we say that children, who can't properly evaluate their actions, aren't morally responsible for what we'd regard as intolerable behavior in adults.

So this approach adheres closely to our customary and relatively trouble-free methods of assigning or accepting moral responsibility. Ordinarily, what matters is whether the agent could control and rationally evaluate the state of affairs in question; considerations about identity seldom (if ever) play a role. In fact, that's true even in the case of dreaming. Generally speaking, when I claim that thoughts or actions during a dream were my own, I make no unusual assumptions about personal identity. On the contrary, questions about identity over time are usually irrelevant to our moral self-assessments, no matter whether we're dealing with the things we do or feel while dreaming or the things we did or felt while awake five minutes ago or yesterday. In both cases, we tend to be straightforwardly concerned with things *we* did or experienced.

The importance of Augustine's dilemma, then, is that it illustrates an apparently major drawback to determining moral responsibility in cases of dissociation on the basis of controversial assumptions about personal identity generally or identity over time specifically. By following our hypothetical Augustinian strategy, it's needlessly (and perhaps insuperably) difficult to account for our quite reasonable remorse, guilt, etc., over things we supposedly didn't do or experience. But as we've just seen, we can avoid this awkward position altogether (rather than simply accept it grudgingly) by assigning responsibility, as we usually do, on the basis of our ability to control and evaluate our thoughts and actions.

RESPONSIBILITY AND DREAMING: A FREUDIAN AMBIGUITY

Freud's approach to the issue of moral responsibility for our dreams leads to a rather different set of insights.[10] Unlike Augustine, Freud wasn't troubled or confused by problems of personal identity. Instead, Freud stumbled over an ambiguity in the term "responsibility." Although it's not clear what Freud's view might have been had he recognized the ambiguity, his discussion raises issues that merit our attention.

First, Freud argued that there's no problem of responsibility for the *manifest* content of dreams. "The manifest content is a deception, a *façade*. It is not worth while to submit it to an ethical examination or to take its breaches of morality any more seriously than its breaches of logic or mathematics."[11] The relevant dream content for which moral responsibility is an issue, he noted, is the set of *preconscious* thoughts that express themselves in the symbolic or otherwise deceptive manifest content of the dream. Then, after arguing that most dreams are either straightforward or indirect "fulfilments of immoral—egoistic, sadistic, perverse or incestuous—wishful impulses,"[12] Freud writes,

> Obviously one must hold oneself responsible for the evil impulses of one's dreams. . . . Unless the content of the dream (rightly understood) is inspired by alien spirits, it is part of my own being. . . . [I]f, in defence, I say that what is unknown, unconscious and repressed in me is not my "ego," then I shall . . . perhaps be taught better . . . by the disturbances in my actions and the confusion of my feelings. I shall perhaps learn that what I am disavowing not only "is" in me but sometimes "acts" from out of me as well.[13]

So according to Freud, we can't disown these evil impulses any more than we can disown the id from which they originate or the behavior caused by and expressing or revealing those impulses.

Finally, Freud made some interesting comments about what it is to have a moral conscience. Evidently, he intended his remarks to apply to ordinary folk who neither desire nor attain Saint Augustine's powers of self-examination and self-criticism. Nevertheless, they extend surprisingly well to Augustine's exalted moral torments. Freud writes,

> If I . . . tried to decree that for purposes of moral valuation I might disregard the evil in the id and need not make my ego responsible for it, what use would that be to me? Experience shows me that I nevertheless *do* take that responsibility, that I am somehow compelled to do so. Psycho-analysis has made us familiar with a pathological condition, obsessional neurosis, in which the poor ego feels itself responsible for all sorts of evil impulses of which it knows nothing, impulses which are brought up against it in consciousness but which it is unable to acknowledge. Something of this is present in every normal person. It is a remarkable fact that the more moral he is the more sensitive is his "conscience." . . . This is no doubt because conscience is itself a reaction-formation against the evil that is perceived in the id. The more strongly the latter is suppressed, the more active is the conscience.[14]

So Freud and Augustine apparently agree on at least one important point. They both hold that we feel regret or remorse for the content of our dreams because we recognize that they're *our* dreams—that is, that the person who feels regret is the person who had the dream. But whereas Augustine (apparently inconsistently) disavows responsibility for the dream content on the grounds that the dreaming and waking selves are *not* identical, Freud maintains that we're responsible for dreams because what is dreamed "is a part of my own being."

But Freud's position suffers from a serious ambiguity, which both his followers and detractors sometimes appear to have overlooked. Consider the following comment by psychiatrist Seymour Halleck. "Freudian therapy . . . [holds] patients to a negligent, as well as intentional, standard of responsibility. The patient in psychoanalysis is repeatedly reminded that he/she is responsible for what he/she forgets, and is even held responsible for slips of the tongue."[15] Whether or not Halleck presents an accurate picture of psychoanalysis (or at least current psychoanalysis), his remarks help bring the relevant ambiguity clearly into focus. First, there should be no doubt that slips of the tongue can reveal one's hidden thoughts and feelings. However, it seems equally obvious that people might be unable to control or avoid making Freudian slips. But if slips of the tongue are outside the agent's conscious control, in what sense can we justifiably hold someone responsible for them?

Undoubtedly there are a number of worthwhile ways to draw distinctions between kinds of responsibility. But for present purposes we need to identify only two forms of responsibility. According to the first, which we may call *weak responsibility*, let's say

- (RESP$_w$) S is weakly responsible for X provided that X is both properly attributable to and is caused by S.

According to the second, which we may call *strong responsibility*, let's say

- (RESP$_s$) S is strongly responsible for X only if S can control whether or not he or she Xs.

These two senses of "responsibility" correspond to two respects in which a mental state or action is (to use Freud's expression) "part of my own being." We could call them *weak ownership* and *strong ownership*, respectively. Presumably, strong responsibility (ownership) entails weak responsibility (ownership), but the latter doesn't entail the former.

Therefore, although it's sufficient for S's being weakly responsible for X that X is properly attributable to and is caused by S, that's not a sufficient condition for strong responsibility. In that case it's also necessary that S be able to control whether or not he or she Xs. That's why a person may be weakly, but not strongly, responsible for Freudian slips or for things experienced or done while dreaming. Moreover, the ability to control whether or not one Xs is still not sufficient for being strongly responsible for X. It's still necessary that the agent possess and be able to use certain reflective or rational capacities. Nevertheless, the criterion of control seems to be the crucial criterion distinguishing strong from weak responsibility. That's because the difference has to do with whether (or to what extent) S should be regarded as an *agent*. Although the inability to evaluate one's actions is clearly important to many legal and moral deliberations, one's moral ignorance, naivete, or depravity doesn't (or at least needn't) *undermine* one's behavioral control. It determines only how, or to what extent, that control is guided by one's values or one's ability to make moral discriminations.

Now it should be clear that although we may be weakly responsible for the content of our dreams or for Freudian slips, that may not be a form of *moral* responsibility. Culpability, blameworthiness, and praiseworthiness are moral categories that seem to apply only to cases in which we're strongly responsible for (i.e., able to control or evaluate) our thoughts and actions. But in that case, the title of Freud's little essay, "Moral Responsibility for the Content of Dreams," is misleading, because the sort of responsibility he identifies is merely weak responsiblity. He doesn't argue that people can control or prevent the impulses of the id, slips of the tongue, and so on. So Freud's position turns out to be closer to that of Augustine than we might have expected. Both Augustine and the Freudian ego feel regret, remorse, or guilt over states for which they may be weakly—but not strongly—responsible.

We can see, then, that the distinction between weak and strong responsibility offers another way of stating the solution to Augustine's dilemma: We may understandably regret or feel remorse or guilt over things for which we're weakly responsible and for which we would rather have been bystanders than participants. But no culpability attaches to dream contents or their by-products (e.g., erections) unless we're also strongly responsible for them. Similarly, one way to clarify Freud's position would be to note that although we may be weakly responsible for impulses of either the id or the ego, we're strongly responsible only for those we can control or prevent.

I should also emphasize that a sufficient condition for weak responsibility is a *conjunction* of two related but distinct conditions—namely, (a) that X is properly attributable to S and (b) that X is caused by S. So it's unclear what to say about a case in which only one of those conditions is satisfied—say, when X is properly attributable to S even though we wouldn't identify S as its cause. For example, suppose we identify a prison cellmate or a scheming lover as the cause of S's homicidal thoughts (i.e., as the person who, so to speak, put those thoughts into S's head). Should we hold S to be weakly responsible for those thoughts? Augustine might say "yes" on the grounds simply that they happened to S, whereas Freud might demur on the grounds that the thoughts weren't so much the product of S's id as they were the products of another person. I prefer to leave this matter unsettled here (and I certainly don't want to become embroiled in matters of Augustinian or Freudian scholarship) because no matter which approach to weak responsibility we accept, our primary concern here is with strong responsibility and the associated issues of culpability and control.

So the value of Freud's view for the present discussion is that it supplements the lesson learned from Augustine's dilemma. By—inadvertently—highlighting the distinction between strong and weak responsibility (ownership) for one's thoughts and actions, it illustrates in a different way how one can disavow moral responsibility for a dissociated state without attributing that state to a different individual.

COMMENTS ON THE CLINICAL LITERATURE

In a moment, we'll consider how the preceding considerations shed light on the problem of responsibility in cases of DID. But first, we should note how the topic has been handled in the clinical literature. Two articles in particular deserve our attention, the first by legal scholar Ralph Slovenko, the second by psychiatrist Seymour Halleck.

In the former, we find the following contentious passage:

> How should multiple personality or other dissociative disorders be regarded under the law? The law is based on the concept of an individual as a unity.

> Whatever the psychological validity, legal theory requires "one body, one person, one personality"; otherwise, society would be unmanageable. Ultimately a person must take responsibility for whatever number of personalities he may have, if for no other reason than that the core personality is dominant in apparently all cases of multiple personality.[16]

This passage is problematic for several reasons, empirical and philosophical. First, it seems to be clinically naive. Slovenko mentions a core personality; but it's unclear whether he's referring to an alter, to some clearly identifiable underlying residue of the predissociative self, or perhaps to some unifying self that undergirds the phenomena of DID. In either case, however, it's false to say that "the core personality is dominant." If by "core personality" Slovenko means an underlying unifying self (e.g., a Kantian ego), *that* self (if there is one) is certainly not dominant in any interesting sense; that's why the person is a multiple. (In a moment, I'll return to the question of what "dominant" might mean here.) Of course, by "core personality" Slovenko might be referring to an alter personality; but if so, the claim is still false. In many cases of DID there simply *is* no single dominant alter personality; contingent and uncontrollable external circumstances often determine which alter is in executive control.[17]

Moreover, there are two coercive reasons for concluding that the notion of a core personality is problematical. First, a multiple's attributes (i.e., the person's pre-dissociative set of skills, capacities, and character traits) get distributed among alters. And second (and even more important), a multiple's inventory of alters may evolve (sometimes more than once) into novel functional divisions.[18] So no alter can reasonably count as a core personality in virtue of having an especially clear link to the predissociative self. In fact, we can only arbitrarily identify a single alter as a unique or privileged descendent of the predissociative self. So if Slovenko's ambiguous claim about a core personality is a crucial presupposition of his overall view on responsibility in cases of DID, that view rests on very thin ice.

Besides, even if the claim were true, it's unclear why anything would follow about the multiple's responsibility. Slovenko says that the multiple "must take responsibility for whatever number of personalities he may have." Now considering that Slovenko is concerned about responsibility for criminal behavior, that claim is at least curious, and it seems to miss the point. One would have expected Slovenko to focus on the multiple's responsibility for the actions of his or her alters, not for the number of alters in the multiple's system of personalities. But it doesn't matter which sort of responsibility Slovenko meant to single out. In either case it's implausible to claim that the multiple is responsible *because* some core alter personality is dominant. For one thing, saying that an alter personality is dominant means only that the alter is in executive control of the body at present or perhaps simply most of the time. But that sort of dominance indicates nothing about whether the multiple could control how many alters he or she has. Similarly, it indicates nothing in particular about the degree of control or influence the dominant alter has (or had) over other alters. In many cases, it appears that no such control exists. In fact, an alter's dominance at a given time may result from nothing more than a fortuitous set of external conditions that triggered the alter's appearance or allowed it to continue. That alter might be relatively unimportant to or ineffectual within the total system of alters. Besides, dominant alters are often dominant only for relatively short periods of time—seldom over the entire period of multiplicity.

Furthermore, it's equally unclear what it would mean to say that an underlying core self (*not* alter) is dominant in cases of DID. The most plausible interpretation of that claim would be that the adaptational nature of DID must be explained relative to an underlying unified self. I'd say that claim *is* correct;[19] but it doesn't presuppose or require that the multiple has any relevant degree of control over the processes of alter formation or switching. It means only that any adequate causal explanation of alter formation and switching must take into account the underlying experiences and needs of the multiple. Although in chapter 4 I argue that these kinds of adaptation often require creativity and resourcefulness, in many cases at least they don't seem to demand the degree of control we exert over most of our everyday behavior. Alter formation seems to be a response to unbearable pressure or pain, and while it undoubtedly engages some of the multiple's cognitive and volitional resources, to a great extent it also seems reflexive, bypassing the deliberation and evaluative capacities many regard as essential for moral responsibility. In fact, in cases where there's reliable evidence for the chronic or ritual abuse of multiples, it appears that alter formation and switching may have been deliberately and coercively controlled by the abusers. So to the extent one can even make sense of Slovenko's claim that the core personality is dominant, it doesn't follow that the multiple has control over and responsibility for "whatever number of personalities he may have." In any case, that conclusion seems plainly false.

It's less clear what to say about the multiple's control over switching and the subsequent behavior of alters. Clinicians experienced in treating DID generally agree that DID patients *can* be induced to control "acting out" or other forms of counter-therapeutic behavior, including (presumably) unsolicited switching and additional alter creation. But it's still unclear which agent(s) are responsible for that control—that is, whether the control should be attributed to one or more influential alters or to the multiple himself or herself. Besides, clinical reports don't suggest that multiples (or their alters) have a similar level of control *outside* the relatively safe therapeutic setting in which the multiple both trusts and depends on the therapist. But in that case, multiples might still not qualify as responsible agents prior to therapy or in forensic or everyday settings, where switching may remain generally spontaneous and uncontrollable, vulnerable to the unpredictable demands of daily life. So in these contexts at the very least, Slovenko's claim that the multiple is in control seems to be unwarranted. But even if that claim were true, it's still a non sequitur; it doesn't follow from the claim that alter formation and switching must be explained in terms of the multiple's needs and interests. The appeal to a background of needs and interests helps explain both controllable and uncontrollable behaviors.

Interestingly, Slovenko's comment about a core personality closely resembles a remark made by French and Shechmeister, about which alters can and should be represented by council. They claim,

> We find no legal basis for exclusion of the second personality as a representable entity . . . it appears that any personality presenting itself for representation before diagnosis of MPS [multiple personality syndrome] may gain at least initial representation but once a diagnosis of MPS has been established, the socially identified primary personality will be represented and all others will be ignored as symptoms of his illness. Indeed, "He who hesitates is lost!"[20]

The trouble with this position is that the very *concept* of a primary personality is suspect and unclear, as many clinicians now realize. As I noted earlier, given both the temporary dominance and short life spans of many alters as well as the interesting fact that multiples often integrate (wholly or partly) and then divide again along novel functional lines, there's no clear way of identifying a personality that counts as historically primary.[21] So there's no reliable way to implement the authors' recommended criterion of representability.

Let's return, however, to Slovenko's article. At the beginning of the passage quoted above, Slovenko seems to be arguing that the concept of legal responsibility (possibly unlike that of moral responsibility) rests on the presupposition that there's only one person to a body. However, Slovenko greatly underestimates the complexity of the issues. For one thing, the concept of a person is hardly unambiguous, even from a legal point of view.[22] Moreover, Slovenko improperly suggests that there's a clearly identifiable entity, *legal theory* (or *the law*), to which one may appeal in this case. Granted, there's a single body of laws which we may consider to be *the* law, although of course different jurisdictions have different statutes. But more important, no set of laws uniquely determines its own meaning; our laws are open to numerous different interpretations. Indeed, it's the job of the courts to continually interpret the laws it enforces, as situations dictate. But in that case, legal theory, perhaps even more so than scientific theory, is an evolving and provisional set of statements whose interpretations are never universally accepted. In fact, one may regard the landmark decision in the Billy Milligan case as one of a number of attempts to refine and reconsider what, exactly, the law requires in connection with DID.[23] And because subsequent court decisions about DID in criminal cases haven't uniformly adhered to the precedent set in the Milligan case,[24] one could argue that *the law* (or legal theory) has no clear requirements at all in this area. So Slovenko's various appeals to "the law," what "the law is based on" and what "legal theory requires" all seem rather naive and simplistic. In fact, they seem to be little more than bare statements of just one of a competing set of legal intuitions.

A later article by Slovenko avoids his earlier contentious claims about core personalities and what the law requires, and it also presents a more balanced and thorough review of legal issues and opinions.[25] However, it indicates little (if any) evolution in Slovenko's grasp of the data of DID. For example, when describing the characteristics of alter personalities, he writes, "In each personality of the multiple personality, there is a distinct id, ego, and super-ego."[26] But Slovenko seems unaware that many (if not most) alters are distinctly lacking in depth and breadth as personalities. So that claim seems patently false, as are others that overestimate the complexity, differences, and relative independence of alters, especially in polyfragmented cases.[27] That's particularly unfortunate, because one would think that the distinctness and independence of alters is relevant to various questions concerning criminal responsibility. But Slovenko doesn't venture beyond the important but unanswered question, "To what extent is a sub-personality allegedly a minor really like a minor?"[28]

A somewhat different set of issues emerges from Halleck's article.[29] On the surface, Halleck seems sympathetic to the position that responsibility is linked to an agent's control over behavior, or (as Halleck puts it) the "capacity or lack of capacity to choose one form of conduct over another."[30] And he argues that "behavior that is highly susceptible to environmental influence . . . [is] under the control of the will."[31] But that criterion for deciding whether behavioral control exists is unconvincing and probably false.

First of all, in defending his criterion, Halleck resorts to a vague illustration of "environmental influence" that (at best) has only limited utility, and which in fact seems to be misleading. He writes,

> If a patient demonstrates noxious behavior only in a permissive, but not in a restrictive environment, we generally assume on empirical as well as on an intuitive basis that the individual has the capacity to control that behavior in either environment (although we may acknowledge that it is a harder choice for him/her to do so in a more permissive environment).[32]

Halleck is probably thinking of various familiar sorts of annoying behavior, and certain moderately permissive or nonpermissive environments in which people probably do have some control over their actions. He seems to be thinking of the sort of behavior we're strongly tempted to indulge in when we can get away with it but which we clearly have the ability to control and which we do, in fact, control when we're pressured to do so. For example, if an unruly child acts in a hostile way toward siblings except under threat of punishment, it's reasonable to suppose that the child can choose to act in a nonhostile way whether or not the threats are made. Similarly, it may be very difficult for some to control the temptation to shoplift when golden opportunities present themselves. Nevertheless, it's reasonable to suppose that such behavior is controllable whether or not those situations arise.

But in other sorts of cases, Halleck's claim seems transparently false. Consider a bad marriage, for example, in which one or both spouses are unable to behave in a loving or sexual way toward the other. It may be true that in a more nurturing relationship they could behave differently. But we can't conclude that within the presently existing repressive (nonpermissive) context of the marriage that either spouse could behave in a more loving or sexual way, even if they desperately wanted to. It would be pragmatically empty to say that control over those aspects of behavior is possible under the circumstances. That would be like the claim one often hears from some religious (and New Age) pundits, that all people are basically good, no matter how evil or reprehensible their behavior has been and no matter how incorrigible they seem. The claim is empty because for many people nothing we could reasonably be expected to do will elicit that alleged goodness and change their behavior.

One problem, then, is that the term "environmental influence" is broad and covers many sorts of cases in which responsibility and control are actually diminished. Both control and permissiveness come in degrees, and (as the above examples suggest) some environments are considerably more nonpermissive than others. In fact, they may be coercive or so restrictive that the individual has little or no control over relevant aspects of behavior.

So perhaps it's not surprising that Halleck fails to note that behavior that can be triggered by external cues is likewise behavior "susceptible to environmental influence." And that behavior may be no more controllable than behavior occurring in other highly repressive environments. Granted, the coerciveness of environmental cues may differ from other forms of coercion—say, being physically forced to fire a gun despite one's best efforts to resist. Nevertheless, as far as moral responsibility is concerned, the coerciveness of environmental triggers is equally significant. They might still be overwhelming in their visceral and emotional impact, and reactions to them might even be involuntary and automatized (as the result, say, of chronic or ritualized abuse or brainwashing).

But perhaps more important, Halleck appears tacitly to endorse an indefensibly skeptical position regarding DID, which he betrays in his emphasis on permissive environments (and apparently rather routinely permissive environments at that). He treats the phenomena of DID as if they were merely types of naughty behavior, as if they occurred in a setting that allows patients to *get away with* behaving like a community of alters. But that approach is antecedently biased against taking DID seriously. It fails to countenance the clear body of evidence indicating that DID is adaptational and that trauma or abuse *impels* subjects to develop the symptoms of multiplicity, at least in the initial stages of the disorder. It also seems to ignore cases in which new alters are created iatrogenically in response to intensely frightening situations arising in the course of treatment, whether competent or incompetent.[33] Granted, once a multiple has entered therapy and the majority of alters recognize that they're alternate personalities, the multiple (or those alters) may be able to exert at least some control over switching and other unacceptable behavior as well as future splitting into additional personalities. At that point, clinicians presumably have some influence over how much self-destructive, countertherapeutic, or simply self-indulgent behavior the patient can "get away with." But that situation is significantly different from times when the patient develops and utilizes alters in a desperate struggle for psychological survival. So it would have been more illuminating, sensitive, and responsive to the data for Halleck to consider the relevance of coercive and other highly *non*permissive environments. In fact, it's ludicrous to think that we permit people to *become* multiples in anything like the way we allow children to misbehave or potential felons to shoplift.

RESPONSIBILITY AND DID

Let's change course, then, and consider whether our earlier discussion of Augustine and Freud guides us toward a sensible position on DID and responsibility. There, we explained the appropriateness of regret for our dreams and slips of the tongue by observing that they're things that happen to *us* even if we can't help ourselves. We noted, in other words, that they're things for which we're at least weakly responsible. We also saw that we can justifiably disavow responsibility for our dreams and Freudian slips without denying that those things are ours and without raising classic puzzles about identity through change or over time. In those cases, it's enough to note that we simply couldn't help ourselves—that is, that we were unable to control the things we now regret. So we've seen that we can determine responsibility in certain cases akin to dissociation without making unusual assumptions about identity. Now let's consider whether we should take a similar position with regard to DID.

On the surface, however, it may seem as if DID demands a different and possibly more radical kind of treatment, because the splits in DID are deeper and more enduring than in dreaming. After all, it's presumably a mere figure of speech to say it was not I who had that dream, or that "I was not myself" when I dreamed those things. Moreover, in some therapeutic and everyday contexts, we *are* justified in treating alters as distinct subjects and agents. So although the possibility of behavioral control may still be important in assigning responsibility for an alter's actions, in the case of DID problems of agent identity seem to loom larger.

Nevertheless, I submit that the familiar criteria of control and rationality are still the main criteria in deciding matters of responsibility in cases of DID, despite the dramatic nature of the phenomena. I suspect we simply tend to forget this in connection with DID and suppose instead that issues about identity matter more. Perhaps that's because DID seems to raise questions about identity *quite apart from* the contexts in which we're concerned about moral responsibility. But those are questions about identity perhaps only a philosopher could love. They're generally too arcane and abstract to play a role in more urgent clinical and everyday deliberations about moral responsibility. At those times, what really matters are refractory empirical questions of control and rationality. For example, can alter A (or the multiple himself or herself) control alter B's thoughts and behavior? Can alter B evaluate its own behavior, or can alter A or the multiple himself or herself do so instead? In fact, these sorts of questions matter *whether or not* we're *ever* justified in identifying A (or the multiple) with B.

But that means only that the similarities between DID and a vast range of other cases (dissociative and nondissociative) are more extensive than some might have thought. In virtually all cases (dissociative and nondissociative), moral responsibility for a certain thought or action X hinges (to varying degrees) on the possibility of being able to control or evaluate X. Granted, it may not be easy to decide when those conditions are satisfied. But that problem is hardly unique to cases of DID. DID is simply one of a large variety of cases in which it's difficult to determine the extent of an individual's ability to control and evaluate his or her thought and behavior.

At any rate, if rationality and behavioral control (rather than identity through change) are what matter in determining responsibility in cases of DID, then we may be in a position to understand the relevance of amnesia to those deliberations. Of course, on the surface it seems as if we must again raise questions about personal identity. Amnesia appears to be a situation in which a temporal stage S_{t1} of a person doesn't recall something done by an earlier temporal stage S_{t0}. But is this important to moral assessments because it suggests that in some crucial respect $S_{t1} \neq S_{t0}$? One might think so, because in the history of philosophy the most ancient concern about identity is whether changes in a thing's temporal stages are changes in the identity of the thing itself. However, if we've been on track in downplaying the importance of identity considerations in connection with moral responsibility, perhaps we should adopt a similar strategy here. But if so, then in what respect can an agent's amnesia for past actions play a role in moral evaluation?

Before answering that question, however, we should note that in cases of DID, amnesia isn't really what's at issue. In fact, the term "amnesia" tends to be used improperly in connection with dissociation, and it certainly isn't the appropriate term to describe the epistemic barriers apparently existing between alternate personalities. As Adam Crabtree observed,

> If dissociation is a sorting process, then the various psychic units or personalities that exist within the individual are *not* subject to "amnesia." In dissociation there is no forgetting, no loss of memory. To forget one has to first be aware of something and then lose the awareness of that thing. That is not what occurs in dissociation. The various psychic units *never had knowledge* of the experiences assigned to the other units and so could not *forget* them.[34]

Crabtree seems to be right about this. Forgetting presupposes losing something one had already—not simply an occurrent state, but a disposition, an ability to recall. However, alters (psychic units) don't seem to stand in that sort of epistemic relation to the mental states of other alters. Instead (judging by approximately one hundred years of clinical scrutiny), an alter's access to the mental states of another alter is more like that of one *person* to another. That's one reason why DID is so interesting and so extreme as compared to other forms of dissociation. It seems that alters don't forget what other alters know any more than I can forget what you know.

Of course, when you and I know the same thing (i.e., a piece of information or proposition), there *is* a sense in which I can forget something you know. But strictly speaking, what I forget in those cases is the information or proposition *I* previously knew. I should add, however, that some alters seem to have knowledge of the *experiences* of other alters as they occur. Moreover, this knowledge seems to be different from the way I can know of your experiences. In fact, descriptions from multiples make it sound more like a kind of telepathy; it's as if another's experiences are had from a different first-person viewpoint. But even in these cases (assuming, perhaps contentiously, that they're described accurately) it would be wrong to say that one alter strictly speaking can forget the experiences of another. That would be possible only if both alters had exactly the same first-person viewpoint.

At any rate, if the term "amnesia" applies at all to cases of DID, it would presumably describe an epistemic relation between the multiple and some (but not all) alters. Suppose alter *A* commits a crime. Suppose also that alter *B* is aware of *A*'s action but that alter *C* is not. We might say that the multiple has amnesia for the crime *with respect to C* but not with respect to *A* and *B*. Although this way of describing things will undoubtedly sound strange to some, perhaps it's really not objectionable. We might simply have to concede that, at least in cases of DID, some of a *person's* epistemic states have an otherwise unprecedented and complex relational structure.[35]

At any rate, the epistemic barriers between alters are similar in a crucial respect to the amnesic barriers occurring between earlier and later temporal stages of a single person. Just as S_{t1} currently lacks epistemic access to certain (past) states of S_{t0}, alter A has no epistemic access to certain states of B. But of course it's precisely that barrier that seems to raise questions of responsibility and also of identity. So whether we call it amnesia or not, our present concern is whether that kind of epistemic inaccessibility plays an important role in moral evaluation.

One reasonable answer it that is raises issues not of moral responsibility but rather of *accountability*. These terms are often used interchangeably in the legal and clinical literature. But there's an important distinction to be made by treating them as distinct technical terms. To see why, let's tentatively accept Jennifer Radden's formulation of the distinction:

> X is accountable for A just when there being reason to believe X did A entitles us to an explanation and justification of A. X is [morally] responsible for A just when it is appropriate to blame X for A.[36]

Now consider how we can apply this distinction. Suppose that S_{t1} now has amnesia for actions performed earlier by S_{t0}, and suppose that S_{t0} had been able to control and evaluate those actions. In that case, we might want to say that if S was responsible at the time for those earlier deeds, S is responsible for them now. But, we might add, S isn't presently accountable for the actions. After all, a person unable to remember a past deed certainly can't explain or justify it. So it would appear that moral responsibility for past deeds doesn't require continuity of memory. By contrast, accountability for one's past actions may be undermined by nothing more than temporary amnesia. (Of course, as Radden correctly argues, accountability might also be undermined by other and sometimes more devastating forms of impairment or incapacitation.) Accountability thus seems to be fragile and potentially intermittent in a way responsibility is not.

However, responsibility and accountability have an important feature in common. Although it's easy to construct imaginary cases (perhaps not plausible ones) in which our attributions of responsibility and accountability depend primarily on considerations about identity, in the vast majority of cases—and certainly real-life cases—concerns over identity play only a peripheral role at best. Generally speaking, we don't have to contend with nagging puzzles about personal identity when we hold a person responsible but not currently (or no longer) accountable for things which *that person* did previously.

If these considerations are on the right track, then we might also want to say that a multiple may be held responsible for actions of which he or she now has no memory, or of which some alters but not others have no memory. Here, too, epistemic inaccessibility undermines accountability only, although how and to what extent it does so is by no means clear. We might say that certain alters aren't accountable for the actions of others, and perhaps we could even say that the multiple himself or herself is accountable with respect only to certain alters. But however interesting these matters might be, our present concern is with moral responsibility and DID. All we need to observe for now is that moral responsibility doesn't seem to be undermined by the epistemic inaccessibility found in amnesia and, in a slightly different way, in cases of DID. Granted, those losses of memory might affect a multiple's ability to testify in court or aid in his or her own defense. But they don't seem to bear on the multiple's guilt or culpability.

So how *do* we determine responsibility in cases of DID? Considering that we sometimes (or often) need to treat alters as distinct agents and subjects, perhaps we should appeal to distinct and possibly conflicting *levels* of responsibility. And we could do that in two obvious ways. We could identify different levels of responsibility either within the system of alters or with respect to the multiple as a whole. In the first case, responsibility for an action might attach to some alters but not others, whereas in the second case the multiple might be responsible *relative to* certain aspects of the case but not others.

The first of these two options is the more straightforward. But we should remember that it applies only to contexts in which we can justifiably treat alters as distinct moral or prudential agents. For example, suppose that alter *A* is either ineffectual or ignorant with regard to another alter, *B*, who behaves very badly. That is, suppose (on the one hand) that *A* can't control *B*'s behavior or (on the other) that *A* is either unaware of that behavior or else too cognitively or morally immature or naive to evaluate *B*'s actions. In that case, we might want to say that *A* isn't responsible for what *B* does. Nevertheless, we might want to hold *B* responsible for its actions and insist that our anger, condemnation, and so on for unacceptable behavior is appropriate when directed toward *B*.

But how, if at all, should we assign responsibility to the multiple himself or herself? This, after all, is the pressing question that clinicians and courts must confront when weighing various penalties or treatment strategies. If the multiple has no influence over which alter is in executive control of the body—for example, if switching is generally an instinctive or involuntary response to contingent and uncontrollable external conditions—we might decide that the multiple can't then be held responsible for what an alter does. That seems to be the thrust of the decision reached in the Billy Milligan case. But one could also adopt what we might call the *luck-of-the-draw* strategy.

That is, we could decide that the multiple's responsibility should be assigned to the alter in executive control at the time of the offense, and therefore that a multiple's responsibility for his or her actions can change over time. So if that alter is morally or conceptually impaired, naive, or unsophisticated or if the alter was the victim of uncontrollable impulses to act, we might say that the multiple isn't responsible for the alter's actions. But if the alter in control can govern and evaluate its own behavior, we could hold the multiple responsible for the alter's behavior. That seems to be the decision reached in the Grimsley case, in which the court ruled:

> The evidence fails to establish the fact that Jennifer [an alter] was either unconscious or acting involuntarily. There was only one person driving the car and only one person accused of drunken driving. It is immaterial whether she was in one state of consciousness or another, so long as in the personality then controlling her behavior, she was conscious and her actions were a product of her own volition.[37]

However, the luck-of-the-draw strategy seems both simplistic and insensitive to the dynamics of the switching process. Most notably, it's difficult to apply to cases in which neither the multiple nor the currently dominant alter can prevent an intrusive alter's appearance and subsequent behavior. If it's true, as it often appears, that the multiple can't govern which personality controls the body at a given time, then it seems unfair to hold the multiple responsible for actions committed at that time. In what respect, we might wonder, could the multiple have done otherwise?

To help clear this matter up, we should note that at least two types of control seem to be at issue. The first is control over the switching process, or (more precisely) control over which alter is weakly responsible for the multiple's behavior. The second is control of that behavior by the alter weakly responsible for it. What needs to be considered, then, is (a) whether the multiple can control switching to alter A and (b) whether A can control its own behavior. Theoretically, at least, there are four options to consider. First, both the switching and the behavior are controllable. Second, the switching is controllable but the behavior is not. Third, the behavior is controllable but the switching is not. And fourth, neither the switching nor the behavior is controllable.

The easiest cases to deal with are obviously the first and last. If both switching and behavior are under control, then (other necessary conditions being satisfied) it seems reasonable to hold the multiple responsible for an alter's actions. And if neither switching nor behavior is under control, it seems equally reasonable to say that the multiple isn't responsible for the alter's actions. Case two is also fairly straightforward. Suppose, first, that the multiple is able to prevent alter A's appearance and, second, that A can't control its own objectionable behavior. In that case (other necessary conditions being satisfied), it seems reasonable to hold the multiple responsible for A's behavior. After all, even if A's behavior is out of control, the multiple could have prevented A from acting by preventing A from emerging or by switching to another alter.

Case three, however, is more troublesome. Suppose, first, that the multiple can't control the comings and goings of alter A and, second, that A can control its own behavior. For example, suppose that A's appearance results from uncontrollable environmental triggers. Suppose, also, that once A has emerged the multiple can't switch to a different alter until A voluntarily relinquishes control or until contingent external conditions trigger the process. In that case, it seems reasonable to conclude (contra Grimsley) that the multiple should not be held responsible for A's actions, even if in some sense or in some contexts A deserves to be held responsible for them. After all, alter A's behavior would presumably not have occurred if the switch to A hadn't taken place or if the multiple could have switched to another alter before A did any harm. But by hypothesis, the multiple had no such control over A's appearance.

Of course, in all these cases we're pretending that we can determine whether a multiple is able to control the switching process or the behavior of an alter. Obviously, real-life deliberations about responsibility would be greatly simplified if only there were a reliable way of figuring that out. But unfortunately, that remains an intractable empirical problem. As I noted earlier, some clinicians argue that when challenged to behave responsibly (say, under threat of cutting off treatment), the multiple's (or renegade alter's) behavior changes accordingly. So they conclude that the multiple as a whole has the ability, and therefore the responsibility, to make the entire system of alters conform to reasonable (or desired) standards of behavior. However, as I also observed, it's still unclear whether (or to what extent) the subsequent compliant behavior should be attributed to the person as a whole (or unity) or to one or more influential alters. But perhaps more important, it's still unclear to what extent the multiple has a comparable level of control outside the therapeutic setting. That level of control may only be possible within the fragile context of trust and dependency with a therapist. And if so, it may be false to say that the multiple is responsible *generally* for what his or her alters do.

Moreover, many of the clinicians who adopt this hard-line approach also concede that it may still be difficult to elicit compliant behavior from the multiple. It may simply be that the strategy of demanding compliant behavior is the best strategy currently known. So we might be justified, from a largely pragmatic point of view, in regarding the multiple as only marginally (or perhaps only theoretically but not practically) responsible for an alter's emergence and subsequent behavior, especially outside the therapeutic setting.

And in that case, we might prefer to determine moral responsibility only at the level of behavior of specific alters.

As if these options and complications weren't enough, another difficulty deserves consideration. Some writers on responsibility argue that people may be so corrupted or impaired by life that they've lost the ability to properly evaluate the moral and nonmoral features of their actions. As Randolph Clarke puts it, they may be "morally malformed" through no fault of their own.[38] For example, some might respond to childhood trauma by becoming insensitive to their own feelings and the feelings of others and therefore also incapable of psychological intimacy. To the extent that people suffer this sort of numbing of sensibilities or character, they seem unable to act on the basis of moral reasons. They seem unable to appreciate fully and take seriously the contexts in which they act and the effects of their behavior on others. Therefore, some would argue that such people aren't responsible for their actions.

However, in the case of DID, it's unclear to what extent *and to which subject or agent* such numbing has occurred. Some alters seem better able than others to appreciate moral reasons and also to evaluate the relevant nonmoral features of their actions. But then it's not clear to what extent the *person* can make those evaluations satisfactorily. One might think (in the spirit of the Grimsley ruling) that if any alter can make those assessments, the person can, since ultimately the alter's abilities are those of the whole person from which they're drawn. But it may be that no alter has an adequate ability to evaluate its actions, no matter how robust its personality might seem over relatively short stretches of time. Although some alters are obviously more clearheaded and aware than others, we must remember that all multiples exhibit what I've termed "attribute-distribution" and "attribute-depletion," in which

> the traits and abilities manifested by or latent in the pre-dissociative personality begin to get distributed throughout the members of the personality system. Moreover, as alters proliferate, they apparently become increasingly specialized, and one is less likely to find any personality having the complexity or range of functions presumably possessed by the subject prior to the onset of splitting.[39]

But in that case, one would think that every alter is likely to be numb along some moral or relevant nonmoral dimension. And if so, there are two reasons for saying that the person as a whole is too morally impaired to be held responsible for his or her actions. First, the multiple can act only *as* or *through* an alter (at least much or most of the time). So if each alter's evaluative capacities are inadequate, then neither the alter nor the multiple should be held responsible for the alter's behavior. Second, and perhaps more important, if the multiple's full repertoire of evaluative capacities is divided among different alters, then it may be that the multiple as a whole can't judge actions in a suitably integrated and comprehensive way.

Indeed, multiples who experience robust integration for the first time as adults often report how novel it is to confront situations with a range of potential responses. For example, one multiple I know told me, with a combination of excitement and apprehension, how she now understood what it's like to experience indecision in everyday life situations. She illustrated this with an example from grocery shopping. Prior to integration, specific alters would emerge at different places in the store (e.g., child alters in the candy and cereal aisles), each perfectly clear about what to buy. But now, she said, she finds herself weighing her options and stopping to consider what to do. Of course, this is a trivial example compared to those of great moral import. But it illustrates nicely how a multiple's ability to act and evaluate situations can be limited by and distributed among alters.

While we're on the topic of a person's ability to evaluate his or her actions and the contexts in which they occur, another issue merits our attention. Consider, first, the following interesting example[40] of acting under a coercive threat. Suppose Pam is kidnapped and then ordered to participate in a crime. At first, she refuses, but then her captors threaten her. Initially, they threaten to harm Pam, and when that doesn't work they threaten to harm her family. Although Pam feels she can tolerate any suffering inflicted on herself, she can't bear the thought of her family being harmed. So she surrenders to her captors' demands and participates in the crime.

Suppose, however, that any outside observer, free from the stress Pam was experiencing, would have been able to tell that Pam's captors were bluffing when they threatened to harm her family. Suppose that the observer would have known from the way the kidnappers were talking that they didn't even know where Pam's family was. But because Pam was under such stress, she missed all the obvious verbal and behavioral clues and couldn't tell that her captors were bluffing. In that case, we may suppose that Pam's decision to commit the crime was based on a rational and intelligent evaluation of her predicament. She did the best she could under those trying conditions. Of course, Pam's assessment of her situation was seriously mistaken. But under the circumstances, it was the sort of mistake for which she could easily be excused.

This is a case in which a person has the relevant rational capacities (or ability to rationally evaluate a situation) but in which it would be unreasonable to expect her to avoid making the evaluative mistake she in fact makes. And if that's right, we're presumably not entitled to hold Pam morally responsible for her participation in the crime. As Clarke puts it, "We expect people to act responsibly in difficult situations, but only up to a point of difficulty. In extremely difficult situations, we sometimes excuse behavior we would ordinarily condemn."[41]

If this is correct, it has interesting implications for many cases of DID in which the multiple behaves objectionably under the pressure of psychological coercion or threat, whether real or imagined (e.g., as the result of expectations formed through a history of abuse or trauma). These, too, are cases in which even rationally well-endowed individuals might have trouble sizing things up properly. Of course, there are reasons for questioning the integrity of an alter's—or multiple's—evaluative capacities. But the importance of the example is that even if multiples *do* have the ability (at least under less stressful situations) to evaluate their behavior, they might not be able to make the right decision under the conditions in which they actually find themselves and that no one would be held responsible for the actions that result from those mistakes.

This reinforces the caveats, mentioned above, in connection with the success of the hard-line approach to therapy adopted by some clinicians treating DID. I noted earlier that even if patients stop acting out when their therapists demand it, that doesn't mean that they can always control their behavior. The dynamics and relative safety of the therapeutic environment might be uniquely conducive to behavioral control. But for similar reasons, that environment might also be one in which multiples are better able to evaluate their behavior rationally. If so, then it would be a mistake to assume that multiples are responsible agents outside of therapy, when they must deal with a wide range of contingent, unexpected, and potentially intimidating situations and environmental triggers.

The possibility that a multiple's evaluative capacities may be systematically impaired raises another pragmatic issue. It complements the considerations underlying the hard-line strategy, and it may also apply to friends or relatives of multiples. Suppose that we can't find any philosophical justification for treating multiples as responsible (whole) individuals, even in the therapeutic setting. Nevertheless, there's a reason why we might be justified in treating DID patients *as if* they're morally responsible individuals. It rests on the distinction between what we could call *causal responsibility* (weak or strong) and *taking responsibility* (i.e., taking charge). To see why, consider a strategy often taken with children as a means of developing their moral instincts and perceptions. We often recognize that small children lack the reflective capacities needed to evaluate and understand their actions and their consequences. But we often treat them as if they had those capacities, and we hold them blameworthy when their actions are objectionable. Usually, we recognize (or at least hope) that this approach helps them to develop the judgmental capacities and perceptual antennae (so to speak) necessary for acting responsibly later on. We assume that our strategy is an effective way of teaching children to *become* morally responsible individuals. We assume, in other words, that by treating children as if they're causally responsible we're helping them learn how to take responsibility.

Perhaps a similar strategy would work with at least some cases of DID. When a child responds defensively to traumatic experiences by developing alternate identities, it's reasonable to think that the trauma might also leave the individual morally and cognitively damaged or immature. So perhaps some multiples need help in developing the reflective capacities and dispositions necessary for acting responsibly, both in and out of the therapeutic setting. Perhaps we can help them to become responsible by treating them as if they're responsible agents now. Of course, successful implementation of this approach would be no easier to interpret than it would be in the case of the hard-line strategy discussed earlier. That is, we may be unable to determine whether success is attributable to one or more alters or to the multiple himself or herself. But that theoretical frustration must take a back seat to more urgent practical matters.

One more point, concerning a rather specific type of moral responsibility. As before, let's begin by considering the topic of dreaming. In many cases, we're justified in treating our dreams as revelations (even if only symbolic) of otherwise hidden needs and impulses. But suppose those dreams indicate the existence of potentially dangerous (e.g., homicidal) impulses within me. Is there a sense in which I might be morally responsible for the dreams, even if I can't control or prevent them? One plausible answer would be that we have a responsibility to acknowledge and in some way deal with or neutralize those impulses. That is, to the extent we're able to control those impulses in the future and prevent them from leading to a wrongdoing, we have a responsibility to see that those impulses cause no harm to another person and perhaps also to ourselves.

It also seems reasonable to adopt a similar position with regard to DID. Although clinicians are divided on the issue, let's grant (at least for the sake of argument) that a multiple (or an alter) might be unable to control or prevent another alter's actions. Even so (we might argue), once a multiple (or alter) has knowledge of, say, a dangerous alter, that knowledge generates the obligation *to do what one can* to prevent harm from occurring. So to the extent that this sort of knowledge is genuinely empowering, a multiple (or alter) might have a kind of moral responsibility for an individual's future— but not past—behavior. But then we're faced once again with a nagging and possibly unanswerable empirical question: How much control does this sort of knowledge actually give a multiple (or alter) over another alter's actions?

IDENTITY AGAIN AND THE RELEVANCE OF METAPHYSICS

I've argued in this chapter that the best way to handle the problem of assigning responsibility in cases of DID is to set aside philosophical concerns over the identity or distinctness of a multiple's alters. I'd now like to approach from a different angle the claim that in order to get clear on DID generally—or at least the related issues of responsibility—we must get the metaphysics right. And getting the metaphysics right means having an account of selfhood or personal identity from which the relevant problems and puzzle cases can be more or less neatly resolved.

Consider, then, how several authors recently have addressed the topic of responsibility and alter identities from the vantage point of a prior view on personal identity. For example, Walter Sinnott-Armstrong and Stephen Behnke claim, with regard to legal responsibility, that "a court's choice cannot be separated completely from metaphysical questions of personal identity"[42] and that it's "crucial to determine whether the alters in a case of MPD really are different persons in a relevant way."[43] Similarly, Steve Matthews and Jeanette Kennett consider the debate over responsibility and DID to be, at its core, a debate over the merits of the multiple persons and single person theses regarding DID. Matthews writes,

> According to the multiple persons thesis, a patient with DID has one body that contains quite literally more than one person. . . . According to the single person thesis, individuals with DID have a disorder that has the effect of fragmenting one's existing personality. The patient is to be regarded morally and legally as a single person whose psychiatric symptoms, among other effects, cause delusions of identity. The alleged alter personalities are not to be thought of as literally separate persons, but rather states in which patients lose control of what they are doing, and are globally deceived about who they are.[44]

I should note that in one paper, Kennett and Matthews state the multiple-persons thesis in a clearly unacceptable way. They claim that the thesis "entails that *each alter* is a separate agent, morally autonomous, a subject apt for praise and blame, a potentially independent social actor with moral and legal rights and responsibilities."[45] Perhaps this was simply stated carelessly, but in any case it's a straw man. No one who knows anything about DID would claim that *all* alters deserve this status, especially in polyfragmented cases where we might find alter fragments apparently created for very specific tasks which at one time the multiple found intolerable and into which she or he dissociated more or less reflexively. Thus, alter fragments may do nothing more than clean toilets, bake cookies, or receive enemas. I'll say more below about Kennett and Matthews's unsatisfactory treatment of polyfragmented cases.

At any rate, Sinnott-Armstrong and Behnke defend the single-person thesis, and Matthews and Kennett do so as well, albeit somewhat ambivalently.[46] By contrast, Kathleen Wilkes, Jennifer Radden, and Elyn Saks seem to be proponents of the multiple-persons thesis, though that, too, is not entirely clear.[47]

But I find it very unhelpful to frame the issues as forcing a choice between the single-person and multiple-persons theses. In fact, I consider both theses to be nonstarters. I've argued elsewhere[48] that personhood is not one thing and, moreover, that there's no context-independent or culture-independent conception of a person. On the contrary, in some cultures, the (to us) familiar one body/one person presumption is not the default presumption even for normal cases. And even in cultures where one body/one person is the default presumption, context plays a central role in determining whether we treat DID patients as one person or many. Granted, it's appropriate to assign DID patients only one driver's license or social security number. But at least for those who have to live (or otherwise interact closely) with a multiple, some contexts require different criteria of individuation—say, promise keeping, gift giving, or deciding whether one should have sex with a spouse's alter. Like the question "How many things are in this room?" the question "Is *S* a single person or multiple persons?" has no answer *at all* apart from a situation in which the question is relevant and certain criteria of individuation seem more apt than others. But in that case, neither the multiple-persons nor the single-person thesis is true generally or in the abstract.

To simplify matters, let's focus just on moral responsibility, and let's consider first the single-person thesis. According to that thesis, we should always treat a DID patient as a single person morally because DID patients merely behave and appear *as if* they are more than one person. So no matter how dramatic the patient's dissociative state—for example, no matter how sharply and broadly characterized an alter might be, Matthews claims that "the patient is to be regarded morally and legally as a single human person."[49] Similarly, Kennett and Matthews write, "We regard alters as persons in altered states, and no more; . . . the person with DID is deluded about who s/he is, and so it is, in the morally relevant respects, merely as if there was another person in control."[50]

However, this seems difficult to reconcile with many urgent contexts in which people feel they *must* treat alters as distinct subjects and moral or prudential agents. Presumably, partisans of the single-person thesis would say that because multiples are merely behaving as if they're more than one person, we can—and, in fact, sometimes do—treat alters *as if* they're distinct persons, knowing all along that they're not. But that would be a kind of *feigned* concern for the alters at best, not the gut-wrenching response that can so easily be provoked by dealing with a multiple.

Consider: when I treat a young child in the disapproving way I'd treat an older person in order to help teach the child correct behavior, it doesn't feel to me *as if* the child is older. Similarly, when I—with good reason—knowingly treat a coworker, spouse, or parent as if (s)he is smarter, or kinder, or more creative, understanding, or reasonable than (s)he really is, my behavior doesn't reflect how I really feel. It's playacting, and I know it. But that's simply not how life is for the husband who feels it's wrong to have sex with a child alter of his wife (but not some other alter), or the person who refuses (perhaps out of fear) to let certain alters drive the car, buy groceries, or handle finances, or the one who sees the need to give alter-appropriate gifts at Christmas, or the person who knows not to discuss certain sensitive issues with particular alters, or the one who withholds certain foods from alters suffering from relevant food allergies. The fears or concerns here are very real and robust. What's striking about real-life interactions with alters is that those situations often compel us to treat alters the same way we treat nonmultiples. Indeed, whether or not we have any view at all about the nature of persons, we often apply the same criteria of individuation to alters as to nonmultiples. This was noted also by Daniel Dennett and Nicholas Humphrey, who wrote, "The grounds for assigning several selves to [a multiple] *can be as good as—indeed the same as—those for assigning a single self to a normal human being.*"[51] I'd say that's because what often matters to us about alters is exactly what matters to us, usually, about ordinary, nondissociated people (I'll say more about this below).

The multiple-persons thesis seems to have analogous deficiencies so long as it maintains that morally and legally, a multiple should *always* be considered as having "one body that contains quite literally more than one person." If so, however, that view errs in the opposite direction (as it were) from the single-person thesis. It doesn't adequately accommodate familiar situations in which it's obviously appropriate, if not mandatory, to treat multiples as single persons. These include the usual candidates, such as issuing driver's licenses and social security numbers,[52] and also the challenge faced by therapists trying to help their patients learn to stop coping dissociatively with problems in life.[53] Interestingly, however, these are cases where our feelings about the multiple may *not* match our behavior. Our everyday interactions with multiples might strongly impel us to treat them as several persons. Still, we might reasonably feel that certain contexts demand something different from us.

That last point highlights an interesting disparity between the multiple-persons and single-person theses. There are clear cases, legally and practically, in which treating multiples as single persons seems obviously to be the proper course of action, even for partisans (such as they are) of the multiple-persons thesis. But there are no such *widely recognized* clear cases requiring us to treat multiples as more than one person or prudential agent—however urgent that course of action might seem to those who interact closely or intimately with the multiple. Perhaps that reflects only the difference between those who, from a comfortable distance intellectually and psychologically, think about what it's like to interact with multiples and those who must contend with that challenge on a daily basis and who inevitably establish different relationships with different alters.

Kennett and Matthews have claimed that it's the "loaded language of 'alter personality' and 'host personality'" that is "partially responsible for the perpetuation of the Multiple Persons thesis."[54] That may be, but it hardly explains why people are often so deeply inclined to treat alters as distinct moral and prudential agents and subjects, even when those people are unfamiliar with the idioms in question. Perhaps Kennett and Matthews simply don't take seriously the exigencies of interacting with multiples. It's clear, though, that they don't appreciate the robustness of character that alters sometimes display. In fact, they make too much of my comments in *First Person Plural*[55] about attribute distribution and attribute depletion in DID and insist that alters are, apparently in every case, diminished to a degree that disqualifies them as distinct moral or prudential agents. They write, "Alter states are grossly abnormal and depleted states of a person."[56] Not only is that a misunderstanding of what I wrote, it also seems inattentive to the literature on DID describing the grubby realities of dealing with multiples in daily life. Contrary to what Kennett and Matthews seem to believe, alters are sometimes as robust personally and in command of their lives (while in executive control of the body) as many nonmultiples whom we would ordinarily consider to be responsible for their actions. (It's not necessary actually to know a DID patient to figure this out—though that certainly would help. It's enough to pay attention to what many have said about their relationships to the alters in their lives.[57]) Some ordinary people, not suffering from any psychopathology, are relatively one-dimensional, affectless, and uninteresting human beings. And some alters are distinctly richer than that as individuals—usually, those who've had some time to develop their character and connections in the world. It's possible (actually, fairly common) to deal with an alter for extended periods and not realize that anything is amiss. Alters may go undetected as such in the workplace, school, and even the intimacy of close friendships and marriages.

Probably, some of my misgivings over the importance some accord the single-person and multiple-persons theses can be traced to a difference in orientation over the philosophical analysis of concepts generally and the concept of a person in particular. Since space is limited, I'll have to wax dogmatic for a moment. To the extent we even have *a* concept of personhood or personal identity, it's loose and elastic, like most of our concepts. Moreover, our ordinary concept of a person (such as it is) is largely *normative* (what Locke called a "forensic" concept). It's important to realize that when we use the term "person" in ordinary life, we're not picking out a *natural kind*—that is, something whose nature scientific inquiry will decide (for example, something that inevitably links persons to the biological species *homo sapiens*). Ordinarily (in our culture, at any rate), we take persons to be (among other things) entities who presumably have (or could have) an inner life relevantly similar to our own, who have various rights and perhaps obligations, and who deserve our respect, consideration, and so on. And we embrace the normativity of this conception of personhood irrespective of our views (if any) about how persons might (or must) be configured biologically or otherwise—for example, whether dolphins, computers, brains in a vat, alters, or even disembodied spirits could be persons. So our ordinary concept of a person fundamentally carries ethical obligations or imperatives along with it. It concerns things we value about ourselves and each other, and it rests on various presuppositions about the ways others should be treated. In fact, I'd agree with Anthony Quinton[58] that what we value most about persons are their psychological traits and that this is why we're often content, in real-life situations, to make judgments about identity (for both DID patients and ordinary folk) on the basis of psychological criteria alone.

In fact, to suppose that abstract considerations about personhood and identity can, do, or should play any role at all in these practical deliberations (as the single-person and multiple-persons theses seem to require) is to elevate philosophy to a prominence in life it never has in fact, and arguably never should have. Indeed, if we had to settle abstract metaphysical issues before deciding how to attribute responsibility to or behave toward a multiple, we'd be no better off than Buridan's ass.[59]

Matthews later clarified his own position with regard to the single-person thesis as follows:

> At the level of philosophical theory we should regard . . . a DID patient as a single person. But obviously the personal, moral, or legal stance we adopt in our relations with others depends on a complex of issues, independent of the theoretical position taken on this metaphysical issue.[60]

Quite apart from whether I agree with Matthews about what philosophical theory requires, this seems right. But it also seems to concede the point I was making. In daily life most of us could care less about, or need to care about, or have any views about or interest in determining *what it is* to be a person. That metaphysical question about identity is either simply ignored or routinely trumped by real-life concerns, including—in the cases at hand—the challenges of interacting regularly with a multiple. What we deal with in life are epistemological or evidential (not metaphysical) questions of identifying and reidentifying others—that is, the grounds on which we decide whether an individual is the same as someone else. Ordinarily, we *need* to make on-the-spot decisions about whom we're dealing with, whether they're DID patients or more ordinarily troubled folk, and most of us make these urgent practical decisions without the aid (or hindrance) of a reasoned or articulated underlying metaphysics, much less proposed abstract criteria of identity.

In fact, most of us satisfactorily deal with these matters without having anything of interest or substance to say either about the nature of personal identity or about the empirical basis for our successful everyday judgments about identity. After all, most people know nothing about the metaphysics of identity, and those who do don't come close to a consensus on the issues. If a metaphysical theory plays any useful role at all, it might merely be to show how we *could* theoretically ground our successful practice of identifying persons. Moreover, most people are largely ignorant of the received medical, biological, or psychological considerations raised in connection with attempts to determine bodily or psychological continuity. Nevertheless, our strategies for identifying others are generally workable, and probably they've remained stable for millennia. At the same time, however, our prevailing philosophies and scientific background theories have changed profoundly. Apparently, then, we haven't been prevented, either by our ignorance, theoretical naivete, or shifting conceptual trends, from making successful judgments about identity.

So if our philosophical or scientific ignorance and theoretical naivete are no barriers to identifying persons, judging identity, and assigning responsibility in everyday cases, it's not clear why they should matter in connection with cases of DID. Granted, the cases are unusual and puzzling both practically and theoretically. But their oddness merely forces us to improvise solutions and strategies as circumstances require. And besides, not every puzzling case needs to be solvable, much less by means of general or abstract criteria. In any case, I proposed a workable strategy earlier in this chapter for assigning responsibility in cases of DID, a strategy that doesn't require settling any big metaphysical issues. Granted, the strategy will not always be easy to implement, but that's because the cases can be very difficult to unravel. However, that strategy is much more manageable than trying to resolve philosophical puzzles that have lasted for millennia.

If I'm right about all this, then it would seem that practical decisions about responsibility require *no general position whatever* on personal identity. But in that case, presumably what matters for determining responsibility in cases of DID are the issues about control and conceptual or moral sophistication that I discussed earlier in this chapter and also the four principal scenarios I outlined there concerning a multiple's control over both switching and behavior.

I should add that I did not, as Matthews alleges, subscribe to the single-person thesis in my book *First Person Plural*. What I defended in that book is a more modest, and I hope a deeper, position—namely, that we need to posit something like an underlying and unifying Kantian ego to explain the multiplicity of selves (or "apperceptive centers" as I called them) displayed in cases of DID. But I never claimed that this unifying subject meets *any* criteria of personhood. Perhaps it does, but if so, that would only be relevant in situations where we can ignore the distinct agendas and interests of specific alters, say, situations where we're focusing on the creativity necessary to maintain a dissociated state (as I discussed in chapter 4) and perhaps some (but hardly all) abstract philosophical discussions about what it is to be a person. And of course, there's nothing privileged about any of these contexts or the perspectives on personhood they require or encourage.

Finally, to avoid misunderstanding, I should mention that I'm not advocating the position articulated by some DID patients and (I would say, naive) therapists—namely, that it's either acceptable or preferable for those patients to resist integration of alters and thus to continue life as a multiple. I would still argue that integration of alters is desirable (when possible) and that it's preferable to face life's difficulties and challenges in a nondissociated state. Of course, life can be hard either way, and in fact integrated former multiples experience indecisiveness and internal conflicts to a degree that still-dissociated patients can often avoid by switching to appropriately focused or unidimensional alters. But multiples always run the risk of spontaneous and disastrous switching in response to uncontrollable external events. And as a result, they can only have a tenuous hold on life's most important relationships and responsibilities. So perhaps the goal of integration will be to attain a degree of psychological cohesiveness that makes it unnecessary to be treated so often as multiple persons.

REFERENCES

Bayne, T. (2002). Moral status and the treatment of dissociative identity disorder. *Journal of Medicine and Philosophy, 27*(1), 87–105.

Braude, S. E. (1995). *First person plural: Multiple personality and the philosophy of mind* (Rev. ed.). Lanham, MD: Rowman & Littlefield.

Clarke, R. (1992). Free will and the conditions of moral responsibility. *Philosophical Studies, 66*, 53–72.

Crabtree, A. (1992, June). *Multiplexity and the legal system: An historical overview.* Paper presented at the XVIIIth International Congress on Law and Mental Health, Vancouver, BC.

Dennett, D. C., & Humphrey, N. (1998). Speaking for ourselves. In D. C. Dennett (Ed.), *Brainchildren* (pp. 31–55). Cambridge: MIT Press.

Duff, R. A. (1996). Commentary on "Psychopathy, other-regarding moral beliefs, and responsibility." *Philosophy, Psychiatry, & Psychology, 3*(4), 283–286.

Fields, L. (1996a). Commentary on "Sanity and irresponsibility." *Philosophy, Psychiatry, & Psychology, 3*(4), 303–304.

Fields, L. (1996b). Psychopathy, other-regarding moral beliefs, and responsibility. *Philosophy, Psychiatry, & Psychology, 3*(4), 261–277.

Fields, L. (1996c). Response to the commentaries. *Philosophy, Psychiatry, & Psychology, 3*(4), 291–292.

Fischer, J. M. (1982). Responsibility and control. *Journal of Philosophy, 79*, 24–40.

Frankfurt, H. (1969). Alternate possibilities and moral responsibility. *Journal of Philosophy, 66*, 828–839.

Frankfurt, H. (1988). Coercion and moral responsibility. In *The importance of what we care about* (pp. 26–46). Cambridge: Cambridge University Press.

French, A. P., & Shechmeister, B. R. (1983). The multiple personality syndrome and criminal defense. *Bulletin of the American Academy of Psychiatry and Law, 11*, 17–25.

Freud, S. (1925). Moral responsibility for the content of dreams. In J. Strachey (Ed.), *The standard edition of the complete psychological works of Sigmund Freud* (Vol. 19, pp. 131–134). London: Hogarth.
Gert, B., & Duggan, T. J. (1979). Free will as the ability to will. *Noûs, 13*, 197–217.
Greenspan, P. S. (1978). Behavior control and freedom of action. *Philosophical Review, 87*, 225–240.
Gunnarsson, L. (2010). *Philosophy of personal identity and multiple personality.* New York: Routledge.
Halleck, S. L. (1991). Dissociative phenomena and the question of responsibility. *International Journal of Clinical and Experimental Hypnosis, 38*, 298–314.
Kennett, J., & Matthews, S. (2002). Identity, control and responsibility: The case of dissociative identity disorder. *Philosophical Psychology, 15*, 509–526.
Kennett, J., & Matthews, S. (2003a). Delusion, dissociation and identity. *Philosophical Explorations, 6*(1), 31–49.
Kennett, J., & Matthews, S. (2003b). The unity and disunity of agency. *Philosophy, Psychiatry, & Psychology, 10*, 305–312.
Keyes, D. (1982). *The minds of Billy Milligan.* New York: Bantam.
Kluft, R. P. (1989). Iatrogenic creation of new alter personalities. *Dissociation, 2*, 83–91.
Lewis, D. O., & Bard, J. S. (1991). Multiple personality disorder and forensic issues. *Psychiatric Clinics of North America, 14*, 741–756.
Matthews, S. (2003a). Blaming agents and excusing persons: The case of DID. *Philosophy, Psychiatry, & Psychology, 10*, 169–174.
Matthews, S. (2003b). Establishing personal identity in cases of DID. *Philosophy, Psychiatry, & Psychology, 10*, 143–151.
Mele, A. R. (1990). Irresistible desires. *Noûs, 24*, 455–472.
Parfit, D. (1973). Later selves and moral principles. In A. Montefiore (Ed.), *Philosophy and personal relations* (pp. 137–169). London: Routledge & Kegan Paul.
Parfit, D. (1984). *Reasons and persons.* Oxford: Oxford University Press.
Perr, I. N. (1991). Crime and multiple personality disorder: A case history and discussion. *Bulletin of the American Academy of Psychiatry and Law, 19*, 203–214.
Putnam, F. W. (1989). *Diagnosis and treatment of multiple personality disorder.* New York: Guilford.
Quinton, A. (1975). The soul. In J. Perry (Ed.), *Personal identity* (pp. 53–72). Berkeley: University of California Press.
Radden, J. (1989). Chemical sanity and personal identity. *Public Affairs Quarterly, 3*, 64–79.
Radden, J. (1996a). Commentary on "Psychopathy, other-regardiing moral beliefs, and responsibility." *Philosophy, Psychiatry, & Psychology, 3*(4): 287–289.
Radden, J. (1996b). *Divided minds and successive selves.* Cambridge, MA: MIT Press.
Rovane, C. (1998). *The bounds of agency: An essay in revisionary metaphysics.* Princeton: Princeton University Press.
Saks, E. R., & Behnke, S. H. (1997). *Jekyll on trial: Multiple personality disorder and criminal law.* New York: New York University Press.
Sinnott-Armstrong, W., & Behnke, S. H. (2000). Responsibility in cases of multiple personality disorder. *Philosophical Perspectives, 14* (Action and Freedom), 301–323.
Slovenko, R. (1991). How criminal law has responded in multiple personality cases. *Psychiatric Times, 3*(11), 22–26.
Slovenko, R. (1993). The multiple personality and the criminal law. *Medicine and Law, 12*, 329–340.
Torem, M. (1989). Iatrogenic factors in the perpetuation of splitting and multiplicity. *Dissociation, 2*, 92–98.
Van Inwagen, P. (1978). Ability and responsibility. *Philosophical Review, 87*, 201–224.
Wilkes, K. V. (1988). *Real people: Personal identity without thought experiments.* Oxford: Oxford University Press.
Williams, B. A. O. (1976). Moral luck. *Proceedings of the Aristotelian Society Supp., 50*, 115–135.

Wilson, P. E. (1996). Sanity and irresponsibility. *Philosophy, Psychiatry, & Psychology, 3*(4), 293–302.
Wolf, S. (1980). Asymmetrical freedom. *Journal of Philosophy, 77*, 151–166.
Wolf, S. (1986). Self-interest and interest in selves. *Ethics, 96*, 704–720.
Wolf, S. (1990). *Freedom within reason.* New York: Oxford University Press.
Zimmerman, M. J. (1988). *An essay on moral responsibility.* Totowa, NJ: Rowman & Littlefield.

NOTES

1. Braude, 1995; Gunnarsson, 2010; Radden, 1996b; Rovane, 1998; Wilkes, 1988.
2. Primarily Radden, 1996b and law professor Elyn Saks (Saks & Behnke, 1997), but also Kennett & Matthews, 2003b; Matthews, 2003b; Sinnott-Armstrong & Behnke, 2000.
3. And they're not alone in holding that view. For example, Tim Bayne considers the metaphysical and moral status of alter identities in connection with the claim that eliminating alters through therapy amounts to their murder. See Bayne, 2002.
4. Slovenko, 1991, pp. 22, 25.
5. J. Radden, 1996b, p. 117.
6. Compare this translation from R. S. Pine-Coffin (Penguin Books, 1961) with that of V. J. Bourke (Mentor, 1963), who renders the passage as follows. "By the very remoteness of our state now and then, [we] discover that it was not we who did something which was, to our regret, somehow or other done in us." The former stresses the concept of responsibility while the latter emphasizes that the dreaming and waking self are not identical. A more recent translation by H. Chadwick (Oxford University Press, 1991) does neither. In Chadwick's version, Augustine says, "From the wide gulf between the occurrences and our will, we discover that we did not actively do what, to our regret, has somehow been done in us." However, Chadwick's translation (like the others) makes Augustine's concerns about identity a few sentences earlier quite clear. Moreover, all three translators seem to agree that Augustine wished to express remorse or regret of some sort for what happened to *himself* during sleep.
7. Williams, 1976, p. 123.
8. For example, Parfit, 1973, 1984; and see Wolf, 1986 for an interesting criticism.
9. See, e.g., Clarke, 1992; Fischer, 1982; Frankfurt, 1969, 1988; Gert & Duggan, 1979; Greenspan, 1978; Mele, 1990; van Inwagen, 1978; Wolf, 1980, 1990; Zimmerman, 1988. For discussions focused squarely on responsibility and psychopathology, see, e.g., Fields, 1996b, 1996c and the commentaries, Duff, 1996 and Radden, 1996a, and also Wilson, 1996 and the commentary, Fields, 1996a.
10. Freud, 1925.
11. Ibid., p. 131.
12. Ibid., p. 132.
13. Ibid., p. 133.
14. Ibid., pp. 133–134.
15. Halleck, 1991, p. 307.
16. Slovenko, 1991, p. 25.
17. Braude, 1995; Putnam, 1989.
18. Braude, 1995.
19. See Braude, 1995 for a defense of that position.
20. French & Shechmeister, 1983, p. 24.
21. Braude, 1995.
22. Ibid., chap. 8.
23. Keyes, 1982.
24. See, e.g., Lewis & Bard, 1991; Perr, 1991.
25. Slovenko, 1993.
26. Ibid., p. 330.
27. Braude, 1995.
28. Slovenko, 1993, p. 338.

29. Halleck, 1991.
30. Ibid., p. 303.
31. Ibid.
32. Ibid.
33. See, e.g., Kluft, 1989; Torem, 1989.
34. Crabtree, 1992, p. 8.
35. Radden appropriately takes a similar view in connection with responsibility. She writes, "To answer the overall question 'Was he responsible?' with 'He both was and was not (responsible)' is to offer an answer that is neither incomprehensible nor inaccurate. . . . It means simply that the public person comprising both selves was responsible, while the separate selves included one or some who were not responsible. This answer becomes unhelpful and incoherent only in the pragmatic context of a legal system, where such judgments must result in legal consequences." Radden, 1996b, p. 118.
36. Radden, 1989; Saks & Behnke, 1997, p. 66.
37. Quoted in Lewis & Bard, 1991, p. 744
38. Clarke, 1992.
39. Braude, 1995, p. 57.
40. Borrowed from Clarke, 1992.
41. Ibid., p. 60.
42. Sinnott-Armstrong & Behnke, 2000, p. 304.
43. Ibid., p. 305.
44. Matthews, 2003b, p. 143. See also Kennett & Matthews, 2002, 2003a, 2003b; Matthews, 2003a.
45. Kennett & Matthews, 2002, p. 510, italics added.
46. In Matthews, 2003b and Kennett & Matthews, 2002, the single-person thesis is stated without qualification. But in Matthews's reply to commentators on the former paper, Matthews, 2003a, and in a later paper with Jeanette Kennett (Kennett & Matthews, 2003a), we find a more nuanced position. There, they endorse the single-person thesis for *modern* highly fragmented cases of DID (i.e., having many alters) but flirt noncommittally with the multiple-persons thesis in some older cases of dual personality. Thus, Kennett and Matthews claim that "the earlier cases in which, as it were, two separate, developed and functioning characters built different lives from a common body, pose a genuine philosophical puzzle and challenge to common sense ideas of individuation," p. 33. And see Matthews, 2003a, p. 171.
47. Radden, 1996b; Saks & Behnke, 1997; Wilkes, 1988.
48. Braude, 1995.
49. Matthews, 2003b, p. 144.
50. Kennett & Matthews, 2002, p. 511.
51. Dennett & Humphrey, 1998, p. 54, italics in original.
52. Interestingly, it's not so easy to prevent multiples from oversubscribing, under different identities, to magazines or other publications. I know the editor of one publication by, for, and about people with DID, who faced this problem routinely.
53. See the final chapter of Braude, 1995.
54. Kennett & Matthews, 2002, pp. 511–512.
55. Braude, 1995.
56. Kennett & Matthews, 2002, p. 519.
57. It's surprising, then, to see how Kennett and Matthews answer the question "How many persons are there in modern cases of DID?" as if one could figure out the matter by pure conjecture alone, as a bit of armchair philosophy. They write, "There are plausibly two possible answers: in general we think one person is present, though in extreme cases, say where more than one hundred personalities or personality states are claimed, the count may be none. Why do we think the count may be none in extreme cases? *It is likely* that an individual body manifesting a psychology so thoroughly fragmented simply could not pass any reasonable test of personhood" (Kennett & Matthews, 2003a, p. 34; italics added). What surprises me is their saying "It is likely that," as if not enough is known about the structure of polyfragmented cases to answer the question. It doesn't take much searching in the literature to know that even in polyfragmented cases, many alters are robust—certainly enough so to pass for ordinary persons

in many contexts. Those polyfragmented cases simply tend to have lots of fragmentary alters in addition to more regular and robust alters. Also, quite enough is known about how people *in fact* deal with multiples on a daily basis to say whether alters pass, *for them*, any reasonable test of personhood.
 58. Quinton, 1975.
 59. Who, unable to choose between two piles of hay, dies of starvation.
 60. Matthews, 2003a, pp. 172–173.

Chapter Six

Parapsychology and the Nature of Abilities

When they're in the stifling heat of theorizing, it's not unusual for philosophers and scientists to appeal, either explicitly or implicitly, to what they claim we know about human abilities. In fact, research in science and philosophy often relies on crucial (and frequently tacit and unexamined) assumptions about what abilities are—for example, which abilities (if any) count as fundamental or theoretically paradigmatic, and whether or how abilities are to be analyzed or explained. I've puzzled over this for many years because it seems obvious to me that the scholarly community is anything but clear when it comes to the nature of human (and other organic) abilities. And it seems equally obvious that gaining this understanding is a prerequisite to doing quality work in several areas of study. Indeed, my varied research interests have required me again and again to reconsider my own assumptions in this general area.

For example, I've examined the nature of abilities in connection with my research into hypnosis and dissociation generally and multiple personality/dissociative identity disorder (DID) specifically.[1] Of course, these phenomena are puzzling in many respects, but three of their features in particular seem to demand careful scrutiny: (1) the partitioning of competencies among alternate personalities, (2) the enhanced levels of functioning that some of those personalities exhibit, and (3) the exceptional performances of nonmultiples in hypnotic and other dissociative states.[2] My interest in the nature of abilities connects also to my study of savants and prodigies, who apparently have much to teach us about the limits (and perhaps also the latency) of human talent. And at bottom, I suppose, it connects to my general and long-standing concern with problems of psychological explanation, particularly in light of the gross inadequacies of trendy computational theories of the mind. (That's a topic I pursue in more detail in chapters 1 and 3.)

I've also spent a great deal of time considering how understanding human abilities is vital to our assessment of the evidence for postmortem survival.[3] And now I want to review the relevance of this topic to the data of parapsychology generally. Actually, I tackled this topic before, in a preliminary way,[4] and I've returned to the issues now thanks in part to a recent comment made to me by a past president of the International Remote Viewing Association (IRVA). He told me that many IRVA members don't like referring to people as "gifted" or "star" psychic subjects. That struck me as an odd position to take, especially since there are persuasive reasons for believing that what little we know about psychic functioning we've learned *only* from people who are clearly star or gifted subjects.[5] So it seemed to me that these IRVA members simply hadn't thought about their position very carefully or critically. In any case, I was determined to give the issues another once-over.

WHAT IS AN ABILITY?

Let's begin by looking at the enormous variety of things we ordinarily refer to as abilities The following list is clearly just the tip of the iceberg, and you'll see easily why the items on the list seem to have no interesting properties in common—much less, something like a set of necessary and sufficient conditions for being an ability. So consider the ability to:

- Play the violin
- Swallow
- Walk
- Draw people out in conversation
- Inspire loyalty in others
- Control pain through self-hypnosis
- Manipulate others through guilt
- Distinguish a curve ball from a slider
- Distinguish an offensive from a defensive basketball foul
- Write a heartfelt condolence letter
- Read acupuncture (chi) pulses
- Remain hopeful in the face of adversity
- Hammer a nail
- Call a hockey game play by play
- Learn new sports with ease
- Digest food
- Stand on one leg
- Read an orchestral score

- Foil a polygraph test
- Speak in front of an audience
- Remember people's names
- Mediate disputes
- Express sensuality
- Carry a tune
- Tell when someone is lying
- Fire an employee
- Learn a new language
- Laugh at oneself
- Laugh at other people's misfortune

A moment's reflection on the items above should make it clear that the term "ability," like most ordinary language expressions, has no single and preferred—much less clear and unambiguous—meaning. That's one reason why there's no interesting set of properties all the listed abilities share and that distinguish abilities from nonabilities. In one appropriate and also very common use of the term, "ability" can stand for rudimentary and more or less universal human (or organic) endowments. For example, we can speak of someone's ability to laugh, experience fear, express aggression or compassion, or merely breathe, blink, or move the muscles in one's arm. In this sense of the term, an ability needn't be any kind of proficiency or skill or disposition to exhibit such a proficiency.

But the term "ability" can also denote the considerable mastery or conscious development of more rudimentary attributes—for example, when we speak of a person's ability to play professional-level tennis, write a string quartet, dock a space capsule, or solve quadratic equations. "Ability" in this sense seems nearly synonymous with what we usually mean by "skill." Ordinarily, the rudimentary attributes enlisted and mastered here would be familiar competencies such as being able to move one's limbs or being able to track moving objects. But they could also be unique or exceptional endowments. For instance, someone possessing a third arm or extra fingers might develop novel and extraordinary abilities in the areas of musical performance or sports.

We can also distinguish an intermediate (and more difficult to characterize) sense of "ability," where we pick out competencies falling between low-level attributes such as the ability to see, wiggle one's toes, or hold one's breath, and the highly developed masteries of being an expert marksman or violinist. And within this intermediate category we can distinguish two principal variants or subsidiary meanings. According to the first, "ability" would denote endowments falling short of what we'd consider mastery but which are still more complex (or of a higher order) than (say) the ability to stand, utter sounds, or chew—for example, the ability to ride a bicycle, make people feel comfortable, deal courageously with one's shyness, remember phone numbers, poach an egg, or respond appropriately in conversation. Moreover, although these abilities may not be as prevalent or common as the more rudimentary endowments mentioned earlier, they may still be relatively widespread.

The second version of this intermediate sense of "ability" we might characterize as *dispositional*. We often speak of people with musical or athletic abilities who haven't yet harnessed those abilities in order to develop musical or athletic skills. For example, people who are musically gifted sometimes develop those gifts only relatively late in life (a good example is the early twentieth-century composer Albert Roussel, whose musical development began only after years spent pursuing a naval career). And in general, those with artistic talents don't exhibit them upon emerging from the womb. They must first mature physically to the point of being able to express those talents, and then usually they must undergo a certain amount of specific training if those talents are to be manifested fully. We could say that such people had artistic abilities, even before those abilities were expressed or developed to a high pitch.

These higher-order attributes, then, are dispositions in a sense similar to what Plato in the *Republic* meant by "natural gift." In this intermediate sense of the term, a person with an ability to x is someone who can acquire the skill(s) of x-ing. Similarly, a person with a talent or natural gift for x is someone who can acquire those skills with considerable ease. And clearly, one can have an ability or natural gift without having yet learned or acquired the associated skill(s).

To make these observations somewhat more systematic, let's now resort to a bit of terminological artificiality and use certain normally fuzzy and elastic expressions as rather specific technical terms. So let's use the term "capacity" to refer to rudimentary and typically universal (or at least very common) human (or organic) endowments, such as the capacity to hear, curl one's tongue, or digest food. Next, we can use the term "ability" to stand for the intermediate but ostensibly higher-level traits or dispositions discussed earlier—for example, the ability to hold a job, cook dinner, iron clothes, install new computer software, and also the dispositional ability to become a highly proficient musician, artist, or athlete. And finally, let's reserve "skill" for a fairly specific kind of proficiency—namely, a notable mastery over certain of one's other organic endowments (abilities *or* capacities). So in this sense of the term, skills are exhibited not only by those who juggle chainsaws, sculpt a lifelike human figure, play the "Waldstein" Sonata, and repair automobiles, but also by yogis who can finely control their heart rate or body temperature and by more ordinary folk who've learned to control pain through self-hypnosis.

Obviously, these different meanings of the term "ability" aren't sharp. They merely identify useful points on a continuum of human endowments (ordered roughly in terms of complexity and refinement). In fact, it's relatively easy to find human competencies that seem to fall at various points in between. For example, the ability to stand on one leg isn't as elementary as the capacity to swallow or smile, and it's not as refined or developed as gymnastic ability. Likewise, the ability to discriminate changes in pitch is intermediate between musical ability and simply being able to hear. We can make similar observations about many other abilities—for example, the ability to manage a retail store, bake a cake, parallel park, haggle over prices with a street vendor, or make people feel comfortable. These seem to fall between (on the one hand) very mundane abilities such as tying one's shoes and counting to ten and (on the other) higher-order endowments such as writing a symphony and playing pro-level basketball. (It should be clear, however, that these intermediate abilities *can* be cultivated thoroughly enough to qualify as a skill and that once again we're not dealing with sharp natural cleavages.)

WHY THIS MATTERS

Armed (or perhaps burdened) with these terminological conventions, we're in a position to make several observations about the data of parapsychology. I've often complained that laboratory research in parapsychology is almost ludicrously premature because researchers have no idea what kind of organic function they're trying to investigate. Not only are we ignorant of psi's finer-grained features, we don't even know what its natural history might be—for example, whether it has an evolutionary role or primary or overall purpose or function (although there's no shortage of speculation on these matters[6]). Of course, there's no reason to think that psychic phenomena occur only for parapsychologists, much less only when those parapsychologists set out to look for them. After all, a major motivation for conducting formal studies is that we have evidence of psi occurring spontaneously in life. But since we're a very long way from understanding the nature and function of everyday psi, we don't know whether psychic functioning is an ability (like musical ability) or whether it's a brute endowment such as the capacity to see or to move one's limbs. Obviously, then, in the absence of this rudimentary knowledge, we have no idea whether (or to what extent) our experimental procedures are even appropriate to the phenomena.

To see this, compare our knowledge and study of psi with our knowledge and study of memory. Memory is something we *can* study formally to some extent (though in my opinion this is usually done very superficially at best). But we have some idea how to proceed because we're already very familiar with the many and diverse manifestations of memory in daily life. Or compare our knowledge of psi with our knowledge of the ability to make people laugh. It's because we're familiar with the latter that we know we *can't* adequately study it experimentally. Or again, a tennis player's ability to return serves is something that—unlike everyday psi—we can systematically and easily examine in real-life, relevant settings. In fact, we can study that ability pretty much on demand and from virtually anyone who claims to have the ability.

It's astonishing to me that many researchers continue to overlook this fundamental methodological issue. It should be obvious that different capacities or abilities, as a rule, demand different modes of investigation. We wouldn't examine mechanical aptitude the same way we'd investigate the ability to produce witty remarks, the ability to babysit, the ability to design and install a patio, the ability to learn a new language, the ability to empathize, or the skill of playing wide receiver or soccer goalkeeper. Similarly, techniques appropriate to studying those abilities will differ from those suitable for examining mere capacities, such as the capacity to blink, swallow, utter sounds, or dream. And, of course, different capacities likewise tend to require distinct modes of investigation.

With all that in mind, we can now look more closely at the methodological implications of conceptualizing psychic functioning along different lines. Suppose, first, that psi is an ability (rather than a capacity). And to see where that takes us, let's consider some conspicuous features of athletic abilities. First, they aren't uniformly distributed throughout the human race. Second, people with athletic abilities have them to varying degrees. For instance, some may be athletic enough to excel at college-level competitions but not gifted enough to turn professional. Third, athletic abilities come in various subvarieties (e.g., the ability to play tennis, golf, football, or basketball). And fourth, a person may have one sub-ability but not another. For example, a gifted baseball player may be inept at track and field events, or—within baseball itself—good at playing shortstop or second base but inept at pitching, good at baserunning but less stellar at hitting. Similarly, a gymnast might be good at rings but not parallel bars. In fact, athletic specialities can be *very* idiosyncratic or specific. For example, a baseball pitcher might have a highly distinctive way of throwing a side-arm curve ball, and only a few pitchers successfully master a knuckleball. Similarly, in American football, a defensive end might be adept at playing (say) only from the right but not the left side of the line (a phenomenon that I've always found perplexing).

Of course, athletic abilities are hardly unique in this respect; in fact, they may well represent the norm. Musical abilities, for instance, have similar characteristics. Musicians can usually play some instruments but not others. They might be able to compose but not conduct (or vice versa). They might master certain idioms but not others (e.g., baroque but not late romantic, jazz and pop but not classical, bebop but not swing or Dixieland). Singers might have a knack or the vocal equipment for Verdi but not Bach or Rossini or for Mozart but not Wagner, Monteverdi, Wolf, or Berio.

In fact, similar observations apply even to more specific musical abilities. Consider the ability to compose music. That, too, can be expressed in many different ways. Many composers notate their compositions; others lack that ability. Some composers have absolute pitch, some only relative pitch, and some neither. Some compose directly onto paper, while others need a piano or some other instrument. Some work best with large forms; others don't. Some write especially well or idiomatically only for certain instruments; others don't have that limitation. Some have a keen ability to set words to music; others lack that sub-ability. Some are especially adept at harmony, rhythm, or instrumental color, and those specialities likewise take different forms and manifest in different degrees and combinations.

So assuming (as I think we can) that athletic, musical, or compositional ability or skill exemplify the variety of expression of abilities or skills generally, two important observations seem indisputable. First, people who possess a general ability (e.g., the ability to compose music, play baseball, sculpt, paint with watercolors) may exhibit it in various ways and to varying degrees. And second, how they express the ability may depend on which subsidiary abilities they possess and the manner in which they express them.

The relevance of all this to parapsychology seems equally obvious: At the very least (given our current and considerable ignorance about the nature of psi), we're in no position to say that psychic functioning is an exception to these rules. On the contrary, there are plenty of reasons for thinking that the manifestation of psi will be as idiosyncratic and variable as any other ability. First, psi-conducive conditions seem to be as personal and individual as the situations people find amusing or erotic. Most subjects don't seem to do their best under intense pressure or when the stakes are high (say, during a live television demonstration), but a few excel under those conditions and even relish the challenge. And some may be able to demonstrate psi only in the presence of select others—for example, investigators they find especially supportive or agreeable, just as most people can sing, express sensuality, or even fart only in the presence of those with whom they feel personally safe. Second, the subjective experience of exercising one's psi varies widely—for example, whether ESP is accompanied by vivid, familiar, or any imagery. And third, the range and specificity of the ability may also vary idiosyncratically (e.g., one may be good at x but not y). For example, one might be good at psychokinetically influencing small objects but not good at affecting random event generators in computerized experiments. Or, one might be good at remote-viewing shapes but not technical details, or colors but not smells, or medium-sized objects but not words on paper (Pat Price, notoriously, was apparently uniquely good at this latter task). In fact, this type of ESP variability would parallel a familiar feature of more ordinary perceptual differences. Some are particularly good at (say) discriminating colors but not sounds, detecting subtle differences in wines or chocolates but not in audio components, or noticing eye color but not manipulative behavior.

It's likely, then, that the context dependency of psi parallels that of ordinary abilities in at least two main respects. The first is that psi-conducive conditions may vary from person to person and from situation to situation. In fact, even idiosyncratic psi-conducive conditions might vary from situation to situation. A subject might succeed most reliably in an experiment only when the experimenter is a comforting and supportive female authority figure—except on really bad days (say, after getting a speeding ticket) or on really good days, when he or she will succeed even with an annoying male experimenter. Analogously, someone might be amused or become sexually aroused under a very distinctive set of conditions (different for different moods or times of day), but not (say) while suffering from a cold, studying for an exam, or mourning the loss of a loved one. Similarly, anger might stifle sexual arousal for some but stimulate it for others (and even then perhaps only some of the time).

And second, many abilities are also context dependent in the sense that they can be expressed or studied properly only under quite specific conditions. Consider again a tennis player's ability to return serves. Clearly, that can be evaluated only in the context of a game. After all, some people play better than they practice, and others practice better than they play. But even if we ignore the ways in which the psychological pressures of a match affect athletic performance, the ability to return serves can be assessed only in actual game situations, when opponents are trying their hardest to win, and then only in relation to the opponents' ability to serve. Similar observations apply widely to athletic abilities—say, a quarterback's ability to read defenses, a base runner's ability to steal second, or a goalkeeper's ability to defend penalty shots. And they apply as well, with appropriate modifications, to a musician's ability to play a sonata without a memory lapse or a comedian's ability to make people laugh. These can vary with confidence level, audience attitude, personal distractions, and many other things.

Now if psychic functioning is analogous to these sorts of organic endowments (as many think and as evidence from both experimental and anecdotal reports suggests), then we'd be entitled to say that not everyone is psychic, that some are more psychic than others (enough so as to count as "stars" or as gifted), and that not all psychics are psychic in the same way.

But what if psychic functioning is analogous to elementary capacities? In that case, psi might be as uniformly distributed among humans as pulmonary or reproductive functioning, or as reflexive and involuntary as nursing behavior or fear responses. Moreover, although some lack these familiar capacities or possess them only in attenuated forms, most people have no such limitations. Analogously, the capacity to function psychically might be robust in all but a few individuals. It might also be the sort of thing we do all or much of the time, and the processes involved may be as removed from conscious awareness and control as those involved in digestion or breathing.

It's tempting to think that research methodology depends critically on which of these two pictures is correct, even if the goal is simply to obtain evidence for the mere existence of psi. In fact, at one time I thought this was an issue of some importance.[7] Now, however, I'm not so sure; I now think that the situation is more complex than I appreciated initially. My earlier concern was that if psi is unevenly distributed throughout the population (like musical and athletic ability), then it would be unwise to seek quantitatively impressive evidence for the existence of psi by testing randomly selected subjects. After all, that's not how to establish the reality of virtuosic mnemonic, calculating, or artistic abilities, or familiar but highly situation-sensitive abilities, or the ability of those who (like yogis) can exert fine control over breathing or vasoconstriction. But in fact, this may not be much of a problem, because competent experimenters will (whenever possible) screen subjects and conduct pilot studies. If so, then no matter whether psi is a capacity or an ability, experimental procedures should help to identify promising test subjects.

Nevertheless, in the context of this discussion at least, a key question remains: If psychic functioning is analogous to either a common capacity or a widespread ability, what distinguishes good subjects (e.g., consistently successful remote viewers or above-chance scorers on PK tests) from others? A plausible answer to that question would be that experimental research tracks not those who can function psychically but only those who have the ability to *demonstrate* psi. And if that answer is correct, then this ability to demonstrate psi would seem to be what we could call a *meta*-ability—that is, the ability to function psychically in specific (and not necessarily all) test situations.

In that case, however, if successful experiments merely track the meta-ability to demonstrate psi, then this provides no clue as to whether psychic functioning itself is a capacity or an ability or whether it's common or uncommon. And so the earlier question remains: Are successful subjects analogous (say) to the yogi controlling breathing (a common human *capacity*) or the musical virtuoso or star athlete displaying exquisite control over *abilities* only some enjoy? But no matter how we answer that further question, the ability to demonstrate psi more or less on demand would undoubtedly be a distinctive endowment, apparently enjoyed by relatively few individuals.

So the moral thus far seems to be this: as long as the goal of psi research is merely to establish that psychic functioning occurs, pragmatically it may matter little whether it's a capacity or an ability or whether it's common or uncommon. At best, our research will only reveal those who have the meta-ability to demonstrate psi under the conditions imposed by the experimenters. And that's precisely why typical psi experiments bring us no closer to understanding just what psi is and how it fits into the general scheme of things.

Earlier, I mentioned some respects in which psychic functioning, like most (if not all) abilities, seems to be context dependent. But notice, that's plausible whether psi is a capacity, ability, *or* skill. After all, in the absence of indications to the contrary, it's reasonable to suppose that psychic functioning is continuous in its broad outlines with more familiar human or organic endowments. And clearly, our normal capacities, abilities, and skills are *all* situation sensitive. For example, our capacity to digest food, sleep, relax, function sexually, and ward off infections will vary (sometimes dramatically) from one context to another. And the reason for those changes may be ordinary alterations either in one's physical environment or in one's mental states. That's why penile erection in the human male (as Arthur Koestler noted) isn't a capacity that can be exercised (for most men, at any rate) no matter what the conditions happen to be.[8] Similarly, the demonstration of our abilities and skills can be inhibited or suppressed by a wide variety of circumstances, physical and psychological. Consider, for example, the situationally variable ability to make people laugh, write a philosophy essay exam, maintain a positive attitude, parallel park, or recite a poem from memory. Or consider the skill of shooting free throws, walking a tightrope, or landing a jumbo jet. So no matter what sort of attribute psychic functioning is, it's reasonable to suppose that its manifestations will likewise vary from one context to the next.

Another familiar and plausible suggestion is that psychic functioning is need-determined. Of course, that hypothesis can be interpreted in various ways (and those options are worth examining on another occasion). But they're all variations on the claim that psychic functioning stands in some sort of lawlike relation to the real or perceived needs of a psi agent. And for now, we need only observe that the presumed relation between psychic functioning and needs (whatever exactly it is) seems compatible with taking psi to be either an ability or a capacity. Many of our normal capacities and abilities are likewise related in a more or less lawlike way to the real or perceived needs of an agent. So if psi is need-determined, it might be analogous either to the capacity to increase adrenalin flow, produce endorphins, or move or respond quickly (I think that last item is a capacity). Similarly, it might be analogous to the ability to act decisively, or be courageous, or be cheerful in the face of adversity, or act selflessly when a loved one needs to be protected. However, there's little reason to regard *skills* or the use of one's skills as generally need-determined. Often, both the development and exercise of one's skills is psychologically optional and relatively trivial. Nevertheless, the *ability* to exercise certain skills might be related in a lawlike way to one's real or perceived needs (say, in the way certain athletes perform optimally only under the pressure of a real game). Apparently, then, the view that psi is need-determined doesn't favor interpreting psychic functioning as a skill. That strikes me as plausible. If there's anything skill-like about psychic functioning, it would seem to be what I earlier called the meta-ability to demonstrate psi. So while some college students might perform significantly above chance on quantitative psi tasks, most will not have exhibited the skill of being able to demonstrate psi. For that, we need to look at people like Mrs. Piper, D. D. Home, or (today) Joe McMoneagle.

PSI, SAVANTISM, AND MEMORY

When I wrote my book on postmortem survival,[9] I intensified my study of the literature on prodigies and what used to be called idiot savants (the trend now is to drop the pejorative first term). Initially, my goal was to explore the relevance of the data only to the topic of survival, and I'll say something about all that shortly. But I soon realized that the study of savants and prodigies connects in intriguing ways to other issues in parapsychology and also to topics relevant to the study of dissociation. The data is particularly significant for our understanding of human *abilities* rather than capacities or skills. What's undoubtedly most striking about savants and prodigies is that despite their handicaps or immaturity, they display unexpected and occasionally astounding musical, calculating, artistic, and other sorts of abilities—that is, higher-order dispositions which (when properly nurtured and cultivated) manifest as skills of various sorts.

One impressive feature of the data is that the abilities (and skills) of savants are often highly circumscribed and idiosyncratic. And those limitations or boundaries are of two sorts. First, savants may be profoundly dysfunctional except for their musical, mathematical, artistic, or mnemonic abilities. For example, one well-known musical savant suffers from cerebral palsy, but his almost constant spasticity disappears when he plays the piano. Another savant can read or write nothing except his name and is just barely able to care for himself; but he can repair virtually any mechanical device presented to him. Others are similarly or more severely disabled, yet they're able to draw, paint, or sculpt works of considerable sophistication and beauty. The second sort of limitation found in savants exists within their special area of expertise. For example, calendar calculators tend to be accurate only within rather clear ranges of years, and those ranges differ from one savant to the next. Moreover, although calculators might be able to perform rapid and complex operations concerning dates or remember extremely long numbers, they might be unable to do simple addition or change a dollar bill. The famous calculating twins, George and Charles, amused themselves by exchanging twenty-digit prime numbers, and they could factor nearly any number presented to them; but they couldn't count to thirty.[10] Another arithmetical prodigy's calculating speed increased if the number twenty-seven was featured in the problem. Still another could rapidly solve complex algebraic problems in his head, but he seemed unable to comprehend even simple principles of geometry.[11]

Of course, everybody's abilities are idiosyncratically circumscribed to some extent, both as compared with their other abilities and also within their particular areas of specialization or competence. For example (as I noted earlier), musicians usually can play some instruments but not others. Similarly, instrumentalists often can neither compose nor conduct, and musicians of all sorts may exhibit (sometimes highly idiosyncratic) limitations in their mastery of musical idioms—or even just specific composers (e.g., some classical musicians just can't play Beethoven well, and some jazz musicians seem stymied by Monk). Likewise, athletes might be able to play some sports but not others or some positions but not others within a particular sport. But the performances of savants bring this familiar phenomenon into sharper relief. They also remind us that if psi is likewise an ability, and even if it's the sort of ability which (as in cases of savantism) is highly developed compared with one's other abilities, it too may appear in extremely circumscribed and idiosyncratic forms.

In fact, savants remind us vividly that *a person good at one task may not be good at what we usually suppose should be a related task*. It shouldn't surprise us, then, or automatically arouse suspicion, when even gifted psychics seem to have some psychic abilities but not others. An all-too-familiar and exasperatingly glib skeptical argument is that if a subject has one psi ability, he should have another; but since he's unable to demonstrate the latter, it's unreasonable to claim that he possesses the former. For example, an old argument against physical mediumship is that if superstars such as Home and Palladino could move tables and make objects materialize, why couldn't they also (say) cure disease or control roulette wheels and slot machines? The implication is that since they didn't (or couldn't) do the latter, they had no psychokinetic abilities at all. This fallacious argument is common and stupid enough to deserve a name; let's call it the *all-purpose-psi* argument.

I've discussed this particular skeptical maneuver at length elsewhere.[12] For now, it's enough to note that it rests on a highly superficial (if not thoroughly moronic) assumption concerning the distribution of and connections between human abilities. We know too little about psi (or even just PK) to have a competent opinion about what a person's repertoire of phenomena or psychic abilities ought to be. In fact, it takes only a minimum of humility and common sense to admit that we have no idea how (or if) having a certain psychic ability affects the probability of having another. Nevertheless, despite our current state of ignorance, it's reasonable to expect psychic abilities to be as variable and individualistic as every other human ability. Under the circumstances, then, claiming that a medium who can levitate tables should also be able to start fires, control roulette wheels, or heal the sick is as foolish as saying that a gifted athlete should also have a talent for medicine, that someone who can play the trombone should also be able to play the violin, pole vault, repair automobiles, or design and build a house, or that a neurosurgeon should also be able to perform a root canal or repair a broken watch. Furthermore, this familiar version of the all-purpose-psi argument shows little appreciation of the psychology of mediumship and why the control of roulette wheels (and other activities) would arguably have been an inappropriate and particularly intimidating manifestion of psi.[13]

Psychologist and parapsychological critic C. E. M Hansel adopted another, inexcusably thick-headed, skeptical gambit similar to the all-purpose-psi argument. In a film produced for the *Horizon* and *Nova* television series, he argued that if people have ESP, they ought to be able demonstrate it on the spot by telling him what he's thinking.[14] Hansel's challenge commits the double-barreled offense of (a) ignoring the obvious fact that human abilities generally are idiosyncratically circumscribed and (b) overlooking the psychology of psi—in this case, the likelihood that psi is as situation sensitive as virtually every human capacity, ability, or skill. In fact, I'm sorry that the film director didn't challenge Hansel to demonstrate an erection then and there, on camera. I'm sure Hansel would have adamantly opposed inferring from his failure that he's simply and always unable to "get it up."

We should also remember that abilities may remain latent and undeveloped and that this may be due to various features of our overall psychology. For example, mathematical abilities might remain undeveloped due to fear of math or the belief that one can't or even shouldn't excel at math.[15] Similarly, musical abilities may remain untapped or undeveloped due to a fear of failure or a fear of criticism (and not just, say, from the absence of available musical instruments). It seems reasonable to think, then, that psychic functioning might likewise be curtailed in quite specific ways in response to various fears and inhibitions or one's overall worldview. And in fact, there are good reasons for thinking that the great physical mediums demonstrated this phenomenon in several ways.[16]

For example, Eusapia Palladino had many unsophisticated beliefs about the nature of mediumship and survival, including which conditions were favorable to the production of phenomena (such as the presence of a curtain or "cabinet" behind the medium and a general preference for darkness or dim light). And in fact, over the course of her career, those were the conditions under which her most impressive phenomena were produced.[17] D. D. Home was less finicky than Palladino about séance conditions, but even he had firm beliefs about the nature of his mediumship. For instance, Home believed that his phenomena were particularly strong beneath the séance table, and perhaps for him they were. Not surprisingly, the most successful and resourceful investigators in both cases took their subjects' beliefs seriously; they simply imposed decent controls within the general sorts of conditions preferred by the medium. In fact, Crookes's accordion test with Home and the 1908 Naples sittings with Palladino illustrate clearly how researchers can respect the medium's beliefs or "comfort zone" and still apply tight controls and obtain compelling results.[18]

The phenomena of Home and Palladino were idiosyncratic in other respects as well. Home, who had some modest normal musical ability (particularly on keyboard instruments), was apparently able to produce musical performances either on untouched instruments or on accordions held at the end away from the keys. Palladino, however, had no apparent musical ability normally, and although in her presence sounds emerged from untouched instruments, she produced no music. Similarly, in Home's case, witnesses often reported the production of written messages (frequently by disembodied hands). Palladino, however, was illiterate, and although witnesses frequently reported touches, pinches, and so on, by limbs (or limb-like "stalks") even while Palladino was under the control of her investigators, I'm aware of no reports suggesting that she was able to read or write mediumistically. In both cases, it seems, the mediums' normal range of abilities was mirrored in their mediumistic phenomena.

There's nothing inherently suspicious in this. Although mediumship may in fact liberate otherwise latent abilities (as seems to have happened in the cases of Patience Worth, Hélène Smith, and others),[19] there's no reason why that must be the case. It seems just as likely that the subject's skills or limitations, if sufficiently profound initially, would manifest in a variety of contexts. For example, if someone is tone deaf and that deficiency isn't simply socially mediated (or practically a form of posttraumatic stress) as some suggest, we'd expect the person to be unable to carry a tune no matter what—even if hypnotized. Similarly, a classical pianist with small hands may not be able to perform works by Liszt and Rachmaninoff, and visual impairments can interfere with or prevent a variety of everyday activities. And again, if someone is short or simply athletically challenged, that person's basketball or track and field skills will be severely curtailed no matter what.

One more point about the differences between Home and Palladino (although this may be pushing things a bit). Although these mediums sometimes produced the same general kind of phenomena, those of Home apparently showed a degree of development and refinement in keeping with his overall character, whereas Eusapia's tended to be as crude or graceless as (by most accounts) she was normally. For example, Home's disembodied hands were reportedly very detailed and lifelike, and witnesses often described them as being beautiful or elegant. Moreover, their deformations and other distinctive features reportedly corresponded on occasion to those of the deceased communicator. By contrast, when Palladino apparently produced visible limbs or appendages, witnesses described them as knobby, ill-defined, and generally lacking in distinctive or clearly identifiable features. Similarly, Home's musical phenomena were frequently described in superlatives and praised for their beauty and exquisite execution. By contrast, no phenomenon of Palladino's was ever described that way.

Similar observations hold for other cases of physical mediumship. For instance, the distinctive ectoplasmic manifestations of Kathleen Goligher and Eva C. may reflect the different ways their investigators influenced their beliefs and actions. Goligher was studied primarily by an engineer, W. J. Crawford, and her extruding ectoplasm apparently raised tables in a way Crawford could well appreciate—namely, in the manner of a cantilever. By contrast, Eva C., under the scrutiny of biological scientists such as Richet, Geley, and Schrenck-Notzing, produced more organic sorts of manifestations (e.g., on one occasion Eva's ectoplasm reportedly grew into a miniature hand).[20] I think it's most plausible to attribute these different ectoplasmic manifestations to expectancy or other experimenter effects. At their most exotic, they would be forms of abnormal or paranormal influence on the medium, caused by the investigators' differing interests and beliefs. However, it's also possible that the differences in the two mediums' phenomena exemplify more familiar and mundane ways in which the presence of others influences our behavior. As everyone knows, different people and different situations elicit different sides of our personalities. That's why we normally adapt our sexuality or style of humor to the company of different persons. In fact, the process of selectively (and, hopefully, appropriately) revealing different aspects of ourselves to different persons is virtually automatic, and it's usually more instinctive than conscious.

Let's turn now to issues concerning memory. The amazing mnemonic displays of savants and some others raise various questions about the nature and function of memory generally, and they suggest some interesting parallels with psychic functioning. First, however, we should consider whether to speak of memory as an ability or a capacity, and I propose that memory can plausibly be regarded as both. Consider: most organisms have some mnemonic capacity, however rudimentary. But in addition, there are specific mnemonic abilities not shared by all who have the capacity to remember—for example, the ability to remember very long digits, nonsense syllables, a complete orchestral score, or even the more mundane ability to remember telephone numbers. Since nothing in what follows seems to hang on whether we regard memory as a capacity or an ability, I'll temporarily use these terms more or less interchangeably.

When we examine the lives of memory virtuosi (so-called mnemonists), we see how it can be especially illuminating to study human performance *in extremis*. In the case of mnemonists, it's tempting to describe their mnemonic ability not as a gift or marvelous endowment but as an affliction or a disability. For example, in Luria's famous study of the subject he called "S," exceptional memory led to overwhelming conceptual clutter and seemed to be profoundly incapacitating.[21] So rather than describe mnemonists as individuals with superb mnemonic abilities or capacities, perhaps we should describe them as people *lacking* a certain useful ability—namely, the ability to forget. From that perspective, then, the ordinary mnemonic abilities of most persons benefit from what we could describe (somewhat paradoxically) as *liberating constraints*. After all (as the case of "S" illustrates), without the ability to forget, life can become virtually unmanageable. So perhaps the normal constraints on our memories make a great deal of sense adaptationally.

Moreover, most (if not all) of what we forget seems to be dissociated from conscious awareness. Nevertheless, under the right circumstances (e.g., hypnosis and other altered states) we can remember what we'd previously forgotten. In fact, that sort of retrievability is an essential feature of dissociative phenomena.[22] Now it's not clear whether all people have (at least latently) the ability to recall consciously virtually everything that's happened to them, as Luria's subject was apparently able to do. But it's clear that most of us remember subconsciously many things which we don't remember consciously. So the familiar and apparently adaptationally appropriate constraints on normal memory seem primarily to be constraints on our ability to remember consciously.

Similar points have sometimes been made about ESP. If people were always and consciously gaining psychic access to *every* recognizable state of affairs (even those within a reasonable physical or psychological distance), their mental lives would presumably be hopelessly cluttered. In fact, our cognitive psi abilities would make little sense adaptationally if they weren't constrained in the way our memory seems to be. So perhaps the inability of even good psychics to use their ESP on demand and without limit parallels the inability of normal persons with decent memories to remember everything. Moreover, we might be psychically active subconsciously, with no conscious indication or awareness of that activity. For all we know, then, the apparently liberating constraints on our psychic functioning may apply primarily to our ability to be psychic in consciously detectable ways or perhaps to the skill of demonstrating psi.

Before leaving the topic of memory, I should mention that our normal mnemonic abilities are as idiosyncratically circumscribed as our other abilities. Some people are good at remembering numbers but not names, while others can remember names but not numbers. Some can easily recall song lyrics but not lecture notes or things they've read but not things they've heard. Musicians are usually able to remember many long pieces of music in every detail, but they might have difficulty remembering directions, birthdays, or visual information generally. Once again, therefore, it would be surprising (if not totally unprecedented) if psi abilities weren't similarly subject specific. In fact, in the absence of clear evidence to the contrary, it's outrageous simply to assume otherwise.

DISSOCIATION AND HUMAN NATURE

Dissociative phenomena (both pathological and nonpathological) are interesting for several reasons. What fascinates me in particular is the way dissociation seems occasionally to reveal a wide range of otherwise hidden aptitudes, capacities, and creative resources.[23] Some of these discoveries are merely unexpected and not especially puzzling. We might simply not have realized that the people in question had these resources tucked away inside them. But sometimes we get a deeper surprise. For example, we might discover seemingly radical—savant-like—discontinuities between the person's previously demonstrated abilities and the ones revealed dissociatively. So, as in the case of savants, we might find an unexpected degree of independence of abilities we'd previously thought to be strongly mutually dependent. And there's another possibility. The newly exposed capacities or resources may be things we don't understand at all or (at best) things we understand only very dimly. In fact, in some of the most dramatic cases, the apparent capacities and resources in question may be things whose very existence many are reluctant to accept.

Of course, the prime examples of that last group are those that at least seem to be paranormal. But for the moment, I prefer to focus on the surprising but apparently nonparanormal abilities revealed by both ordinary and more exotic forms of dissociation. Even so, much of the most interesting data comes from paranormal case investigations. But I'm interested now in the abilities people reveal in cases where we can reasonably *reject* explanations in terms of psychic functioning (as we often can). In fact, these are precisely the cases that I believe raise some of the most interesting issues about human nature. And they, too, illustrate nicely why, in order to understand human nature, we must often study behavior in its more extreme forms.

The most consistently intriguing of these exotic cases are instances of apparent mediumship or channeling and also some cases of apparent reincarnation. But let's forget (for now) cases that seem most strongly to suggest postmortem survival as well as those that seem only to indicate psychic functioning among the living. That still leaves a huge pool of ostensibly postmortem survival cases seemingly explicable, nonparanormally, in one of two ways. Some, which we can also ignore for now, we can clearly account for in terms of what I call "The Usual Suspects" (fraud, mistakes in observation or reporting, or hidden memories). That leaves the cases that interest me here: those we seem best able to explain in terms of what I call "The Unusual Suspects"—that is, by positing the operation and possibly the combination of rare or abnormal nonpsi abilities. These might be similar to the abilities demonstrated by savants and prodigies, or perhaps just remarkable displays of memory, or perhaps previously hidden creative abilities liberated in dissociative or other altered states.[24]

As it happens, some cases of apparent postmortem survival (whether of mediumship or reincarnation) really do seem explainable, and plausibly so, in terms of The Unusual Suspects—specifically, a combination of dissociation and latent abilities or capacities.[25] And when those cases are taken together, they seem to reveal certain intriguing trends or regularities. They suggest, first, that the existence of hidden capacities may be the norm rather than the exception, and second, that the more extreme cases seem merely to be extensions of cases that are easier to accept initially. Of course, that makes the extreme cases seem a bit easier to swallow.

To keep matters simple, I'll focus for now just on cases of mediumship or channeling and forget about the subtle variants we find in cases of apparent reincarnation. In good mediumistic cases, subjects demonstrate at least one of two main types of anomalous knowledge. The first is sometimes called *knowledge-that* (or propositional knowledge, knowledge of information). Here, mediums offer bits of information known (normally, at least) to no one present at the séance. But for present purposes, a different type of mediumistic knowledge is more important. This is often called *knowledge-how*, and it's the manifestation of skills or abilities.

Many consider this to be the more intriguing form of mediumistic phenomena, especially when mediums exhibit talents or skills they'd never displayed before, or at least never displayed to the extent they do when in a mediumistic trance. Typically, these abilities present themselves as coming from a deceased communicator, as if that entity is acting through the medium. So, for example, the medium might exhibit an artistic ability associated with a deceased individual, or the medium might speak a presumably unlearned language which was the deceased's native tongue.

We'll look at some crucial background conceptual issues in the next section, but for now, consider a sample case—that of the late Rosemary Brown, a British medium who ostensibly channeled compositions from famous composers (e.g., Liszt, Chopin, Debussy, Berlioz, Schubert). The works are primarily for the piano, and they've been studied by a number of very prominent musicians. Those musical authorities have disagreed over the merits of the compositions, but some judged them to be similar in both style and quality to the known works of their alleged composers. However, we have to take all these assessments with a grain of salt. The critical appraisals of Mrs. Brown's works have all been made by people who know the circumstances surrounding their production and who undoubtedly have biases or predispositions concerning the possibility of survival. So it's difficult to know to what extent their assessments of Mrs. Brown's production reflect those predispositions.

At any rate, I don't think we need to worry much at this point about the quality of Rosemary Brown's channeled compositions. Unlike some mediumistic cases where subjects apparently display both knowledge-*that* and knowledge-*how*, the Rosemary Brown case offers no evidence for the personal survival of famous composers *except* the compositions themselves. Granted, the mediumistic portrayals of the composers' personalities are consistent with what we know of the composers. But those portrayals offer no revelations of information. Mrs. Brown didn't provide, in addition, obscure bits of information about the composers to which she had no normal access and which later had to be confirmed by investigators. So although nothing in the Rosemary Brown case rules out survival as an explanation, nothing strongly favors that hypothesis either. In my view, the most plausible and parsimonious hypothesis is that Mrs. Brown was a naturally gifted impressionist, a musical version of those who can mimic the speech and mannerisms of famous actors and other performers. And of course, that hypothesis isn't undermined by the apparent originality of some of Mrs. Brown's compositions. In fact, it's precisely what one would expect of a good impressionist. Although stage impressionists copy the verbal and behavioral style of other people, the best of the lot do this not simply by copying their subjects' *exact* words, inflections, gestures, and so on, but by producing *original* and sometimes worthwhile performances in the appropriate style.

Also, it's important to note that Mrs. Brown knew how to play the piano and read music before she began channeling musical compositions. We don't detect, in her case, the (perhaps only superficial) gap between background knowledge and creative ability that we see in more puzzling cases. So it certainly looks like Mrs. Brown's mediumship was an outlet for musical talents that might otherwise have remained hidden.

Of course, some think Mrs. Brown genuinely channeled deceased composers. They'd argue that her productions can't simply be first-rate musical mimicry because that kind of mimicry requires extensive musical training or experience—that is, training that Rosemary Brown didn't have. And so they claim that her compositions can be attributed *only* to the deceased composers. But I have to disagree. For one thing, as prodigies and savants demonstrate, impressive musical abilities don't have any such prerequisite. Besides, it's as implausible to claim that training or experience are necessary for musical mimicry as it is to make a similar claim about the verbal mimicry of gifted impressionists. Impressionists don't have to attend impressionist school; some people simply have what it takes. For that matter, musical training and experience don't, by themselves, enable people to play or compose in the style of various composers. In fact, relatively few musicians have that ability (just as relatively few speakers of English can successfully imitate major movie stars). What *is* required is a good memory and a certain kind of good "ear." Just as some people have an ear for accents and dialects or an ability to discriminate idiosyncratic speech patterns and bodily movements, others have an antenna (as it were) for musical styles. And that musical ability is just one of many musical abilities that not all musicians (including extremely talented musicians) enjoy. Moreover, it's one that is relatively independent of musical training.

Perhaps Rosemary Brown's state of mind resembles those reportedly elicited by Vladimir Raikov, who claims to have improved subjects' artistic skills hypnotically by suggesting to them that they're famous artists.[26] Raikov's experiments were intended to explore the possibility of "developing latent creative potentials by means of the psychological stimulation of hypnosis."[27]

Unfortunately, the experiments aren't described very carefully (in translation, at least) or thoroughly. And it's unclear how well controlled they were—for example, how well they guarded against experimenter expectancy effects or whether experimenters were blind as to which subjects had been hypnotized. But they're nevertheless suggestive and provide a decent (albeit rough) template for follow-up studies.

Raikov investigated the effects of hypnotic suggestion on improving musical and artistic performance, doing mathematical sums, and playing chess. His subjects were university students. Fifty of them could respond to deep hypnosis, twenty-eight were only slightly hypnotizable, and seventy-eight were apparently not hypnotizable at all. He found that "while the high hypnotizable group showed significantly real improvement in hypnotic creative performance, the slight hypnotizable group showed significantly less success and those who were unresponsive to hypnosis failed to achieve any improvement."[28] Performances were evaluated by "experts" in each task.

For example, the fifteen subjects who played musical instruments were from the Moscow Conservatory. Performances before and after hypnosis were tape-recorded (presumably audio, although it's never made clear), and experts and participants evaluated the quality of the performances. Subjects were given suggestions to simulate an active and talented person, capable of coping quickly and successfully with the task presented to them. Over the course of twelve sessions, twelve of the fifteen subjects under hypnosis showed significant improvement with the self-images of outstanding performers such as Rachmaninoff and Kreisler. Ten of those showed real improvement very early in the series of sessions, and Raikov reports that the improvement in subjects' performances was retained "to some degree" in the waking state.

Raikov also had four control subjects who performed without hypnosis in eight sessions (presumably also trying to simulate active and talented musicians), and experimenters and experts observed no significant improvement. Moreover, Raikov reported similar results in drawing experiments, where only highly hypnotizable subjects markedly improved their drawing ability under the suggestion that they were famous past masters such as Raphael.

Before moving on, we also need to consider briefly the case of Hélène Smith (pseudonym of Élise Müller). This case raises questions about linguistic facility, to which we'll return in the next section and which many consider a key to evaluating the evidence for postmortem survival. But we can ignore those issues for the moment. In fact, this case will help put the later discussion into perspective.

Mlle Smith was studied by the Swiss psychologist Theodore Flournoy,[29] and while there's reason to think that something paranormal might have been going on in connection with certain of her phenomena, what matters here is the linguistic fluency demonstrated during her mediumistic trances. The most dramatic example of this was when Mlle Smith ostensibly channeled messages from residents of the planet Mars, which she delivered fluently in a Martian language of her own invention. These messages claimed to present information about the human, animal, and plant life on Mars, and apparently they were a response to someone commenting casually at a séance that it would be interesting to know about activities on other planets. Mlle Smith's Martian communications were conveyed both in speech and in writing, and they employed a thoroughly consistent Martian alphabet whose written form was attractively ornate. Analysis of this language showed that, grammatically and phonetically, it corresponded closely to French.

Flournoy concluded that the Martian language, as an intellectual achievement, was as "infantile and puerile" as other features of the Martian phase of Smith's mediumship. Nevertheless, he regarded the language as an impressive feat of memory and subconscious creativity. And I think we have to agree. Also, considering that Hélène's father (a Hungarian merchant) had a facility with languages, I think we can also wonder, along with Flournoy, "whether in the Martian we are not in the presence of an awakening and momentary display of an hereditary faculty, dormant under the normal personalty of Hélène."[30] And we can only wonder how many other people might conceal a rich vein of linguistic facility just waiting to be unleashed by an appropriate trigger.

An amusing footnote to this aspect of the H. Smith case: Mlle Smith had an interesting response to Flournoy when he expressed his doubts about the genuineness of the Martian language and the truth of her descriptions of life on Mars. She invented an ideographic Ultra-Martian language, in which strange hieroglyphs represented words rather than letters, but unlike some hieroglyphs, they didn't resemble the objects for which they stood. Flournoy regarded this development as a somewhat childish attempt to construct a language he would be unable to analyze. He thought it "brilliantly corroborates the idea that the whole Martian cycle is only a product of suggestion and autosuggestion,"[31] to which we should probably add latent linguistic and mnemonic ability. As if to reinforce that conclusion, the Ultra-Martian cycle was quickly followed by a series of messages from the inhabitants of Uranus, and the Uranian language and writing differed greatly from the Ultra-Martian. But Flournoy found that the Uranian language copied the phonetic and alphabetic system of the original Martian language. In fact, he said it differed less from French than French differed from the languages of neighboring countries. Mlle Smith also inaugurated a Lunarian phase of her mediumship, introducing several different lunar languages about whose authenticity F. C. S. Schiller wryly commented, "Mr. H. G. Wells does not yet seem to have been consulted."[32]

SURVIVAL AND THE NATURE OF SKILLS

These reflections bring me to a different and much more thorny set of issues, having to do with the literature on postmortem survival. Even the best and most sophisticated writings in defense of the survival hypothesis rely on questionable assumptions about human abilities and skills. But when those assumptions are replaced by more cautious (or obviously true) alternatives, the case for survival seems to weaken considerably. (To avoid misunderstanding, I should emphasize that I'm not opposed to the survival hypothesis. On the contrary, as I chronicled in gory detail in my book on the subject, I'm very much on the fence with regard to this issue.[33] I'm also disappointed that advocates of survival typically consider alternative explanations only in their weakest or least plausible forms. And while I think it would be tremendously exciting and clearly momentous if we could make a good case for survival, when I'm tilting toward the nonsurvivalist side of the fence I simply think we have a very long way to go. The arguments which follow illustrate some reasons why.)

As I noted earlier, survivalist interpretations of the evidence compete with a set of exotic explanatory alternatives I call "The Unusual Suspects." In the previous section, I mentioned only one main subset of that class of explanations—those positing the operation and possibly the combination of rare or abnormal *nonpsi* abilities. And as I noted then, these might be similar to the abilities demonstrated by savants and prodigies, or just remarkable displays of memory, or perhaps creative abilities liberated in dissociative or other altered states. The other and more notorious type of Unusual Suspect is often called the "super-psi" or "living-agent-psi" explanation, framed in terms of relatively high-level psychic functioning on the part of living persons. According to this latter alternative, psychic functioning among the living masquerades (presumably unconsciously) as evidence suggesting interaction with the deceased. This isn't the place to explore the extensive and tangled web of issues involved in that debate. Rather, I want to examine what many have found to be an unusually compelling argument for survival, partly in virtue of its alleged resistance to living-agent-psi or other nonsurvivalist alternatives. The argument concerns cases apparently demonstrating the persistence of a deceased person's skills or abilities—that is, knowledge-*how*.

Generally speaking, for a case to suggest postmortem survival, two main conditions must be satisfied. First, some living person must display knowledge closely (if not uniquely) associated with a deceased individual, and second, we must have good reason to believe that this knowledge couldn't have been obtained by ordinary means. As I mentioned earlier, the knowledge in question falls into two broad categories: knowledge-*that* (information or propositional knowledge) and knowledge-*how* (abilities or skills). As an example of the former, suppose a medium channels accurate information, known normally to no living person, about the existence of the deceased's secret will hidden in a secret desk compartment. Impressive as that might be, many consider cases of the latter sort to be more impressive still. Suppose, for example, that a living person (say, a professional medium or a child) displays an ability or skill she never manifested before (e.g., the ability to speak German or write music) or perhaps an ability or skill uniquely associated with a deceased person (e.g., a distinctive style of humor or musical composition). Many writers believe that nonsurvivalist explanations (including living-agent-psi explanations) fail for the best of these cases, even when they admit that living-agent-psi explanations are always live options for cases of other sorts (in particular, those suggesting apparently paranormal knowledge-that). That is, even if we grant that people can paranormally "perceive" or acquire remote bits of information, these writers argue that it's implausible to suppose they can paranormally acquire someone's abilities or skills, especially in forms as idiosyncratic as the person's fingerprints. Thus, they conclude, the apparent persistence of a deceased person's skills is especially difficult to explain away along nonsurvivalist lines.

Superficially at least, that position seems credible. But it lacks relevant detail; we need to ask the survivalist: "What, *specifically*, is the problem with claiming that the knowledge-how seen in survival cases might have manifested by means of one or more of the Unusual Suspects?" The answer to that question, which some survivalists seem to think is state of the art, is as follows. Mere information or propositional knowledge is the sort of thing which we can acquire simply through a process of communication (normal or paranormal). But skills, such as playing a musical instrument or speaking a language, are another matter. Granted, obtaining information may be a necessary part of skill development; but it's hardly sufficient. That's because we develop skills only after a period of *practice*. But since the subjects in survival cases who display anomalous skills had no opportunity to practice them first, it's reasonable to reject explanations in terms of living-agent ESP and accept survivalist explanations instead.

As I said, this familiar argument has at least superficial appeal, but it's defective nevertheless. I've considered the relevant issues in great detail elsewhere;[34] so for now, a brief survey will have to do. And to simplify matters, let's ignore for the moment issues arising in connection with the persistence of a deceased person's *idiosyncratic* abilities, such as a distinctively quirky sense of humor or highly specialized technical expertise. At this point, it's enough to focus on more general abilities, such as the ability to write or speak in a foreign language, play a musical instrument, compose music, discuss theoretical physics, or solve mathematical problems, never mind the singular forms the abilities might take. If a nonsurvivalist hypothesis can't account for these general competencies, we needn't worry about their more highly specialized forms. However, I believe the Unusual Suspects have more going for them here than writers on survival have realized. In fact, I believe that on this general set of topics (and on others, for that matter), the literature on postmortem survival has been both superficial and confused.

So consider first how the argument above has been applied to the evidence for *responsive xenoglossy*, the ability to understand and respond appropriately in an unlearned language. Many have felt that if a medium can carry on a conversation in a language never learned through normal means and if the language is that of a known deceased person apparently expressing himself through the medium, then this would constitute good prima facie evidence for survival.[35] As Ian Stevenson once argued, this bit of reasoning rests on a crucial and usually tacit principle—namely, that "if skills are incommunicable normally, it follows that they are also incommunicable paranormally."[36] (I believe Stevenson here uses the word "skill" primarily in the way I've proposed using the term "ability"—that is, as intermediate between rudimentary capacities and the masteries I'm calling "skills." Fortunately, nothing major hangs on this terminological indeterminacy right now, but since much of the time Stevenson's arguments seem to pertain to *either* abilities or skills, I'll occasionally refer to this disjunctive target as "competencies.")

Anyway, according to Stevenson, it was the philosopher C. J. Ducasse[37] who first applied this principle to the evidence for survival, and Stevenson apparently considered it to be self-evident, or at least not in need of a defense. But first of all, it's not clear that the argument above does rest on this principle because it's not clear that *communicating* (or somehow conveying) competencies to the living is at issue. All we know is that some individuals *manifest* anomalous abilities. *How* they got them remains a mystery, and in fact (as I'll explain shortly), nonsurvivalist explanations needn't appeal to a process of transmission or communication. In any case, Ducasse's principle isn't nearly as obvious as Stevenson suggests, and if it's really an essential step in the survivalist argument, it may be more a liability than a virtue.

Consider: if Ducasse's principle is true, that isn't because it's an instance of the more general principle, "If any bit of knowledge x is incommunicable normally, then x is incommunicable paranormally." That general principle, in fact, seems quite clearly to be false. And ironically, if we accepted it, we'd have to conclude that ESP is impossible, because in ESP people gain access to data which at the time is inaccessible through all known normal channels of communication. So it's reasonable to assume that Stevenson (and other survivalists) don't accept this more general principle. And (among other reasons) that's because mediumistic communication actually *presupposes* ESP between communicator and medium or sitter or between communicator and physical states of affairs.[38]

But then if Ducasse's principle is true, presumably it's true only of competencies. But why? Actually, there are several crucial issues here. One concerns the possibility of expressing, developing, or acquiring abilities by circumventing our usual blocks or impediments to learning or training. Another concerns the relationship between competencies and practice. And a third concerns the legitimacy of generalizing about competencies, including the ability to speak a language. These issues overlap, but I'll try to keep them distinct.

Consider first some familiar obstacles to competency development. When we learn a new ability, we usually do a certain amount of unlearning, if only of acquired motor and cognitive habits that would interfere with manifesting that ability. For example, this process is a well-known and annoying feature of switching to a new spreadsheet or word-processing program after many years of familiarity with different software. Similarly, musicians and athletes might have to unlearn long-ingrained habits in order to advance to a higher level of expertise. Moreover, learning of any kind (whether of abilities, skills, or information) is often highly resistance laden; it can be hampered by an endless number of interfering beliefs, insecurities, and other fears. But as we considered in the previous section, some can overcome these physical, cognitive, and emotional obstacles relatively easily during hypnotic or other profoundly altered states. In fact, learning an ability might even be *facilitated* if the process bypasses the normal states in which our impediments to learning are strongest. That's why I argued it's important to consider the rich and suggestive literature on dissociation.

In fact, cases of DID reinforce the sorts of cases I mentioned in the previous section. They illustrate how dissociation facilitates the development or appearance of personality traits and abilities which might never be developed or displayed under normal conditions. Alternate identities (alters) exhibit wide varieties of behavioral and cognitive styles that can't be explained simply in terms of propositional knowledge and which seem highly unlikely in light of the multiple's previously observed capacities, repertoire of abilities, and level of achievement.[39] Those cognitive styles encompass various abilities and skills, such as mathematical facility, mechanical aptitude, and the skills of drawing, sculpting, and writing poetry. Differences also manifest commonly as changes in handedness and handwriting. (And of course these capacities, abilities, and skills might occur in distinctive or idiosyncratic forms, just as they do in nondissociative individuals.) But since alters appear quite suddenly and sometimes evolve quickly, their distinctive traits might emerge without any practice. (I realize we're very close here to the third issue mentioned above—namely, whether Ducasse's principle applies to *every* competency or just certain kinds and whether there are, accordingly, relevant differences between kinds of competencies. I'll return to that topic shortly.)

Moreover, the ostensibly mediumistic case of Patience Worth poses a serious challenge to a survivalist interpretation of xenoglossy, even though the case doesn't concern the apparent mastery of a foreign language.[40] Rather, the case closely resembles those mentioned in the previous section, but it's even more dramatic. It raises crucial and more general questions concerning the anomalous appearance of any kind of skill. The medium in this case, Pearl Curran, with only an eighth-grade education, no apparent literary ability, and no apparent interest either in literature or in arcane areas of scholarship, suddenly began producing a steady stream of poetry, novels, and remarkably pithy and witty conversation through a Ouija board. The material purportedly came from a personality named Patience Worth, who claimed to be a seventeenth-century Englishwoman. But there's little reason to think that the evidence supports the hypothesis of survival. Although "Patience" offered several (but not many) clues regarding her origin and identity, careful investigation has failed to uncover any indication that a Patience Worth ever existed.

A more reasonable interpretation of the case is that it demonstrates, even more dramatically than the usual good cases of hypnosis, the power of dissociation to liberate otherwise hidden or latent abilities. Although all the Patience Worth communications exhibit a distinctive and consistent personality as well as common verbal traits, Patience expressed herself in several different linguistic styles. In fact, one of her works was a Victorian novel, despite the fact that (as the book's dust jacket wryly noted) Patience was a pre-Victorian author. Most of the time, however, Patience communicated in an unprecedented style rooted in archaic Anglo-Saxon idioms. Much of her vocabulary was appropriate to the seventeenth century, but some of it seemed to belong to a period several centuries earlier. And some of the words Pearl used on those occasions were tracked down by contemporary scholars only *after* they appeared in the Patience Worth scripts.

Many consider Patience's literary works to be of exceptional quality, easily the best literature ever produced in a case of mediumship. But we needn't plunge into the murky waters of literary criticism. What matters here is that Patience Worth's poems and novels—and, indeed, her entire vivid personality—betray an intelligence and psychological style profoundly different from that displayed by Mrs. Curran. Furthermore, Patience's abilities and skills go well beyond anything Mrs. Curran (and, arguably, anyone else) ever exhibited. In fact, Pearl/Patience's compositional and improvisational abilities seem unprecedented in literary history. Patience was able to compose (often exquisite) poems on the spot in response to requests to write on particular topics. She could compose several works (sometimes in distinct literary styles) on the same occasion, alternating passages of one with those of another. She could write part of a novel for a while, leave off in mid-sentence to converse or work on something else, and then days later return to the novel exactly where she'd left off. More impressively still, with almost the sole exception of a beautiful child's prayer written haltingly and with a few revisions, Patience produced her entire corpus of thousands of poems and several long novels (one was over six hundred pages) without ever making a correction. She also performed astonishing compositional stunts. On one occasion she was asked to compose a poem with each line beginning on a different letter of the alphabet, from A to Z (omitting X). After a pause of a few seconds, the poem came through the Ouija board as fast as the scribe could take it down. There's much more to this remarkable case than my brief description suggests; I strongly encourage readers to study it closely.[41]

What I believe we can learn from this case and other cases of dissociation is that a person may apparently acquire, develop, or manifest novel abilities and skills under various kinds of abnormal—but not necessarily paranormal—circumstances and a variety of altered states. And since we obviously don't understand how these achievements are possible, we're hardly in a position to assert that the sudden appearance of new abilities and skills is impossible in the extraordinary circumstances generally found in ostensible survival cases. In fact, we have no choice but to admit our ignorance. We simply don't know what human beings are capable of under conditions we can scarcely comprehend.

Another (possibly deeper) set of problems concerns the way even sophisticated writers on survival (such as Stevenson and Gauld) generalize about skills. For example, Stevenson asserts, "Practice does not just make perfect; it is indispensable for the acquisition of any skill."[42] There are at least two related problems with that claim. First, abilities and skills differ from each other, often dramatically, in many respects, one of which is precisely the importance of practice in their development. The second problem (as I noted above) is that the *acquisition* of these competencies isn't clearly the issue. All we're entitled to discuss, strictly speaking, is their *manifestation*. We have no idea when, whether, or to what extent new abilities or skills were acquired by mediums or by the subjects of reincarnation investigations. In fact, we might interpret mediumship or reincarnation cases as examples of *possession* or control of the living by the deceased. And in that case, the knowledge-how exhibited in these cases would still be possessed by its original owner. The living subject would no more have acquired a new competency than a video or audio system has the competencies of the artists whose works they express during a live feed.

For now, though, let's focus on a different issue—namely, the obvious and critical point that practice is clearly not always needed in order to manifest abilities or skills for the first time. To see this, we need only consider child prodigies and cases of savantism. In fact, typical musical prodigies, such as Mozart, Mendelssohn, and Schubert, and mathematical prodigies, such as Gauss, manifest exceptional abilities *prior* to their being perfected or developed through practice. It's not simply that prodigious abilities are rudimentary at first and then simply evolve with amazing rapidity. The abilities of prodigies can be amazing even at the beginning, and the same is true of savants. For example, one fascinating musical savant was reportedly able to read music without ever receiving instruction. She was also able to improvise in the styles of various composers at the piano the first time this feat had ever been requested. In fact, she found that she could play in different composers' styles at the same time, the right hand playing in one style and the left hand playing in the other.[43] Similarly, Mozart could write down a complex piece of music while composing another one in his head; and to my knowledge there's no evidence that he first had to practice that skill. But more important, most subjects in survival cases demonstrate levels of expertise considerably less impressive than (say) Mendelssohn's initial displays of musicianship. In fact, the suddenly emerging abilities of child prodigies typically far exceed anything displayed by the subjects investigated in xenoglossy cases or in other cases suggesting survival. This can only reinforce the concern expressed earlier. Given our current and considerable level of ignorance about the processes involved, we have no idea to what extent certain unusual conditions (e.g., dissociation, trauma, specific physical impairments) may unleash prodigious competencies latent in many (or all) of us.

Of course, it's not just prodigies and savants who can manifest a new competency without practice. Ordinary folk demonstrate this all the time. Consider, for example, the ability to play tennis. Many people are naturally athletic, even though they may not be prodigiously gifted. And to the occasional consternation of those who are less precocious athletically, natural athletes can, on their first try, play a game of tennis reasonably well—at least without looking hopelessly foolish. In fact, on their first try they might even play as well as or better than others who've played for years, taken lessons, and so on. But more important, the natural athlete's beginning level of tennis would arguably match, if not exceed, the rather unimpressive linguistic abilities displayed in the best cases of responsive xenoglossy.

Probably, some will protest that the ability to play tennis is much simpler than speaking a new language. But that's doubtful. For one thing, competency difficulty is relative to a person's native capacities; there's no absolute standard of difficulty to which we can appeal. Consider: Is learning to play tennis more difficult than learning multiplication or learning to play the piano? Obviously, it depends on the individual. Moreover, there's even an interesting parallel between conversing in a language and playing tennis. Responsive xenoglossy involves more than the ability to form sentences in a new language; it also involves understanding and responding appropriately to sentences in that language. Similarly, the ability to play tennis goes beyond being able to get the ball over the net and in bounds. It also requires being able to return shots and place them appropriately.

Behind these various considerations lurks a more sweeping problem, one that stands in the way of *ever* concluding confidently that mastering one ability is more difficult than mastering another. First of all (as we noted at the beginning of this chapter), we have—at best—only a rudimentary understanding of what abilities are. Indeed, we saw that the various things we call abilities may not be similar enough to permit useful generalizations, much less of the kind made in the literature on survival. In fact (as we also observed earlier), we don't even know to what extent we can generalize about *individual* abilities. The things we identify as specific abilities (e.g., the ability to speak a language or compose music) typically *consist* of other competencies and capacities. But those subsidiary competencies may also be organized collections of other competencies, and so on, and at no point along the way is there some preferred set or arrangement of lower-level endowments necessary for exhibiting the more general capacity. Recall, for example, my previous illustration of how the ability to compose music can be expressed in a great variety of ways.

But in that case, certain familiar arguments in the survival literature seem hopelessly simplistic. For example, when Stevenson argues that skills can't be communicated or manifested without practice, he mentions riding a bicycle, dancing, and speaking a foreign language as examples. Similarly, Gauld writes,

> The ability to play bridge well is not simply a matter of learning (whether normally or by ESP) the rules (considered as a set of facts together with the precepts given in some manual). It can only be acquired by practising intelli-

gently until things fall into place. And it is the same with learning a language.[44]

But if there are serious disanalogies between linguistic competence and these other abilities, they may be deep enough to prevent us from generalizing usefully across them. And if we can't say how difficult or easy it is, *generally*, to learn or develop a new ability (including learning a new language), then this sort of survivalist argument is dead in its tracks.

Let's take second things first and consider some aspects of language learning. Language use, like musical composition, encompasses a variety of other capacities or abilities and manifests differently in different contexts. So it's not surprising that we can't say, *in general*, how difficult it is to learn a new language. The degree of difficulty seems to depend on many things, including linguistic aptitude, a good "ear," the context in which the language is learned, and how different the language is from one's native tongue.[45]

Furthermore, studies suggest that learning a second language is a significantly different process from learning a language for the first time, and also that a second language will be most difficult to learn in those respects in which it differs significantly from the first language. And since formal tests of linguistic aptitude don't measure real-life linguistic adaptability, we can't expect to be enlightened by administering such tests to subjects in xenoglossy cases (e.g., as Stevenson did in the Jensen case).[46] Contrary to what Stevenson claims, it seems false that the best tests measure "the ability to learn a modern language easily."[47] Moreover, even if there's no shortcut for learning words, we can't specify, in general, how much and what sort of exposure to a new language is necessary for low-level linguistic proficiency. As common sense would suggest anyway, that seems to vary widely from person to person and context to context. In fact, it seems reasonable to assume that, as in many other areas of life, some people learn much more quickly than others. Given the right combination of needs and natural aptitudes, some people might require only a very brief exposure to elements of a language, while others might require repeated exposure over a long period. And as cases of DID demonstrate dramatically, it may only be under very special circumstances that we exceed our ordinary capacities or demonstrate otherwise latent natural gifts.

But in that case, the crude linguistic competence displayed in most cases of xenoglossy may not be all that impressive. The context of answering simple questions put to a medium (probably in a dissociated state) differs in many respects from, and seems far less demanding than, real-life social situations where important personal and professional relationships are at stake, where the need and motivation to develop linguistic competence is especially high, and (of course) where complex issues are being discussed. So if the new language isn't radically different from the subject's native language, the low-level linguistic competence found usually in mediumistic xenoglossy may require little more than some native (and possibly latent) linguistic aptitude and also rudimentary knowledge (-that) of vocabulary and grammar, at least some of which could be learned paranormally. After all, once a person already speaks a language, a major part of learning a new language is exposure to it, whether it's through listening to actual conversations, watching movies, or listening to audio recordings in one's sleep (or while falling asleep). So since we're considering exotic explanations, we can't rule out the possibility that subjects gain the needed exposure to the new language nonconsciously as well as psychically. And of course, if those subjects have a knack for this sort of thing, they might be able to learn a surprising amount with only the most meager information. Sharada's mastery of Bengali, T. E.'s command of Swedish (or Norwegian), and certainly Gretchen's German[48] don't seem outlandish for an adult who might have been exposed to those languages extensively but nonconsciously, especially if it's possible for linguistic skills to be enhanced under dissociative or other unusual conditions.

Interestingly, Stevenson himself seems to make a crucial concession related to all this. Citing a case reported by Dreifuss, he says that it shows "that an ability to speak intelligibly (not merely to recite) a foreign language may remain dormant and emerge later in life."[49]

I should note that there are cases in which mediums speak in languages (e.g., Hungarian, Chinese) that are quite different from their own and to which they presumably had no normal exposure. But quite apart from serious questions concerning the reliability of the data in those cases, in every case I'm familiar with, some sitter present knew the language, and either they or someone else benefitted in rather obvious ways from receiving communications in those languages. So the possibility of telepathic sitter influence (including sitter PK) and unconscious sitter collaboration in these cases would be so strong that we're not justified in making much of the medium's apparently surprising linguistic competence.

Generally speaking, in addition to thwarting appeals to living-agent psi, what would be impressive prima facie evidence for survival isn't merely the manifestation of a novel (and, ideally, an impressive) ability or skill associated with some deceased person, but rather an ability or skill substantially different from and discontinuous with those one has already displayed. And in that light, the evidence for responsive xenoglossy isn't as impressive as some claim. The linguistic skills demonstrated are (a) typically very minimal, (b) not conspicuously beyond what we'd expect from someone with a possibly latent talent for language, (c) arguably continuous with abilities already demonstrated, and in the most florid cases, (d) vulnerable to charges of telepathic contamination from a sitter (not to mention other failings).

One intriguing recent case—but not of xenoglossy—may avoid some of the weaknesses of the language cases. It concerns the manifestation of very high-level (and, arguably, grand-master) chess played by someone with (as far as we can tell) little or no knowledge of the game and similar to that of a deceased Hungarian grand master.[50] Because I have only the most rudimentary knowledge of chess, I must defer to others for a full evaluation of the case. However, if telepathic leakage or influence from a sitter (or other interested parties) is a live option in the most dramatic xenoglossy cases, it should be an option in this case as well. In fact, nonsurvivalists can point to several relevant considerations. After all, the subject was playing chess with an opponent who had grand-master skills; the idiosyncratic moves of the deceased were verifiable and therefore available through ESP to both players; and both the grand-master opponent and others were aware of the deceased's presumed ignorance of chess strategies developed after the deceased's death (in particular, a strategy used to counter an opening variation attempted by the medium).

Nevertheless, Vernon Neppe argues that we can rule out a living-agent-psi interpretation of this case. He claims that a survivalist interpretation of the case tells a relatively straightforward causal story, positing nothing but interaction between a medium and a deceased communicator retaining at least some of his former embodied faculties. By contrast, he argues, "super-ESP . . . would require the repeated and active cogitation of a master chess player or players while alive, extended over a prolonged period of time with 47 different responses (47 moves in the game)."[51] This looks like a wholesome appeal to parsimony, and that's how Neppe presents it. But in fact it's merely a variant of the old and defective argument that a living-agent-psi interpretation presupposes an implausible degree or refinement of psychic functioning and (in particular) *more than would be required by the survivalist*. Now I admit, I've run out of patience with this line of argument. Contrary to what Neppe and others claim, the survival hypothesis *requires* virtually the same degree of psychic functioning as is posited by the living-agent alternative, and this is not a difficult point to grasp. According to the survivalist, the persisting intelligence of the deceased communicator is causally responsible for the forty-seven chess moves in question. But for that to occur, the deceased would need extended, accurate ESP (either telepathy with the medium or an onlooker or else clairvoyance of the chessboard) to know what the state of play is and then ongoing and effective ESP (presumably telepathic influence on the medium) to convey the desired next move. Neppe's oversight here is all too common, and since the error has been noted in the literature for some time now, at this stage of the survival debate I consider it inexcusable.[52]

Nevertheless, this remains a very intriguing case—possibly the best ever. But what's frustrating generally about the evidence for survival is that we have nothing close to the slam-dunk ideal cases that we can construct relatively easily.[53] Granted, this may not be the fault of those arguing the case for postmortem survival. For all we know, some survivalists may be correct that the transition to "the other world" involves some loss of cognitive function, or perhaps only that it erects various obstacles to communicating through a "clear channel." So long as we're both seriously entertaining the possibility of survival and also playing fair, we're in no position to rule that out.

However, that concession doesn't alter the status of the argument for survival. Most cases are disappointing in some crucial respect or another. When it comes to knowledge-how, what would be completely coercive would be a subject doing something comparable to composing music in a deceased composer's style and at a similar level of quality, never before having played a musical instrument or exhibited any musical ability, and doing it in a context where sitter or onlooker contamination is completely out of the question and, in addition, where the ability is also conspicuously foreign to the subject (geographically and culturally). By that standard, the survival evidence for knowledge-how still has a long way to go.

CURMUDGEONLY POSTCRIPT

Before bringing this chapter to a close, I feel I must register a final concern—or complaint, actually—for the reader's consideration. This, too, has to do with the nature of abilities, in particular the strategies appropriate to studying them.

In this case, I'm focusing on parapsychologists. And to be clear, the people I have in mind are some (and sometimes the most high-profile) fellow members of the Parapsychological Association (an affiliate organization of the American Association for the Advancement of Science) and Society for Scientific Exploration (a worthwhile organization devoted to the study of a broad range of scientific anomalies), as well as a small number of others outside the PA and SSE, all of whom have published serious and peer-reviewed research in the field. I'm not concerned here with those who think they're parapsychologists simply because (like laughable TV ghost hunters) they're interested in the phenomena and make ignorant and amateurish attempts to study them. My target here is a subset of those who ostensibly know what they're doing and who've contributed to the scientific and scholarly literature in the field. Despite parapsychology's position on the margins of scientific respectability, that field of research has a rich and complex history and also a reasonably well-defined set of issues, problems, and areas of expertise. People lacking the relevant background knowledge and competencies simply aren't worth the time of day.

What's bothering me is this. Although exceptions aren't hard to find, parapsychologists can be rather pretentious scientifically and at the same time disappointingly meek. In part that's because they suffer from various misconceptions about what it is to be scientific and clear headed. And in part it's because they're often beleagured by stupid, incompetent, or dishonest attacks, usually from critics who know much less than they do about psi research. It's hardly surprising, then, that parapsychologists tend to be defensive about their activities. They take pains to demonstrate that they follow recognizably careful procedures and methods endorsed (in word if not in deed) by other branches of science. And thanks in part to many decades of criticism, both from within and outside their own ranks, they do this unusually well. In fact, experienced psi researchers are arguably more careful and sophisticated methodologically than most mainstream scientists.[54] But this conventional methodological obsessiveness sometimes conceals a suspicious motive. Many parapsychologists want to downplay the apparently radical nature of their enterprise and show that they're honest-to-God scientists who operate exactly the way their peers do in more established fields. So they proceed as if they're doing nothing more than legitimately extending tried-and-true scientific techniques to a new and largely ignored domain of phenomena.

Although that conservative strategy may be understandable, it hasn't proved to be especially useful in undermining skepticism about parapsychology. Skeptical responses to even first-rate and inventive experiments are as strong now as they ever were.[55] Moreover, the strategy may not be ultimately defensible rationally. At the very least, it ignores an obvious point noted at least as long ago as Aristotle and reiterated throughout this book—namely, that different domains require different methodologies (i.e., different investigative procedures and modes of explanation). What saddens me about this is that these methodologically conservative parapsychologists are squandering an opportunity to be on the cutting edge of scientific inquiry. They *could* be genuine trailblazers with respect to their data *and procedures*. But in fact, these parapsychologists don't operate as much on the frontiers of science as they'd like to think; they're not quite the pioneers they often fancy themselves to be (and others expect them to be). Rather, they tend in important ways to be methodologically myopic and disappointingly unimaginative and shortsighted. They follow meekly in the already misguided footsteps of traditional experimental psychology by slavishly conforming to methods canonized in physics. They strive to make their work technically crisp and fail to notice that it remains conceptually crude.

I find this profoundly disheartening. It's preposterous to suppose that the behavioral sciences are analogous to the physical sciences in all but the phenomena. It's naive and professionally chauvinistic to think that the principles and methods of certain "hard" sciences are inherently deeper than those of other sciences, especially the behavioral sciences (for more on this, see chapter 8). And it's simply foolish to think that the secrets of psi phenomena will be unraveled by pretending it's not (at least in part) a behavioral science, much less to assume that psi phenomena will conform neatly to the few rigorous experimental procedures that have proved useful in psychology. Indeed, as I've argued in detail elsewhere,[56] the so-called source-of-psi problem—that is, the problem of sneaky or naughty psi—is insuperable. We have every reason to think that psi functioning, by its very nature, can be triggered unconsciously and no reason to think we can develop a "psi meter" to detect either those unconscious triggers or lines of causal influence in a psi experiment. But then, since no conventional experimental controls can prevent people from using whatever psi abilities they can muster to achieve whatever result they want, experimenters can only pretend to know the full details of what occurred, and they'll never know for certain whether (or to what extent) the final results should be attributed to the under-the-surface psi activities of someone other than the official subject.

So as I see it, the real trailblazers of parapsychological research will be those who recognize that conventional experimental methods and controls may be practically useless in psi experiments and that laboratory work has little, if anything, of interest to tell us about the nature (rather than the mere existence) of psychic functioning. In fact, I suspect that the most valuable attributes a psi researcher can have are those that (ironically) seem to be in short supply in psychology—namely, perceptivity and sensitivity. Parapsychologists need to be good observers; they must perform a role similar to that of the biological naturalist who can record and systematize the subtleties of broad ranges of organic behavior. For one thing (as I mentioned earlier), that sort of work is a vital preliminary to doing anything with psi in a laboratory setting. Until we have some sort of empirically justified idea of what psi is doing in the world (and it's no more than a conceit to think we have it now), we don't even know what it is we're looking at in the lab. But equally important, playing the psychic naturalist might be about all we can *ever* do with psi phenomena. As I noted above, there seems to be no way, in principle, to apply conventional experimental controls to the study of psychic functioning, even to determine conclusively or exhaustively whose psi (if any) is responsible for (or contributes to) the observed result.[57]

If parapsychologists are to be conceptual pioneers, they must take a bold and pluralistic stand on the nature of science. They must repudiate the idea that only the methods of a few physical sciences yield genuine scientific understanding. They must recognize that there are different legitimate forms of understanding and explanation and different ways of systematizing a domain of phenomena, no one of which is inherently privileged over the others. Contrary to what some opportunistic parapsychological skeptics say on the matter, experimentation and experimental repeatability aren't essential to the scientific enterprise; rather, their success and utility vary greatly from one domain to the next. Experimentation is appropriate and essential in physics, chemistry, and microbiology, less so in astronomy, geology, and meteorology, and less so still in the behavioral sciences. Of course, what we need from science is *systematicity*, some way of converting an otherwise motley and disorganized collection of observations into an orderly and intelligible whole. But ultimately the domain guides and limits our attempts to systematize and understand it. It's almost comically arrogant to think that nature should conform to our favorite modes of investigation or that we should dictate to nature the forms in which we're willing to accept its secrets.

But parapsychologists do that all too often. Rather than concede that psychic functioning, like most human competencies, should be studied in real-life contexts where those competencies have genuine dynamic relevance, they attempt to study psi in artificial settings which (at best) are deeply significant only to the experimenter. Rather than accept the limitations of vertical explanations in the case of human abilities, they stubbornly theorize about their subjects as if they were biocomputers analyzable in mechanistic terms. And rather than recognize that psychological and parapsychological laws and regularities may not translate without residue into the language of another science, some assume that only physics can uncover the deepest facts about psi. That's why parapsychology is so often boring and unilluminating. And that's why most parapsychologists, despite their protestations to the contrary, have no greater understanding now of psychic abilities than they did when J. B. Rhine arrived at Duke.

REFERENCES

Bem, D. J. (2011). Feeling the future: Experimental evidence for anomalous retroactive influences on cognition and affect." *Journal of Personality and Social Psychology, 100*(3), 407–425.

Bialystok, E., & Hakuta, K. (1994). *In other words: The science and psychology of second-language acquisition.* New York: Basic.

Braude, S. E. (1992). Psi and the nature of abilities. *Journal of Parapsychology, 56,* 205–228.

Braude, S. E. (1995). *First person plural: Multiple personality and the philosophy of mind* (Rev. ed.). Lanham, MD: Rowman & Littlefield.

Braude, S. E. (1997). *The limits of influence: Psychokinesis and the philosophy of science* (Rev. ed.). Lanham, MD: University Press of America.

Braude, S. E. (2002). *ESP and psychokinesis: A philosophical examination* (Rev. ed.). Parkland, FL: Brown Walker.

Braude, S. E. (2003). *Immortal remains: The evidence for life after death.* Lanham, MD: Rowman & Littlefield.

Braude, S. E. (2007). *The gold leaf lady and other parapsychological investigations.* Chicago: University of Chicago Press.

Braude, S. E. (2009a). The concept of dissociation from a philosophical point of view. In P. F. Dell & J. A. O'Neil (Eds.), *Dissociation and the dissociative disorders: DSM-V and beyond* (pp. 27–36). New York: Routledge.

Braude, S. E. (2009b). Perspectival awareness and postmortem survival. *Journal of Scientific Exploration, 23*(2): 195–210.
Cory, C. E. (1919). Patience Worth. *Psychological Review, 26*, 397–407.
Dreifuss, F. E. (1961). Observations on aphasia in a polyglot poet. *Acta Psychiatrica et Neurologica Scandinavica, 36*, 91–97.
Ducasse, C. J. (1962). What would constitute conclusive evidence of survival after death? *Journal of the Society for Psychical Research, 41*, 401–406.
Edwards, T. (Writer). (1984). The case of ESP. In T. Edwards & T. K. Rockefeller (Producers), *Nova*. Boston: WGBH/BBC.
Eisenbeiss, W., & Hassler, D. (2006). An assessment of ostensible communications with a deceased grandmaster as evidence for survival. *Journal of the Society for Psychical Research, 70*, 65–97.
Eisenbud, J. (1982). *Paranormal foreknowledge: Problems and perplexities.* New York: Human Sciences.
Eisenbud, J. (1992). *Parapsychology and the unconscious.* Berkeley, CA: North Atlantic.
Flournoy, T. (1900). *From India to the planet Mars: A case of multple personality with imaginary languages.* Princeton, NJ: Princeton University Press.
Gauld, A. (1982). *Mediumship and survival.* London: Heinemann.
Litvag, I. (1972). *Singer in the shadows.* New York: Macmillan.
Luria, A. R. (1987). *The mind of a mnemonist.* Cambridge, MA: Harvard University Press.
Neppe, V. M. (2007). A detailed analysis of an important chess game: Revisiting "Maróczy versus Korchnoi." *Journal of the Society for Psychical Research, 71*(3), 129–147.
Prince, W. F. (1927). *The case of Patience Worth.* New Hyde Park, NY: University Books.
Prince, W. F. (1929). A note on "Patience Worth." *Bulletin of the Boston Society for Psychical Research, 10*, 16–19.
Putnam, F. W. (1989). *Diagnosis and treatment of multiple personality disorder.* New York: Guilford.
Putnam, F. W. (1997). *Dissociation in children and adolescents: A developmental perspective.* New York: Guilford.
Raikov, V. L. (1976). The possibility of creativity in the active stage of hypnosis. *International Journal of Clinical and Experimental Hypnosis, 24*, 258–268.
Ross, C. A. (1997). *Dissociative identity disorder: Diagnosis, clinical features, and treatment of multiple personality.* New York: Wiley.
Sacks, O. (1985). *The man who mistook his wife for a hat.* New York: Summit.
Schiller, F. C. S. (1902). Professor Flournoy's "Nouvelles observations sur un Cas de Somnambullisme avec Glossolalie." *Proceedings of the Society for Psychical Research, 17*, 245–251.
Sheldrake, R. (1998). Experimenter effects in scientific research: How widely are they neglected? *Journal of Scientific Exploration, 12*, 73–78.
Stevenson, I. (1974). *Xenoglossy: A review and report of a case.* Charlottesville: University Press of Virginia.
Stevenson, I. (1984). *Unlearned language: New studies in xenoglossy.* Charlottesville: University Press of Virginia.
Sudduth, M. (2009). Super-psi and the survivalist interpretation of mediumship. *Journal of Scientific Exploration, 23*(2), 167–193.
Treffert, D. A. (1989). *Extraordinary people: Understanding "idiot savants."* New York: Harper & Row.
Viscott, D. S. (1969). A musical idiot savant. *Psychiatry, 32*, 494–515.

NOTES

1. As noted elsewhere in the book, "dissociative identity disorder," or "DID," is the designator du jour of this condition.
2. I've explored these matters in considerable detail elsewhere. See, for example, Braude, 1995, 2002, 2003.
3. See Braude, 2003 for the fruits of those labors.

4. Braude, 1992.
5. Braude, 1997.
6. For some of the best, see the essays in Eisenbud, 1992.
7. Braude, 2002.
8. My students charmingly like to think of this as the *fart factor*. They understand that while the capacity to fart is presumably universal, being able to do so is constrained by a wide variety of situational and psychological factors. That's why most people can fart in the presence of only select others (if they can do so in another's presence at all).
9. Braude, 2003.
10. Sacks, 1985.
11. Treffert, 1989.
12. Braude, 1997.
13. Braude, 1997, 2007.
14. See, e.g., the Nova/Horizon film "The Case of ESP" (Edwards, 1984).
15. I used to see this often in female students early in my career (especially when I taught logic), but I'm pleased to note that it seems far less common now.
16. Braude, 1997, 2007.
17. However, in the 1908 Naples sittings and with three experienced debunkers of physical mediumship (two of whom were accomplished magicians), Eusapia's best phenomena occurred under the most stringent controls. For a summary of the case, see Braude, 1997.
18. Ibid.
19. Braude, 2003, chap. 4. Also this book, chap. 4.
20. See Braude, 1997, for details of these cases.
21. Luria, 1987. I should add, however, that "S"'s difficulties were exacerbated by his synesthesia.
22. Braude, 2009a. This refines somewhat the analysis offered in Braude, 1995.
23. See chapter 4 for more on the creativity of dissociation.
24. See Braude, 2003 for details.
25. Braude, 2003.
26. Raikov, 1976.
27. Ibid., p. 259.
28. Ibid., p. 261.
29. Flournoy, 1900. See Braude, 2003 for a more detailed discussion.
30. Flournoy, 1900, p. 163.
31. Ibid., p. 168.
32. Schiller, 1902, p. 247.
33. Braude, 2003.
34. Ibid.
35. Gauld, 1982; Stevenson, 1974, 1984.
36. Stevenson, 1984, p. 160.
37. Ducasse, 1962.
38. Braude, 2003, 2009b; Sudduth, 2009.
39. Braude, 1995; Putnam, 1989, 1997; Ross, 1997.
40. Braude, 2003; Cory, 1919; Litvag, 1972; Prince, 1927, 1929.
41. Or, of course, failing that, to read my summary in Braude, 2003.
42. Stevenson, 1984, p. 160.
43. Viscott, 1969.
44. Gauld, 1982, p. 102.
45. Bialystok & Hakuta, 1994, and see the discussion in Braude, 2003.
46. Stevenson, 1974.
47. Ibid, p. 50.
48. Stevenson, 1974, 1984.
49. Stevenson, 1974, p. 53; Dreifuss, 1961.
50. Eisenbeiss & Hassler, 2006. For commentary, see Neppe, 2007.
51. Neppe, 2007, p. 147.
52. For more on this classic error, see Braude, 2003, 2009b; Sudduth, 2009.

53. For examples, see the final chapter of Braude, 2003.
54. See Sheldrake, 1998.
55. For example, Daryl Bem's very ingenious recent series of experiments created a lot of noise but no noticeable change in people's beliefs about psi. See Bem, 2011.
56. Braude, 1997.
57. See also Eisenbud, 1982, 1992.

Chapter Seven

Some Thoughts on Parapsychology and Religion

One common theme in the world's great religions is, to put it roughly and colloquially: you can't fool God. The general idea is that if you do something reprehensible, you might fool others into thinking that your behavior was acceptable, and you might even fool yourself (at least superficially) into thinking the same thing. But, according to this view, there's a sense in which you're really not getting away with it. The major religions all have something to say about the price we ultimately pay for our earthly transgressions. It may have to do with the place where we're eventually forced to reside (and I don't mean New Jersey), or it may concern the number of times we must live again before we get our act together and stop screwing up, or it may simply concern the humiliation of being confronted in the afterlife with a litany of our sins (possibly presented by our victims). But whatever the scenario is supposed to be, the underlying common theme is that sooner or later, we'll pay for our wrongdoing, even if we reap some transitory benefits in the short term.

Many undoubtedly find this religious admonition very handy. It encourages them to remember that the universe is much bigger than they are and that there are implacable and morally relevant forces we're powerless to subvert but which we unwisely ignore during all-too-frequent times of hubris and carelessness. Thus, the admonition can help keep our behavior in line by helping us maintain an appropriately humble and ethical perspective on our activities.

Interestingly, even atheists and agnostics occasionally advocate something arguably close to the theme that you can't fool God, although of course they state this theme (and other religious views) without referring to a deity. So instead of saying "you can't fool God," some nondeists might argue that people know in their hearts when they're doing wrong, even if they can't articulate exactly what they feel is improper about their actions and even if they manage to deceive themselves into thinking they've acted ethically. According to these nondeists, the price we pay for our wrongdoing is internal. Echoing a viewpoint as old as Plato, they claim that in some sense our minds will be disordered or unsettled or that we'll otherwise be profoundly agitated or unhappy, no matter what sorts of superficial or temporary rewards we enjoy.

A somewhat different nondeistic approach would be to say that there are natural laws or regularities governing behavior. Presumably, these laws would be statistical rather than universal; that is, they have exceptions. But, like statistical generalizations about the dangers of certain foods, or of unprotected sex, or of taking philosophers too seriously, we ignore them at our peril. So nondeists of this sort might argue that people eventually pay for their wrongdoings, whether it's in terms of how they suffer psychologically, make themselves ill, alienate others, or engage in various forms of self-defeating behavior. Of course, some nondeists simply reject the notion that there's *any* secular analogue to the claim that you can't fool God. For them, that's simply one of many religious superstitions we should reject. Perhaps members of this group should read no further, especially if they also reject (as some do) the claim that psychic phenomena are genuine.

Nevertheless, for the more intrepid, we can note how the evidence from parapsychology adds an interesting wrinkle to this issue. It suggests ways in which our psychic interactions may intimately link all conscious beings and all objects (no matter how physically distant) into a kind of global community. In fact, one intimidating way of understanding the evidence for ESP and PK is that we have more than the normal ways of gaining information about and affecting—even taking action against—one another. So the data of parapsychology suggest that people might sometimes pay for their wrongdoings through various kinds of psychic interventions. If telepathic interactions occur, then perhaps our real motives can't be as easily concealed as we'd like to think. And if PK occurs, then perhaps psychic vendettas are a genuine option. In that case, then, we can apparently interpret the claim that you can't fool God in a way consistent with both deism and nondeism (or at least forms of those positions open to the existence of psychic functioning). And on a related but somewhat less sinister (or at least less unsettling) note, the data of parapsychology might also help us understand the apparent (if only sporadic) efficacy of prayer.

WHAT THE EVIDENCE SUGGESTS

In previous works, I've had much to say about the relative merits of experimental and nonexperimental evidence in parapsychology.[1] Although I've expressed my admiration for some of the experimental work, I've also noted that it's of very limited utility. In particular, I've argued (contrary to the classical view inherited largely from J. B. Rhine) that quantitative laboratory experiments are unlikely to convince even open-minded skeptics of the reality of psychic functioning, and that even if that unlikely event happened, such formal experiments in principle tell us virtually nothing about the nature of psychic functioning.

This is not the place to rehash my arguments for that general position. What matters is this. It's clear to me at least that some of the most interesting, compelling, and illuminating parapsychological data comes from venues outside the lab, and I submit that some of this data (particularly from the best cases of reported large-scale PK from late nineteenth- and early twentieth-century physical mediumship) is at least as clean and well controlled as evidence gathered from traditional and formal experiments. In fact, I believe that nonlaboratory evidence promises insights into the nature of psychic functioning far greater than anything we could conceivably learn from laboratory research. Granted, that's hardly the received view, even within parapsychology. But few people (parapsychologists included) either know what the best nonlaboratory evidence is or have taken a close and clear-headed view of the relevant issues. (I'll speculate briefly below on why that is.)

So let's suppose (if only to see where it leads) that I'm right and that nonlaboratory evidence must be taken seriously, both for its ability to establish the reality of psychic functioning and for the light it can shed on the nature of psi. And let's consider what that body of evidence suggests about the scope of human intention and the possible purposiveness behind even seemingly impersonal events.

First of all, if we accept the best nonexperimental evidence for observable (or macro) PK, then we have reason to believe that humans can intervene in day-to-day occurrences to an extent that most people (in the West, at any rate) would find deeply intimidating. To see this, suppose (if only for argument's sake) that psi can occur in real-life situations. In that case, then, it's also reasonable to suppose that those occurrences might go undetected. After all, there's no reason to think that all instances of observable PK must be as obvious or incongruous as (say) table levitations or other movements of ordinarily stationary objects. On the contrary, if everyday PK can insinuate itself into our daily lives—say, by affecting the cycle of traffic lights, foiling radar traps on the highway, messing with our computers or other electronic gear, aggravating a coworker's arthritis, or hiding our socks, it could easily go unnoticed. Moreover, there's no reason to think that occurrences of everyday PK must be preceded by some sort of overt precursor or warning (a paranormal counterpart to a flourish of trumpets). So since the nonexperimental evidence for observable PK seems to demonstrate that PK does really occur in naturalistic settings outside the lab, then for all we know, everyday PK might blend smoothly and imperceptibly into ordinary surrounding events, and real-life PK might affect or cause events of a sort that we usually believe are independent of PK (e.g., heart attacks, car crashes, good or bad "luck," ordinary decisions and volitions, and both healing and illness).

Further considerations reinforce this picture. For one thing, both laboratory and nonlaboratory studies suggest that psi phenomena can have both conscious and unconscious causes.[2] And since human intentions are all-too-frequently malevolent, it may be that not all psi effects are innocuous or benign. Moreover, large-scale effects needn't have large-scale causes. For example, a heart attack, mine collapse, or car crash can be triggered by a small event happening in just the right place (e.g., a ruptured fuel line or weakened strut). But in that case, it's clear that the magnitude of PK required for these effects is no greater (or at least not substantially greater) than that for which we already have both experimental and nonexperimental evidence. So we can't rule out the possibility of massive, unconsciously caused, and unwanted PK effects on the grounds that those effects require psi to operate on an implausibly large scale. Furthermore, the only difference between a normal car crash and one caused by PK might be in their unobservable underlying causal history, and so there's no way to determine conclusively whether psychic interventions played a role in that history. As I've noted before, it's not as if we can go around with a PK "meter" to detect its presence before the ostensible PK event occurs. But in that case, it looks like it's impossible in principle to distinguish conclusively a psychically caused or influenced event from one that occurred in the absence of psychic influence. All these considerations point us, probably uncomfortably, toward accepting the possibility of what many unfortunately call "super psi."

There's also a more abstract reason for taking seriously the possibility of psychic functioning of much greater scope and refinement than what laboratory studies suggest. Given our present and considerable state of ignorance concerning the nature of psi, it's methodologically indefensible to open the door to the paranormal (even as a mere thought experiment) and then decide a priori that it can be opened only a crack. If even modest ESP and PK indicate that we can bypass the usual constraints on acquiring information and influencing our environment, then as far as we know, anything goes. For example, in the case of PK, since we have no idea how agents affect remote physical systems, we're in no position to assume that PK effects are inherently limited in magnitude or refinement. After all, we don't understand how even the smallest-scale PK violates or circumvents the usual constraints on influencing other physical systems. So we're in no position to set limits in advance on how far those apparent violations may go. The only way we could ever be entitled to insist that psi effects have inherent limits would be on the basis of a thoroughly developed and well-supported theory, one that embraces *all* the available evidence for psi (not just the laboratory evidence) and explains how or why psi functions both in and out of the lab. But at present, no decent theory forbids large-scale or super psi (most simply ignore it), and (as I've argued elsewhere) no scientific theory renders any form of psi improbable.[3] At our current (in fact, pathetic) level of understanding, super psi is as viable as puny psi.

If this view of things is on the right track, then we might have to take seriously what most westerners would consider to be a "magical" worldview, one commonly associated (usually and conveniently condescendingly) only with so-called primitive societies. According to this picture of reality, our conscious and unconscious desires can surreptitiously influence a broad range of events, both local and global, including those we think we're merely observing rather than causing.

Needless to say, in industrialized countries at least, this suggestion is typically greeted with alarm. It proposes a view of reality which most people find profoundly repulsive or frightening, conjuring images of superstitious, prescientific cultures that take seriously hexing or the "evil eye." So, of course, many resist this picture; they feel that accepting it is tantamount to taking a giant step backward in our intellectual development. Not surprisingly, then, the resistance to this picture is often passionate, and it takes many forms. One strategy is to knowingly adopt specious reasoning when arguing against the reality of PK.[4] Another is to pay no attention to one's own inconsistencies. Here, I have in mind those who know that no force can be used exclusively for the good but who nevertheless simultaneously reject the possibility of malevolent PK and defend the efficacy of (say) psychic healing or meditation for world peace.

At any rate, the foregoing observations about PK in life can be extended to the forms of ESP. Just as occurrences of PK might, for all we know, inconspicuously permeate everyday events such as car crashes and heart attacks, our mental lives might conceal a rich vein of telepathic and clairvoyant interactions. Occurrences of ESP, like occurrences of PK, needn't announce their paranormal ancestry beforehand or in some other way display their paranormal nature. For example, although some of our psychic experiences might stand out like a sore thumb, in general there needn't be anything about psychic experiences that—like a marker or label—distinguishes them from ordinary experiences.

I realize this runs against a common, but I believe unreflective, view. Many believe that ESP experiences would have to be qualitatively distinctive or exceptional—say, by being peculiarly vivid or by being incongruous relative to our other experiences. But I see no reason why that must be the case.

For one thing, the vividness of an experience may have more to do with the background against which it occurs than with any intrinsic property of the mental event. For example, it may be a function of the relevance of the experience to our current interests, just as we might be able to pick out our name spoken softly amid a noisy crowd. And there's no reason why ESP experiences must be personally relevant or even notable, especially if we can interact psychically with strangers.

Granted, the vividness of the experience might also result from the contrast between it and the rest of what's going on in our mind at the time. But it would be foolish to assume that the contrast could only be due to the experience's paranormal origin. Most of us have more than one thing going on in our minds at any given time, even if we're not consciously multitasking. We're all steaming, stinky cauldrons of issues and concerns, most of which bubble furtively below the threshold of conscious awareness, but any of which might rise to the surface with little or no provocation. So disruptions to (or contrasts with) the flow of our mental lives are likely to result from all sorts of nonparanormal and thoroughly humdrum ordinary mental processes. The problem remains, then: both in principle and certainly in practice, there may be no way to distinguish ordinary thoughts and feelings from those that have an underlying paranormal causal history.

Furthermore, the nonexperimental evidence for ESP—particularly the evidence from mental mediumship and precognition—suggests that the cognitive forms of psi are considerably more extensive and refined than we might have thought simply on the basis of laboratory studies. The nonexperimental evidence also reinforces laboratory data suggesting that telepathy and clairvoyance are at least two-stage processes. First, there would be a stimulus or interaction stage during which subjects are affected telepathically or clairvoyantly. And second, there would be a manifestation stage during which subjects consciously experience or express the causal influence of the remote mental or physical event. The initial interaction occurs *pre*consciously, and then later the received information rises to the surface in a form that's both convenient and appropriate (e.g., a dream, a feeling, an image, or an urge or impulse to act). So, for example, telepathic influence needn't—and arguably seldom does—manifest immediately. Indeed, so-called *telepathic deferment* is a well-known feature of many apparitional cases.[5] In fact, the enormous body of carefully documented anecdotal material suggests that, like posthypnotic suggestions, the effects of telepathic influence might be delayed considerably until an appropriate time.[6]

These considerations pose a very clear cognitive and psychological challenge. If it's possible for ESP to infiltrate our lives in subtle and undetectable ways, that's as potentially unsettling as the prospect of sneaky and naughty PK. For in that case, our most private thoughts and feelings might not be so private after all. Instead, they might be transparent to anyone and therefore vulnerable to indiscriminate psychic snooping. And if so, although we might fool ourselves into thinking that our sinister motives are benign, the real fact of the matter might still be open for public inspection and condemnation.

Of course, it's easy enough to understand why that's disturbing. Probably everyone likes to feel they have *some* private thoughts and feelings, including inner demons or sins of the heart. In fact, even if we wrestle successfully with our less savory impulses and desires, and even if we feel our victories are morally praiseworthy, we're still likely to prefer that those inner battles remain hidden. A dramatic illustration of something like this *telepathic transparency* or lack of mental privacy was portrayed in Alfred Bester's science-fiction novel *The Demolished Man*, about an attempt to commit a perfect crime in a future society whose police had highly developed ESP ability. Another potent illustration of the noxious side of telepathic leakage—from the other end of the causal chain—was a memorable *Twilight Zone* episode in which a man spent a horrific day privy to the thoughts of everyone around him. Those revelations, it turned out, were much more than he wanted to know, and they made his life a living hell.

Ironically, once we grant the possibility (in fact, the likelihood) that psi occurs outside the lab or séance room and plays a role in everyday life, we must also grant that it could be an unrecognized causal factor in ordinary scientific experiments. After all, it's absurd to think that PK, for example, could occur only in experiments conducted by parapsychologists. But in that case, it's easy to see how conceding the reality of PK complicates the interpretation of normal and apparently straightforward scientific research. If PK occurs in laboratory situations and can affect the sensitive and delicate equipment designed to test for it, *and* if it can occasionally occur unconsciously in those situations (as some studies suggest[7]), one would expect this to be possible—if not probable—in nonparapsychological laboratory work as well. Presumably all scientists are interested, and interested deeply, in their experimental outcomes, whether or not they're working in parapsychology. So if we grant that motivation or motivation intensity can trigger the operation of PK, then one would think that conventional scientific experiments are no less vulnerable than parapsychology experiments to psi-mediated experimenter (or observer) effects.

Moreover, if ESP occurs, then there's no such thing as a genuinely blind or double-blind experiment. The ordinary control procedures in these tests block only normal channels of information. In fact, the possibility of both uncontrollable telepathic leakage and telepathic influence might go a long way toward explaining some of the more puzzling evidence from psychology for experimenter expectancy effects—that is, evidence that the experimenter's expectations concerning research results affects the experimental outcome.[8] For example, in one famous series of tests, experimenters were provided with groups of rats which they were told had been bred to be maze- or

Skinner box–bright or maze- or Skinner box–dull; and the experimenters believed that their tests were designed to confirm the success of this selective breeding. But in fact that was false; the rats hadn't been selectively bred for their dullness or brightness. On the contrary, the groups of rats assigned to the different experimenters were selected so as to *minimize* differences between them, and which groups were to be labeled dull or bright was decided randomly. Nevertheless, the rats believed by their experimenters to be bright outperformed those believed to be dull.[9]

Another study compared the performance of brain-lesioned rats to that of rats who received only a sham surgery in which the skull was cut through without damaging brain tissue. The rats were labeled as either lesioned or nonlesioned. But randomly, some of the really lesioned rats were labeled accurately, and some were falsely labeled as nonlesioned. Similarly, some of the unlesioned rats were randomly and falsely labeled as lesioned. The results again clearly indicated the effect of experimenter expectancy. In the case of genuinely lesioned rats, those mislabeled as nonlesioned outperformed those labeled as lesioned. And for the genuinely unlesioned rats, the correctly labeled rats outperformed those falsely labeled as lesioned.[10]

Of course, not all expectancy effects noted in the literature are as potentially exotic as these. In other experiments, with human subjects, observed expectancy effects can easily be attributed to mundane types of interpersonal interactions. But in the experiments just described, it's an open and interesting question how the experimenters' expectations were conveyed to (or otherwise influenced) the rats. In any case, whether the processes involved are ordinary or exotic, all scientists must assume that their interests or expectations might be causally relevant to their experimental outcomes. They certainly can't pretend that as experimenters they're merely neutral participants in an objective search for scientific knowledge. Nevertheless, mainstream science (especially non-behavioral science) almost never takes the possibility of expectancy effects into account (even to the extent of using blind methodologies).[11] But then for all we know, (a) expectancy might have been contaminating the results of centuries of scientific experimentation, (b) some of the effects might be psychically mediated, and (c) we haven't a clue how extensive that contamination might be. And that possibility might be one reason many scientists resist taking a serious look at the evidence from parapsychology.

In fact, this would be one instance of a more general concern extending well beyond the scientific community. Many people seem to think that by admitting the reality of psychic functioning, especially day-to-day and inconspicuous (sneaky and naughty) psi, we're conceding that things could really get out of hand. It's not simply that scientific experimentation might be deeply polluted and unreliable. As I mentioned earlier, for all we know, we might be living in a world where we need to fear a profound lack of mental privacy, the direct psychic influence of others' malevolent thoughts, and the potential and daunting responsibility for the psychic efficacy of our own uncontrollable unsavory impulses and desires.

The problem of the resistance to psi is extremely subtle and complex, and some writers have made worthwhile and provocative observations about it.[12] But for now, we need only note that this resistance exists on a broad scale and that much of it may plausibly be attributed to the fears and concerns just mentioned. For present purposes, though, what matters is how the basis for those concerns also fuels a secular interpretation of the claim that you can't fool God.

SNEAKY PSI

So how might an appeal to psychic functioning help flesh out the claim that you can't fool God? One approach, suggested above, would be to regard telepathic transparency as the secular version of God's access to our thoughts and feelings. Deists who sin only in their hearts might take comfort in believing that only God knows about their moral struggle, at least so long as they also believe that a forgiving God would recognize the virtue of resisting temptation and defeating one's inner demons. Nondeists, by contrast, lack that particular invisible means of support. So if they believe in telepathy, they'd consider *other potential sinners* to be the ones who know what's really in their heart of hearts. From their perspective, it's only other mortals who would be in a position to pass judgment on their moral struggles. But what would be the moral status of that earthly court of appeals? I suppose nondeists would consider a divine tribunal to be a greater source of solace than any collection of mortal and telepathically intrusive peers. But they'd possibly find it to be more sternly judgmental as well, and more cosmically intimidating. So perhaps they might find the judgment of other sinners to be a viable alternative to the divine tribunal and still enough to keep them on the straight and narrow.

Another approach would be to view psi as a psychologically safe way of expressing certain feelings (for example, guilt and anger) that have other and probably more familiar negative consequences. Consider guilt first. Most of us are probably all too familiar with the usual ways in which guilt can prevent us from "getting away with" our shameful acts. Guilty feelings may prevent us from lying convincingly or successfully feigning innocence in some other way. Or we might simply be overcome with remorse and confess our sins. Or we might unconsciously sabotage some later activity and thereby atone symbolically for our earlier behavior. Or we might make ourselves sick, utilizing destructively the impressive control of our bodies noted in cases of placebo effects, hypnosis, and biofeedback.

But what if we manage to surmount or avoid these ordinary obstacles to successful sinning? Let's assume (perhaps without justification) that placebo effects, hypnotic control of bodily functions, and psychosomatic ailments aren't expressions of PK. How (or how else) might we psychically express our guilt?

Perhaps the most obvious tactic would be to subject ourselves to various difficulties or calamities that appear to originate from external sources. We could have an apparently inexplicable run of "bad luck"; or we might simply find ourselves confronted with a single major nuisance or tragedy (e.g., a serious accident, expensive car repair, lost wallet, etc.). By externalizing psi influence—that is, by obscuring its emotional origins and making our misfortune appear to emanate from outside us, we make it easier to view ourselves as victims of simple impersonal bad luck at best and cosmic—or divine—justice at worst. In either case, however, we'd be attempting to deflect responsibility, both for our original shameful behavior and for our psychic retaliation against ourselves.

If these suggestions are on the right track, they might alter our perspective on a view of humanity captured by the Yiddish distinction between a shlemiel and a shlemazel.[13] According to one familiar version of that distinction, a shlemiel is someone who spills soup on himself; a shlemazel has it spilled on him. So a shlemazel is someone who seems to be the victim of impersonal forces or the universe at large. Shlemazels exemplify the "unlucky soul," and as I know from personal experience, they really exist. I was once married to one member of an entire family of shlemazels, and I also lived next door to a married couple of shlemazels a number of years before that. For reasons of personal harmony, I'll limit my comments to the latter case. I don't know if my next door neighbors were shlemazels before they met (and I wish I could now find that out). But their life as a married couple was undoubtedly a nightmare of annoyances and accidents. For example, they felt as if they were living in consumer hell; it seemed that nearly everything they bought was defective. Appliances and other electronic equipment almost invariably failed to operate out of the box; an apparently solid wooden rocking chair fell apart within their first week of ownership (with their infant sitting on it), and their cars were always in the shop, even though they owned brands noted for their reliability.

But my favorite incident was when the wife enthusiastically invited me over to see the large poster-sized photo she'd just purchased, framed, and hung proudly on her living room wall. She told me the photo was of the Golden Gate bridge. But when I saw it, I had to inform her that it was actually a picture of the Brooklyn Bridge. My neighbor, in other words, had both symbolically and (in a sense) actually purchased the Brooklyn Bridge. This, as many readers will realize, is a classic—although now quaint—image of the "sucker" or "loser."

What I'm proposing, then, is that my neighbors and shlemazels generally might not merely be unlucky. Instead, their misfortune might be a psi-mediated expression of their own negativity, guilt, or self-hatred. Through the use of psi, they might be arranging their lives covertly to punish themselves or reinforce their own negative self-image, and they might accomplish this with the same degree of refinement found in more familiar forms of self-destructive behavior. Moreover, like other types of unconsciously driven self-destructive behaviors (for example, the way many find themselves repeatedly in the same kinds of unhealthy romantic entanglements), all this would be accomplished in a manner that deflects responsibility away from themselves.

The parallel with psychosomatic ailments seems obvious enough. Similarly, acts of psychic self-aggression might be analogous in certain respects to results observed in some biofeedback studies. For example, Basmajian found that subjects could learn to fire a single muscle cell without firing any of the surrounding cells.[14] Of course, those subjects had no idea *how* they accomplished this feat. But for all we know, our psychic expressions of guilt or self-hatred might exhibit a similar degree of precision or refinement, and we might execute them with a similar degree of ignorance concerning the processes involved. Moreover, just as conscious willing often interferes with success in biofeedback tasks, it may likewise thwart our attempts at psychic influence. And the specter of responsibility may, again, be one reason why it's advantageous for us to remain consciously ignorant of our roles in the process.

Having said all this, it's now easy to see how we might psychically (and unconsciously) express our anger not just toward ourselves but toward others as well. Instead of expressing hostility overtly, we might help arrange an accident or other nuisance for our victim. In fact, the more obscure the connection to us, the better. If a total stranger hits our victim in a car crash, we can conveniently deny any complicity in the event. After all, we didn't know the offender. This scenario reminds us that shlemazels might be victims of conveniently untraceable remote influence by people who know how wretchedly they've behaved and who accordingly wish them harm.

Perhaps these unsavory options will be clearer when we recall that expressions of hostility might be *symbolic*. People often express their hostility toward surrogates in order to deflect responsibility for what they're really feeling. This is a familiar fact; we might be angry at a spouse, for example, but adopt the less risky course of venting our anger toward a coworker or an unsuspecting cashier at the supermarket. So let's suppose we're feeling very angry, say, toward a parent, and suppose that instead of expressing our anger directly toward the parent, we psychically target someone who stands in symbolically for the parent. This could be someone who has the misfortune of resembling the parent or having the same initials; but it might just be some poor randomly selected shlemazel. We might therefore cause a complete stranger (someone who, for the moment at least, represents the parent) to suffer an accident. And of course, because we don't know the victim, we can easily convince ourselves that we had nothing to do with it.

It may be, then, that at least part of the force behind the claim that you can't fool God concerns the way in which psychic influences make it difficult to escape the anger of others or the wrath or contempt we feel toward ourselves. At least that's one way some atheists or agnostics could accommodate an analogue to that belief.

THE EFFICACY OF PRAYER

On a slightly more positive note, if telepathic leakage, telepathic influence, and PK can occur, then we can see how to explain the apparent (if only occasional) efficacy of prayer causally but without reference to a deity. The potential psychic strategies are obvious enough: (1) Relevant people could come to know our prayers through ESP and respond consciously or otherwise. (2) We might telepathically or psychokinetically influence others to carry out needed actions. Or (3) we could psychokinetically bring about relevant physical states of affairs (e.g., a change in someone's health). Obviously, psi-sympathetic atheists or agnostics could maintain that it's through these forms of psychic influence that our prayers are sometimes answered. Even deists could hold that at least on some occasions, prayers that seem to be answered by God are in fact answered through human psychic intervention. But if the efficacy of prayer results from psi rather than from divine influence, the underlying causal story would seem to be anything but straightforward, and the prospects may not be quite as cheery as one might have thought.

I imagine most readers would argue that prayers are frequently (and perhaps usually) *not* answered. For example, when both teams or contestants in a sporting event pray for victory, at least 50 percent of them will not have their prayers answered (I suppose a tie game could be viewed as divine mischief). So if an apparently efficacious prayer isn't simply a coincidence, what needs to be explained is not simply why prayer occasionally succeeds but also why it sometimes (or usually) fails. It's at this point that a secular explanation of prayer as psi mediated might have certain theoretical advantages over conventional deistic interpretations. Here, too, I'll be covering ground I've gone over elsewhere.[15] However, the current discussion widens the scope of my previous observations.

The problem is this. For any attempt at psychic influence to succeed (whether or not it's a prayer), it must presumably navigate through an unimaginably complex causal nexus—a web of underlying and possibly countervailing psychic interactions and barriers. On the assumption that people do function psychically, it's reasonable to assume that their psychic activities have a natural setting—in fact, a natural *history*, a larger stage of operations in which psychic activities happen more generally. Analogies are easy to come by. For example, good hypnotic subjects can raise welts on the skin in response to suggestion. It's a neat trick, of course, and one that we likewise don't understand. But whatever exactly the mind-body connection might be in such a case, presumably the hypnotically induced welt effect exemplifies a process that exists more broadly. Presumably, related or similar events occur more widely—and probably less conspicuously—in more naturalistic or less contrived settings as well (e.g., in psychosomatic ailments or spontaneous remissions). Analogously, psychic functioning wouldn't be the sort of thing we call forth just to meet the demands of psi research or other overt solicitations, such as police investigations, séances, or for the purpose of entertainment, and it certainly didn't emerge for the first time when psi research began. Ostensibly psychic events have been reported throughout recorded history, long before investigators arrived on the scene. So if psi has a natural history, then it's reasonable to suppose that it evolved along with other organic coping mechanisms and that it's typically (or at least often) driven by our deepest genuine or perceived needs and interests. That's why it's implausible to regard psi as the sort of capacity that's likely to be elicited (or elicited in a full-blown or illuminating form) in response to the contrived and superficial needs created by formal experimentation.[16] (See chapter 6 for more on psi and the nature of abilities.)

Moreover, if people can use their psychic capacities unconsciously, then it's reasonable to assume that they might be attempting to use them continually. In fact, it's also reasonable to assume that people will (again, possibly unconsciously) erect psychic barriers or defenses against the psychic interventions of others, just as we ordinarily go about our daily affairs with a normal armor of defenses against the more familiar and overt activities of our peers. In that case, there's no reason to believe that our attempts at psychic influence are likely to succeed. Even if there's no limit in principle to what we can accomplish psychically, those activities might be subject to and defeated by serious case-by-case practical constraints.

An example I've used on other occasions should make the point clear. Consider, first, what must happen to carry out an ordinary nonpsychic plan of action. Suppose I'm a virtuoso assassin, and suppose I'm contracted to carry out a "hit" on Mr. Jones. No matter how good I am at my profession, a number of factors can confound even my best efforts. In particular, I could be caught in the crossfire of other activities having nothing directly to do with me. Of course, Mr. Jones might anticipate my actions and go into hiding, hire bodyguards and make other security arrangements, or even put out a contract on me. But more important, others will be going about their daily business, and even though these people don't have me or my job on their minds, some of their actions might inadvertently get in my way. Similarly, any number of natural processes will be unfolding, some of which may be unpredictable and probably all of which I'm powerless to prevent or divert. In general, I can be stymied *indirectly* by an indefinitely large number of events and activities. My attempted hit could be thwarted by elevator repairs, airport weather delays, traffic jams, a power failure, a flat tire, a broken water main, a faulty telephone, pedestrians getting into the line of fire, a sudden storm, an attack of hiccups or the flu, an allergic reaction, food poisoning, police rushing to the scene of a nearby crime, and so on.

Now if we can continually and unconsciously exercise our psi, imagine how dense the total underlying nexus of potentially countervailing activities and interactions will be. Actually, I don't think we can really imagine this, especially if psychic causation isn't subject to typical spatiotemporal limitations. Our prayers (or any other attempted psychic influence) might be limited not only by ordinary "above-the-surface" activities and events. They would also have to successfully penetrate or navigate through a vast array of other *psychic* causal chains initiated in principle, and perhaps with little or no interruption, by every other human being (at least). And presumably any one of those causal chains could interfere with or neutralize our own psychic efforts. So the potential obstacles to exerting psychic influence might be so numerous and so great that it might be the exception rather than the rule if our efforts succeed. Certainly, it would seem to be impossible to predict when our psychic efforts would succeed. So even if our successes are not fortuitous (because, after all, like those of the assassin, they'd be related causally to real volitions and efforts), they might nevertheless seem quite random. Moreover, the prospect of collective prayer doesn't seem appreciably better. Both a lone assassin and a team of assassins can be thwarted by an enormous number of countervailing influences.

Of course it's not just underlying psychic activities that could frustrate attempts to fulfill our prayers. That's just icing on the cake—or perhaps better, it's the cake beneath the icing. Our failures might be largely homegrown and result in part from the familiar and natural unreliability of our capacities and the inevitable difficulty of summoning our own best efforts. Analogously, athletes, musicians, and actors can't always perform as well as they'd like (or as well as they usually do), stand-up comedians don't always elicit the laughs they desire, and the best writers sometimes suffer writer's blocks and temporary failures of eloquence. Here, too, there's no shortage of reasons for our failures, although they're presumably far less numerous than what an underlying paranormal causal nexus can provide. For example, we might be sleepy, sick, nervous, preoccupied, bored, overconfident, or underprepared.

But as daunting as the totality of potential obstacles to success (both normal and paranormal) might be, there's no reason to think that our attempts at psychic influence are doomed to fail. And when they succeed, it might be due to a combination of normal and paranormal factors—for example, the resoluteness of our volitions along with a temporary and possibly fortuitous clearing in the underlying causal nexus (e.g., perhaps merely good navigating, or perhaps something analogous to proposed "wormholes" in spacetime). If so, then the secular interpretation of prayer as a ritual for invoking our psi capacities actually makes some sense of prayer's mixed and rather underwhelming record of success. By contrast, if we try to explain the efficacy of prayer in terms of divine intervention, then many might feel that we need to tell a variety of ad hoc, convoluted, and antecedently implausible stories about why a presumably loving God withheld his grace from us all those times our prayers were not answered—not to mention why the prayers of apparently conspicuously wretched persons seem to have been answered instead.

Of course, these considerations don't clinch the case for a psi-enlightened secular humanism. For example, I realize that the so-called problem of evil is very complex. But I believe they do show that this position has more explanatory power and empirical support than some might have thought. More generally, whether we're deists or nondeists, I believe the reflections in this chapter show that appeals to psychic functioning can play a useful and plausible role in the interpretation of religion.

REFERENCES

Basmajian, J. (1963). Control and training of individual motor units. *Science, 141*, 440–441.
Basmajian, J. (1972). Electromyography comes of age. *Science, 176*, 603–609.
Braude, S. E. (1997). *The limits of influence: Psychokinesis and the philosophy of science* (Rev. ed.). Lanham, MD: University Press of America.
Braude, S. E. (2002). *ESP and psychokinesis: A philosophical examination* (Rev. ed.). Parkland, FL: Brown Walker.
Braude, S. E. (2003). *Immortal remains: The evidence for life after death.* Lanham, MD: Rowman & Littlefield.
Braude, S. E. (2007). *The gold leaf lady and other parapsychological investigations.* Chicago: University of Chicago Press.
Braude, S. E. (2008). The fear of psi: It's the thought that counts. In G. Taylor (Ed.), *Darklore* (Vol. 2) (pp. 99–111). Brisbane: Daily Grail.
Burnham, J. R. (1966). *Experimenter bias and lesion labeling.* (Unpublished manuscript). Purdue University, West Lafayette, Indiana.
Eisenbud, J. (1970). *Psi and psychoanalysis.* New York: Grune & Stratton.
Eisenbud, J. (1982). *Paranormal foreknowledge: Problems and perplexities.* New York: Human Sciences.
Eisenbud, J. (1992). *Parapsychology and the unconscious.* Berkeley, CA: North Atlantic.
Gurney, E., Myers, F. W. H., & Podmore, F. (1886). *Phantasms of the living.* London: Society for Psychical Research.
Martin, M. (1977). The philosophical importance of the Rosenthal effect. *Journal of the Theory of Social Behavior, 7*, 81–97.
Myers, F. W. H. (1903). *Human personality and its survival of bodily death.* London: Longmans, Green.

Rosenthal, R. (1976). *Experimenter effects in behavioral research* (Enlarged ed.). New York: Irvington.
Rosenthal, R. (1977). Biasing effects of experimenters. *et cetera, 34*, 253–264.
Rosenthal, R., & Rubin, D. B. (1978). Interpersonal expectancy effects: The first 345 studies. *Behavioral and Brain Sciences, 1*(3), 377–415.
Sheldrake, R. (1998). Experimenter effects in scientific research: How widely are they neglected? *Journal of Scientific Exploration, 12*, 73–78.
Society for Psychical Research. (1894). Report on the census of hallucinations. *Proceedings of the Society for Psychical Research, 10*, 25–422.
Tart, C. T. (1986). Psychics' fears of psychic powers. *Journal of the American Society for Psychical Research, 80*, 279–292.
Tart, C. T., & Labore, C. M. (1986). Attitudes toward strongly functioning psi: A preliminary survey. *Journal of the American Society for Psychical Research, 80*, 163–173.

NOTES

1. See, in particular, Braude, 1997.
2. For illustrations of apparently unconscious laboratory psi, see my discussion of Schmidt's RNG PK tests in Braude, 2002.
3. Braude, 1997, chapter 1.
4. See Braude, 1997, 2007, 2008 for a discussion and examples.
5. See the discussions of apparitions in Braude, 1997, 2003.
6. See, e.g., Gurney, Myers, & Podmore, 1886; Myers, 1903; Society for Psychical Research, 1894.
7. See, for example, the discussion of Schmidt's PK tests in Braude, 2002.
8. I've discussed the so-called Rosenthal effect more fully in Braude, 2002. See also Martin, 1977.
9. Rosenthal, 1976, 1977; Rosenthal & Rubin, 1978.
10. Burnham, 1966.
11. In this connection, readers should look at Sheldrake's paper on the almost shocking neglect of blind methodologies in most scientific disciplines. See Sheldrake, 1998.
12. For example, Eisenbud, 1970, 1982, 1992; Tart, 1986; Tart & Labore, 1986. Also Braude, 2008.
13. I discuss this distinction and its relation to parapsychology in Braude, 2007, in connection with the topic of synchronicity.
14. Basmajian, 1963, 1972.
15. Most extensively in Braude, 2003, but also in detail in Braude, 1997.
16. I discuss this more fully in Braude, 1997.

Chapter Eight

Credibility under Fire

Advice to the Academically Marginalized

I've had the good fortune to spend most of my scholarly life considering issues that the majority of academics treat with disdain. In the process, I've learned a number of important lessons, some of which I hope are worth passing on to others in the academy and elsewhere who likewise find themselves assailed for their interests and beliefs. So this chapter will be unlike the others in this volume. It will be distinctively personal, more conversational and informal, and (I hope, at least for some readers) therapeutic. It will also be decidedly more polemical than the other chapters (although the rest of this book is hardly polemic-free). I make no apologies for any of this, including the polemic; under the circumstances, I believe that my tone and approach are both fitting and long overdue. Actually, I even hope I can offer something at least modestly inspirational here, despite the fact that we (appropriately) don't usually expect philosophers to have an inspirational arrow in their quiver.

The areas of research that have drawn the fire of my colleagues have been (a) parapsychology and (b) dissociation generally and multiple personality/dissociative identity disorder (DID) specifically. Both of these broad areas of study have been treated as illegitimate or at least questionable by many others, and the style and substance of the attacks have been remarkably similar. I want to explore those similarities and offer some counsel and support to readers who dare to tackle topics that expose them to intense criticism at best and ridicule at worst.

Chapter 8
PHILOSOPHICAL CRITICISM

First, some relevant background information to explain why I feel I can speak with authority about being criticized. It's not just because I was raised in a home where sarcasm was regarded as a familial obligation. And it's not just because I was married at one time to someone listed in the *Guinness World Records* under "Consecutive Insults." What matters here is that I'm very familiar with the experience of being attacked by my academic colleagues for the topics I've chosen to study and for the views I've held on those topics. Of course, to some extent, fielding vigorous criticism is simply part of the experience of being a professional philosopher. It's what we in philosophy learn to do to one another, and purportedly it helps weed out false propositions from the true ones. The true ones, supposedly, are those that can withstand the blistering assaults of philosophical argumentation. I grant that this technique is at least somewhat effective; sloppy thinking often gets exposed as such. Ostensibly, this dialectical weeding process works because we philosophers are generally hardy sorts who can withstand forceful and sustained criticism from our colleagues; and in part that's supposed to be because our egos play no role in the views we hold. In fact, we're supposed to know that we're engaged in a search for truth; and if we stumble, we should even be *glad* to discover that we were wrong, especially so long as that revelation brings us closer to the truth.

At least that's the official view. Not surprisingly, I haven't met too many people who fit that idealized profile. In fact, I was shocked early on, during my undergraduate philosophical studies in London, to realize that philosophical debate often had more to do with scoring points than with getting things right. I'd been under the impression that philosophy was important and noble and that its aim was to be deep, not clever. Admittedly, I was appallingly naive, and even in graduate school I was still somewhat surprised to see how ugly, personal, and too often shallow philosophical argumentation could be. Only gradually did I appreciate how widespread that phenomenon was. But I also observed that many philosophers handled the broadsides from their colleagues rather well. Apparently, like combat veterans, they went about their jobs with their armor on, relatively impervious to the unpleasant side of philosophical argumentation, and as a result they remained somewhat oblivious to the personal side of philosophical disputes. Perhaps it's part of a more general insensitivity to interpersonal dynamics; academics in abstract disciplines are often accused of that. But in some still-flickering optimistic corner of my mind, I also think it's because many realize that however nasty or silly the arguments may get and however much some of them may sting, it's *important* to subject one's philosophical views to the toughest criticism. If our views can't pass that test, they don't deserve to survive. Even if our fears and personalities get in our way, we still *want* to get at the truth.

The same holds—or at least should hold—for our theoretical views in science, every one of which rests on numerous (usually unrecognized) abstract or philosophical presuppositions. However, whereas philosophers deal with tough criticism as a matter of course, I've learned that people outside of philosophy don't handle it with the same sort of equanimity. In fact, many find its tone to be downright rude and offensive. When I began criticizing the theoretical speculations of scientists working in parapsychology, I was alarmed initially to learn that those scientists felt that I'd attacked them personally and savagely. That wasn't how it had seemed to me. As far as I was concerned, I was simply employing the argumentative strategies I'd used for years previously but only with other philosophers. And when I became deeply involved in the study of dissociation, I discovered that mental health professionals had their own distinctive—and clinically appropriate—perspective on this. Not surprisingly, they, too, found my theoretical criticisms needlessly and unexpectedly harsh, and I'd like to think that I eventually learned to moderate my tone. At any rate, I appreciated the perspective of my clinician colleagues. Quite understandably, they felt that it's important for people to validate and support one another, not tear each other down; life's difficult enough as it is. Of course, we philosophers don't generally excel at that sort of activity. I believe most of us genuinely love to argue, to challenge one another, and to examine issues from all sides. This is a deep and dominant philosophical character trait, which professional training often exacerbates by turning us into intellectual attack dogs.

So I really do sympathize with those who recoil from strongly worded philosophical criticism. No one likes to be told that they hold views that are unintelligible, nonsensical, or confused. Nevertheless, there's a danger in soft-pedaling one's criticisms and in overmoderating one's tone. I see it all too often in fields other than philosophy. If criticism is too polite, it becomes too easy to brush off. And the fact is, within their own fields at least, nonphilosophers are seldom held as accountable for their theoretical abominations as philosophers are. However, it should be obvious that if you're going public with your views, you should be prepared for others to subject them to intense scrutiny, and you should be prepared to defend them if necessary. I've been amazed to see scientists and clinicians get flustered and even very angry at sincere and respectful questions from people who were simply unwilling to accept their assertions at face value. Now I know that those sorts of defensive reactions are complex; I know that they often betray various insecurities or fears; and for that reason they might merit our sympathy and concern. But sometimes they merit our contempt instead, because the inability to entertain criticism can also reveal a lack of seriousness and intellectual honesty.

It's also important to keep in mind that there's no disgrace in being confused about deep and abstract issues. Not all confusions are foolish, and not all forms of theoretical nonsense are examples of stupidity. Nonsense is something that literally makes no sense. Of course, some forms of nonsense *are* pretty stupid. But (as I've noted in other chapters and elsewhere) there's another kind of nonsense, which is easy to fall into and which is easily obscured, and which also takes real effort to uncover. This is *deep nonsense*. Often, it's hidden beneath assumptions we're not aware of making; at other times, it's built into the language we speak. All I want to say about this now is that I see the job of a philosopher as being, at least in part, that of deep nonsense police. And if I or others play that role with you, try to remember that nonsense of this sort is nothing to be ashamed of. Some of our greatest minds have been guilty of it, going back at least as far as Plato. In fact, I'd say that one of the most exciting things about philosophical or conceptual criticism is the occasional revelation that something which looked reasonable on the surface is actually highly problematical. (Of course, I suppose one reason I'm a philosopher is precisely that I get excited about such things.)

THE GOOD, THE BAD, AND THE UGLY

But there's another and perhaps more pertinent reason why I feel I know something of value about professional criticism. As I noted earlier, it has to do with the areas of research I chose once I moved beyond my early and professionally safe interests in philosophical logic and the philosophy of language. For it was at this point that criticisms of my work frequently morphed from typically vigorous dialectic into ridicule and abuse. And it was at this point that I had to confront more instances and varieties of intellectual cowardice and dishonesty than (in my naivete) I'd previously thought possible—at least from a philosophical and scientific community I'd at one time revered for its presumed devotion to free and serious inquiry.

For some time now, I've been struck by similarities between research in parapsychology and the study and treatment of DID. These similarities extended to the argumentative strategies deployed against researchers in those fields, and I found that lessons learned from my study of the paranormal carried over into the study of dissociation. Probably much of what I'm about to say will not be news to veteran researchers in parapsychology, but perhaps it will be of some value to parapsychological newcomers, mental health professionals studying dissociation, and researchers in other areas of anomalistics or so-called frontier science (e.g., ufologists and cryptozoologists). Moreover, I realize that many of those researchers are defensive enough already about the scientific or intellectual legitimacy of their areas of study, and so I realize that offers of help from a philosopher/parapsychologist might not exactly seem like manna from heaven. Still, I hope readers will bear with me, because one of the things I want to discuss is the pointlessness of allowing irresponsible critics to put you on the defensive.

But one more preliminary, concerning an important difference between attacks leveled at mental health professionals treating dissociative disorders and those directed toward parapsychological researchers. In the former case, clinicians have been forced to deal not only with criticisms of their ideas and attacks on their professional competence but also (in the United States at least) with the threat of lawsuits and crippling legislation. And since I believe that many competent clinicians have been unjustifiably condemned along with those who were genuinely irresponsible,[1] that's a matter for which I have considerable sympathy. But it's also a matter in which I have no expertise. After all, philosophers aren't your usual prime candidates for legal action. (What would it be for? Conceptual assault? Reckless superficiality? Can you imagine a False Profundity Syndrome Foundation?) Anyway, the legal assaults on clinicians *are* connected with something about which I believe I can offer help, because the lawsuits at least tacitly involve attacks on the clinician's *thinking*. Behind the attempt to constrain some clinicians' behavior is the assumption (or the overt assertion) that they're confused or mistaken on matters of theory or of fact. And it's at that point that the mental health professional and parapsychologist have more in common than many realize.

So let's consider what I find to be the striking similarities between research in parapsychology and the study and treatment of DID. Three in particular stand out for me, and I believe many of my observations carry over smoothly to other areas of anomalies research.

(1) In both parapsychology and the study of DID, researchers deal with phenomena whose existence other professionals deny; and as a result, members of both fields are often labeled as naive, credulous, or simply sloppy in their thinking.

(2) Related to (1), critics claim that people who report ostensible occurrences of psi phenomena (especially those taking place outside strict laboratory settings) do so because they're in the grip of biased or motivated misperceptions. Similarly, critics have often charged that clinicians treating multiples don't *really* see switching between alter personalities/identities; at best they see subtle forms of role playing or social compliance, and at worst they don't see anything at all worth mentioning. The problem, according to these critics, is that both areas of research illustrate on a grand scale how people merely see what they want (or are disposed) to see and how their observations are contaminated by their theoretical biases and conceptual confusions.

(3) In some ways the most interesting similarity, critics express their views with an intense hostility uncharacteristic of and inappropriate to an objective scientific inquiry. In fact, critics often engage in obviously shoddy (if not sleazy or dishonest) dialectical tactics whose weaknesses they know perfectly well, which they wouldn't resort to in other contexts, and which

they'd protest loudly if they'd been the target of the attack instead. To me, this suggests strongly that these critics are moved by something deeper than an impartial, clear-headed, and nonegocentric quest for the truth.

These three general similarities are all closely related, and they rest on a common set of problems and issues. Let's begin by considering the last point first—that is, the intensity with which critics deploy transparently weak arguments. In parapsychology, critics often like to charge that the evidence can all be explained away as due to fraud or malobservation. Although I happen to think that claim is false, it's not an *inherently* implausible position. What *is* unacceptable, however, is the way the claim often gets defended. And one standard skeptical tactic is to base one's evaluation on the least impressive or simply irrelevant bits of evidence and generalize from those. Of course, a more honest and fruitful approach would be to look instead at those cases which seem, prima facie, to be most *resistant* to skeptical counterexplanations. Those are the ones, obviously, that count. To dismiss all the evidence in parapsychology by arguing from anything but the strongest cases is, clearly, to set up a straw man.

Critics tend to do something similar in connection with the study of dissociation and the treatment of dissociative disorders; they, too, generalize from the weakest or from irrelevant cases, or else they attack clinicians for views they don't hold. For example, Nicholas Spanos waged a prominent campaign against the reality of hypnosis as an altered state distinct from engaged role playing or social compliance. And he did this by focusing on experiments which *at best* would illustrate only very modest or relatively uninteresting forms of hypnosis—that is, which even those sympathetic to hypnosis would regard as marginal and relatively easy to simulate unconsciously.[2] Spanos systematically either ignored or passed quickly over the phenomena he *should* have discussed, the dramatic phenomena of hypnosis (e.g., hypnotic anesthesia of the sort reported by Esdaile and others).[3] These are precisely the cases most difficult to explain away as forms of social compliance.

There's no point in mincing words about this. For one thing, straw-man reasoning is an elementary and often transparently dishonest dialectical trick which every philosophy student learns to identify in introductory courses in critical thinking and logic. And in Spanos's case, its deployment had to be either dishonest or jaw-droppingly stupid. (Spanos was clearly not stupid.) The studies by Esdaile and others demonstrating the efficacy of hypnotic anesthesia are well known, and it's simply ridiculous to maintain that surgical patients who don't react to (say) limb amputations, removal of hundred-pound scrotal tumors, or removal of toenails by the roots are merely complying with the wishes of the surgeon by feigning a lack of pain. These are *paradigm* cases of genuine and profound altered states and quite different from the nonreactions to relatively mild pain (e.g., hands in ice water) considered by Spanos. In the same vein, Ray Aldridge-Morris based his skeptical appraisal of DID on a case which by no stretch of the imagination should have been taken as a paradigm case of multiplicity or as a strong case from an evidential point of view—namely, the Bianchi ("Hillside Strangler") case.[4] What's needed instead is a case for which malingering is not a plausible counterexplanation.

Much of the literature on so-called false memories is equally disgraceful. For example, Richard Ofshe and Ethan Watters, in their wretched paper "Making Monsters," set up a straw man by attacking clinicians for holding a "recorder" view of memory (the idea that the mind records and stores everything perceived). But that picture of memory is simply not presupposed by clinicians who believe that patients may recover hidden memories of abuse, and in fact most dissociation researchers seem quite aware that the recorder view is antecedently implausible. Ofshe and Watters adopt this tactic again when they attribute to clinicians and then attack the gratuitous and false assumption that amnesia always results in the *conscious experience* of lost time.[5]

And again, Elizabeth Loftus and other luminaries of the False Memory Syndrome Foundation discuss memory distortions in situations whose psychodynamics differ profoundly from those of the therapeutic contexts in which the allegedly insidious memory reports were elicited. So Loftus and others make unwarranted extrapolations from apparent memories of merely awkward or unpleasant situations to memories of traumatic events. Or they make unwarranted extrapolations from the influence on memory of a trusted family member to the alleged influence of a therapist.[6]

In parapsychology, similar straw-man gambits have been tried countless times—for example, dismissing the entire corpus of well-documented accounts of the mediumship of D. D. Home by focusing exclusively on reports of phenomena observed by uncritical witnesses under poor conditions and no or inadequate controls. Perhaps the most egregious example is Trevor Hall's obsessing over Home's alleged Ashley House levitation, one of the most poorly documented incidents in Home's twenty-five-year career.[7] Hall devotes nearly one-fourth of his book to this case but says nothing whatever about William Crookes's detailed work with Home (e.g., his accordion-in-the-cage or spring-balance tests) or about other studies conducted under much better conditions and documented with much greater care.

Although it's important to remember how weak this familiar form of criticism is, I'd say the major lesson to learn here is that in some important respects, it doesn't matter what critics of this caliber say. For example, it really won't matter in the long run, and it probably doesn't matter that much now, whether Spanos, or Aldridge-Morris, or psychiatrist Paul McHugh at Johns Hopkins Hospital regard hypnosis or DID as fictions. Similarly, it doesn't matter how superficially Trevor Hall or Peter Lamont deal with the case of D. D. Home or what Martin Gardner, Ray Hyman, James Alcock, Richard Wiseman, and (for the love of God) magician James "The Amazing" Randi say about psi phenomena generally. In my view, researchers simply can't allow themselves to worry about such people. The critics will always be there; they're part of the academic ecology. In fact, history might have a lesson to teach us here. We should remember how the study of hypnosis outlasted the considerably more prominent and influential criticisms of the French commissions investigating animal magnetism. After all, research into hypnosis survived the attacks of such luminaries as Lavoisier and Benjamin Franklin. By contrast, Spanos, Aldridge-Morris, McHugh, Gardner, Hyman, Alcock, Wiseman, and (for the love of God) James Randi are very minor figures at best (in my view, merely blackheads on the complexion of intellectual history).

Psi researcher Charles Honorton spent years debating critics (primarily Ray Hyman) over the merits of ganzfeld experiments, time he could have devoted productively to further experimentation or (say) the search for superstar subjects. I seriously question whether this was time well spent. Hyman never identified problems with the ganzfeld experiments that could be linked to those experiments' positive results. After much wrangling, Honorton and Hyman eventually jointly endorsed a revised, autoganzfeld (i.e., computerized) experimental design that was supposed to avoid the methodological "flaws"—including the risk of sensory leakage—Hyman claimed to have identified in the earlier series. But (presumably contrary to what Hyman expected) the new tests achieved scores at virtually the same level of significance as that yielded by the earlier series. So my take on the overall result of Honorton's efforts to engage Hyman in a real and honorable dialogue is that there was no positive outcome even remotely commensurate with the effort.[8] There's no reason to think that many (if any) skeptical opinions about ESP were revised as a consequence, and there's no reason to think that Honorton or anyone else learned anything new or important about ESP from all that work.

So it seems to me that the only thing that will matter in the long run is the quality of work one does, and I believe the truth will out. Although scientific research may (and apparently does) get off course theoretically from time to time, I believe that human inquiry overall produces increasingly more satisfactory ways of understanding the world.

I also believe that anomalies researchers should take seriously the almost evangelical fervor of some of the criticism often directed against their work. They suggest that parapsychologists, hypnosis or DID researchers, and other anomalists aren't simply confronting opposing theories when they're under such emotionally charged attack. Instead, they're in conflict with articles of faith; they're engaged in something closer to a religious battle than to an honest and dispassionate appraisal of rival hypotheses.

Another telltale sign is that critics sometimes state their disagreements, their differences of *opinion*, as dogma, and they do this with a certitude totally disproportionate to their knowledge of the facts. I've often seen this in parapsychology, where people declare authoritatively that the evidence can all be explained in terms of fraud, incompetence, and so on. I ran out of patience with that maneuver long ago, and it's easy to make such people look like fools. Just go on the offensive and force them to display their ignorance of the data. It's not hard to do. In many cases, you know your critics lack even a rudimentary command of the evidence. So when you're confronted with that sort of posturing ignoramus, go for the jugular. Expose those people as frauds. They're only bluffing.

Of course, that kind of justifiable aggression has only limited utility. And that's because in the case of some critics, researchers are up against a type of personality and behavioral style that reason has no power to change. So although researchers often can't afford simply to ignore their critics (after all, they may stand in the way of funding), I would urge them not to invest too much energy in responding to their charges. In parapsychology critics have sometimes goaded really creative scientists into devoting the lion's share of their time to responding to shallow and inept criticism (Honorton's case is by no means unique; it's simply a prime example). This can happen, and to some extent it has happened, in the DID field. So my advice is this: if you're not careful about how you use your time, critics can keep you occupied forever with formulating responses to them. It's a very effective way to prevent you from doing any useful work or making progress of your own. So I feel it's important to maintain a broad perspective. Reply to critics when you must. But I'd suggest that you not bend over backward to reason people out of positions they haven't been reasoned into, and I'd suggest you remember that, in the long run at least, feeble and dishonest criticism usually gets recognized as such.

Incidentally, Spanos's strategy of focusing on laboratory studies of small-scale forms of hypnosis commits another error (regrettably common in psychology)—namely, extrapolating from the laboratory to life. That is, Spanos assumed, like many others, that what's true of human behavior in the artificial and contrived context of a laboratory study is a reliable guide to what human beings can do in the context of more meaningful situations in real life. This is part of a general theoretical approach that downplays the viability and importance of field- or nonlaboratory-based observations of human behavior. It's one sweeping way of dismissing the sort of evidence that *must* be marshaled in favor of positing DID and other dissociative disorders, and which arguably is also critical in the case of psi research and other anomalies. And nobody should fall for it (I'll have more to say on the topic shortly).

THE ARGUMENT FROM HUMAN BIAS

Now let's consider the charge that field parapsychological reports and clinical observations of dramatic dissociative phenomena merely illustrate the power of biased or motivated misperceptions. There are several points worth mentioning here.

First, note that this charge of bias is a double-edged sword. Biases cut two ways: against reports by the credulous and also against reports by the incredulous. For example, the negative testimony of DID critics (e.g., that there are no signs of alter switching) is no more inherently reliable than clinicians' testimony that such things *do* occur. By the same token, reports by credulous witnesses that a psi phenomenon occurred are no more inherently suspicious than a passionate or resolute skeptic's insistence that nothing paranormal happened. And in parapsychology at least, there's ample evidence from the history of the field that both extremist viewpoints are unreliable.[9]

So my advice on this matter is as follows: don't let critics get away with pretending that their alternative descriptions of a DID patient's behavior or their alternative skeptical assessment of an ostensibly paranormal event are inherently more objective than your own. Here's one time when I feel researchers and clinicians should be feisty like a philosopher. Don't simply allow critics to put you on the defensive; turn the tables on them. If they charge you with motivated misperception, challenge them to explain why they aren't equally afflicted. Make them defend their unstated assumption that they've somehow managed to transcend the grubby predispositions that we all carry around as part of our conceptual baggage. Remember that there's no such thing as genuinely objective science; the only truly emotionally or conceptually neutral scientist is a dead one. So force your critics to acknowledge that their observations must be scrutinized just as carefully as your own; remind them forcefully that they don't deserve any antecedent presumption of accuracy or objectivity.

And in cases where skeptics dismiss the evidence of parapsychology, challenge the critics to demonstrate that they really know what the evidence is. As I mentioned above and have noted on several other occasions, critics of parapsychology often engage in little more than ignorant posturing and bluffing. If they want to be taken seriously, it's mandatory that they demonstrate their mastery of the data and the issues.[10]

And for the record, I'd question whether (or to what extent) clinical descriptions of the features of DID *can* be explained away in terms of observer bias or expectation (that is, a predisposition to see certain signs of psychopathology), which then gets communicated in subtle ways to patients. For example, even if clinicians now have such biases and expectations, it's unlikely that most of them had the same predispositions when they started out—for example, when many were surprised to discover their first multiple.

And I question how biased turn-of-the-twentieth-century pioneers of the field were, especially in connection with some of the more subtle or fine-grained and unexpected signs of multiplicity, which only later got described in the literature.

Of course, there's no doubt that many parapsychologists, dissociation researchers or clinicians, and other anomalists have been *open* to the possibility of the phenomena under investigation or that they've been open to certain specific manifestations of the phenomena. But being open to the possibility of a phenomenon isn't the same thing as being biased in its favor. For example, I can be open to the possibility that members of an alien civilization have visited the earth, but still think that the probability of its having occurred approaches zero. In fact, a person can be open to the possibility of a phenomenon and be biased *against* it. That's why many parents fail to observe that their children have been doing drugs, and it's why victims of poltergeist disturbances often feel strongly that although the phenomena are empirically possible, they're things that happen only to others.

REMARKS ON PERCEPTIVITY

In this connection, I'd like to say a few words about human perceptivity. This is commonsensical stuff probably all readers know but which is all too easy to lose sight of, especially while being attacked. Also, it's generally considered unfashionable, quaint, and perhaps a bit intellectually perverse to reply to purportedly scholarly criticism with handy bits of common sense.

First of all, many facts or phenomena become apparent to us only after a process of perceptual education. We learn to refine our observational skills as our experiences accumulate and also as our conceptual framework develops or evolves. For example, consider manipulative behavior. That's something we must learn to recognize. Of course, we first need some native discriminatory abilities. But I think we can safely assume that most people have what it takes. So what else is needed to be able to identify manipulativeness? Well, for one thing, people must be able conceptually to parse reality into the appropriate pieces and see the right connections between the diverse things we regard as manipulative. And these two stages of conceptual development go hand in hand. Acquiring the concept hinges on learning to identify certain behavioral regularities—a kind of pattern recognition; we grasp the concept when the patterns become clear and fall into place for us. Often with the help of conceptual coaching from someone who already can pick out the relevant connections, we come to see that a loosely knit set of common features underlies and unifies a great variety of subtle behaviors. And of course, as with any learning process, some people do this better than others. As a result, the ability to recognize manipulativeness comes in degrees; some people are more perceptive (or more impaired) in that way than others.

So the ability to recognize manipulative behavior requires (among other things) certain conceptual preliminaries, a certain degree of conceptual sophistication. That's why children can't begin to identify behavior as manipulative until they acquire the concept (or grasp the patterns) in at least a rudimentary form. Until then, they may be puzzled and upset by behavior others recognize as manipulative, but they won't really be able to explain why. That behavior won't stand out as distinctive for them—that is, as a regularity they can discern. It won't fit into any descriptive or conceptual category they currently possess. Even if they're aware of the word "manipulation" and its cognates, they won't understand what the words mean. And of course, the same is true of adults: they won't grasp the words until they learn to see the patterns.

We should also keep in mind that there are many ways of being *blind* to the forms of manipulativeness (or whatever it might be). For example, a person can be blind to manipulativeness generally, or just with respect to certain people, or possibly just in oneself. In fact, we can impose these blinders on ourselves for any number of reasons, and those blinders may be quite specific in their range. Moreover, even if these perceptual deficits don't result from something we do to ourselves (that is, in one of the many ways we interfere with our own lives and thwart our best interests), manipulativeness (or whatever) may simply be a dimension of human experience for which we're not particularly acute, however perceptive we might be in other respects.

In this connection, we should also recall my earlier remarks about biased or motivated misperception. We shouldn't forget that genuine perceptivity can nevertheless be clouded, distorted, or misinterpreted according to one's prevailing attitudes or assumptions. Perhaps that's why Freudians may fail to diagnose patients as dissociative, even though they perceive all the behavioral nuances seen by clinicians working within a more dissociation-friendly theoretical framework. And of course, a similar process can corrupt diagnoses made by clinicians accustomed to treating dissociative disorders. For example, the clinician may see a patient apparently "space out" for a couple of minutes during therapy and see it as a dissociative symptom when in fact the patient experienced a partial complex seizure.[11]

So I would say that both empirical (especially field or clinical) researchers and their critics need to remember that perceptivity is not an all-or-nothing sort of ability. It seldom (if ever) occurs in equal measure in all areas of life or with regard to every kind of event or phenomenon. Researchers and their critics must remember that even perceptive people are bound to have their limitations. They won't be equally keen observers of everything a person can observe. They may still lack the appropriate emotional, conceptual, and experiential background or perceptual education to recognize what others already detect quite clearly.

Now when you encounter someone who's blind to manipulativeness (or whatever), there may be any number of reasons why there's nothing you can do to change the situation. As everyone knows, people can be firmly entrenched and invested in their perspectives—either their distinctive ways of seeing the world generally, or perhaps just in some blindness or viewpoint in particular. When we deal with such people in our daily lives, it's important to be able to recognize when it's futile to try to change them. For example, I'm firmly convinced that there are aspects of manipulativeness which certain members of my family will never grasp (I can't be the only one ever to have had *that* experience). And I've had to recognize that it's a losing battle to try to change them in that way.

Similarly, I once dated a woman who was a first-grade teacher. She was a warm and generous person who apparently perceived and behaved toward all people the way she dealt with her students. As a result, she seemed to think that practically everything I did was *cute*. She experienced me through the same sort of perceptual and conceptual grid she applied to her occupation as a teacher. She would constantly (and I believe quite sincerely) say to me, "Isn't that cute?" or "That's precious." (I think she even patted me on the head once or twice.) Of course, I like to be appreciated as much as the next person, and I'd like to think that I can be cute once in a while. But I refuse to believe I was ever so relentlessly cute. And I knew that my friend wouldn't change her general way of seeing me or any other adult for that matter. I also think there was no reason why she had to. So in that respect, this case probably differs from that of critics of DID research who don't see the signs of switching that are so apparent to clinicians or who see those signs only as indications of something else (say, malingering or social compliance). Similarly, it would differ from the case of parapsychological skeptics for whom any experience of a table levitation would seem inherently suspicious, no matter how cleanly it had been demonstrated, or for whom no psi experiment would ever be accepted as evidential, no matter how many times it had been replicated successfully. But apart from that difference, the similarities between the two sorts of cases may be instructive. As with my family members and former lady friend, it may simply be that there's nothing one can do to get the critics to change.

So what *should* one do in those cases? In my own life, and especially in my role as a student of the ostensibly paranormal, I've found it helpful to remember a delightful Zen image. When a seedling trying to push its way out of the ground encounters an obstacle such as a rock, it doesn't simply continue to push against the rock and accomplish nothing. Rather, it grows around it. Like the seedling, researchers often really have no choice. So they might as well take the necessary detour and do it with as much grace as they can muster. For example, when dealing with unscrupulous critics of psi research or the treatment and study of dissociative disorders, there may be little point in engaging the critics directly. If they're irrevocably entrenched in their opinions and have no reservations about engaging in dialectical dishonesty, don't waste your time with them. There will always be other avenues for publishing your responses to their criticisms and other audiences who are genuinely open to appraising the evidence and letting the chips fall where they may. Respectable specialist journals exist just for that reason. Parapsychologists have several peer-reviewed journals dealing exclusively with psi research; dissociation researchers had *Dissociation* (now, the *Journal of Trauma and Dissociation*); and the *Journal of Scientific Exploration* deals courageously and at a very high level with a broad range of scientific anomalies which more mainstream publications typically shun.

One last point about perceptivity. I've been using an example from everyday life (manipulativeness). But the sort of perceptual education I've been considering happens also in science, and in some sciences it happens more conspicuously than in others. Although to some extent I consider experimental psychology to be a systematic retreat from developing or cultivating real-life perceptual skills, one would expect this sort of perceptual education to occur in the behavioral sciences. At least ideally, behavioral scientists will sharpen their observational skills with practice, as they learn to attend to the subtle features of the phenomena under investigation. We see a similar process occurring conspicuously in professional sports and also in sports broadcasting—for example, in learning to call a hockey game on the radio. That's an ability which constantly amazes me; I can scarcely believe people actually do it. It requires not only a mastery of the subtleties of the sport but great perceptual quickness as well. Additional sports examples are easy to find—for example, learning to identify different pitches in baseball or distinguishing offensive from defensive basketball fouls. These, too, take both perceptual acuity and practice.

Moreover, this kind of perceptual education occurs in nonbehavioral sciences as well. You see it in physicists who've honed their skills at reading tracks in cloud chambers; you see it in the archaeologist who's adept at finding subtle clues on a dig; you see it in the geologist who can easily spot outcroppings and structural features of the terrain. I vividly recall my geology field trips in college. I was impressed and intimidated by the perceptual keenness of my mentors, who would easily pick out distant distinctive features in land which seemed undifferentiated to me.

Now I'd say that there's every reason to think that many of those who study and treat dissociative disorders (and DID in particular) undergo the same sort of perceptual education. I'd say they've quite probably—and no doubt gradually—become attuned to things (specifically, certain types of pathological behavior) to which others are oblivious to varying degrees. So why isn't this readily acknowledged by their critics, even as a likely possibility? This brings me to the last of the similarities I see between this field and the field of parapsychology. In particular, it raises the issue of what Sherry Turkle has described as physics envy.

PHYSICS ENVY

This concerns yet another respect in which some parapsychologists and dissociation researchers have been unjustifiably defensive. It has to do with the allegation that the study of these domains is unscientific unless it satisfies the canons of "real" hard science.

There are several points I'd like to make about this. First, that allegation has plagued the social sciences (and psychology in particular) for some time, and it's led to a number of prominent intellectual abominations, including behaviorism and the more recent and quite trendy field of so-called cognitive science (insofar as it's founded on the belief that humans are types of biocomputers whose behavior can be explained mechanistically). Regrettably, when behavioral scientists found themselves confronted with the charge that their "soft" sciences aren't genuinely scientific, many yielded much too easily. Instead of defending the observational skills and exquisite sensitivities that *should* be the pride of their fields, they adopted experimental methods and terminological conventions that belong more appropriately to other areas of research (typically, physics and chemistry). So instead of defending the obvious point that different domains of phenomena might require different investigative procedures and modes of explanation, they emulated the technical jargon and formal techniques of some physical sciences, and they substituted laboratory studies and artificial experimental protocols for penetrating field or real-life investigations. Clearly, this was a desperate and wrongheaded attempt to cultivate the facade of being careful and tough minded, unlike those who embraced more informal and naturalistic modes of investigation. Never mind that this required importing techniques used in some (and *only* some) physical sciences into domains where those techniques are almost wholly inappropriate. And never mind that this required the foolish pretense that one can usefully extrapolate from the straitjacketed and limited menu of behaviors we can observe in the lab to the infinitely richer and more varied things people do in the real world.

Human beings, after all, display a dazzling palette of behaviors and character traits, and the traits are indispensable both for explaining and for predicting human behavior (see chapter 3 for more on this). People can be charismatic, whimsical, candid, ironic, manipulative, self-deceptive, diplomatic, consoling, generous, empathetic, opportunistic, finicky, adventurous, grouchy, dependable, industrious, timid, shy, impulsive, adaptable, demanding, greedy, shrewd, confident, gentle, jealous, secretive, serious, faithful, thoughtful, sneaky, lazy, bossy, reliable, sentimental, respectful, resourceful, cruel, opinionated, narcissistic, rude, proud, pretentious, taciturn, sullen, pessimistic, callous, dogmatic, polite, stingy, diligent, pensive, touchy, efficient, tenacious, warm, cautious, playful, tender, obsequious, superstitious, courageous, humble, responsible, decisive, caustic, facetious, immature, tolerant, curious, mischievous, neat, sensual, loyal, uninhibited, reckless, coarse, vulgar, unfriendly, trustworthy, trusting, stubborn, careless, childish, obedient, happy-go-lucky, and countless other things. And we can't even begin to get a handle on these traits by trying to harness and study them under controlled conditions. Moreover, this isn't true just of personality traits or characteristics. Not even the ability to sing or the ability to endure pain can be properly evaluated under controlled conditions. The former is something many people can do only in the presence of select others (if they can do it at all in the presence of others), and the latter may vary considerably, depending on what's at stake in real-life situations (e.g., childbirth, battlefield conditions, or athletic competition as opposed to a routine medical exam or an accident at home).

In fact, since most of our character traits manifest only during our interactions with others in contexts of real needs and interests, they're analogous to athletic abilities that can be studied *only* during the pressure of actual contests. If we want to assess a basketball player's ability to hit free throws or a tennis player's ability to volley, we must see how well the player performs during a game. As everyone knows, some people practice better than they play, and others play better than they practice. So a basketball or tennis player's ability is partly a function of how the player deals mentally with the pressures of an actual match. But even if we ignore the ways in which psychological pressures affect athletic performance, many athletic abilities still can be studied only in the context of a game. Only in actual playing situations, in which opponents are trying their hardest to win, will we be able to evaluate a linebacker's ability to sack the quarterback, a tennis player's ability to play the net, or a baseball batter's ability to bunt.

All this strikes me as painfully obvious, and in certain respects I find it inscrutable that people actually need to have it explained. But since it's clear that some do, in fact, need it explained, it's worth considering why that is and why some behavioral scientists in particular have gotten so far off track. I think there are two general underlying reasons for this state of affairs. The first is philosophical; many have been deeply confused about the nature of explanation generally and psychological explanation in particular. The second is more political than conceptual: many have simply succumbed to a kind of intellectual bullying. Let me comment briefly on each.

Let's start with the conceptual confusions. One reason so many behavioral scientists genuflect in the presence of physicists and cognitive scientists is that they uncritically accept an unwarranted assumption about the nature of explanation. Elsewhere[12] (and also in chapters 2 and 3) I've dubbed this the *small-is-beautiful assumption*. The problems with it are complex and far-reaching, and I can only hint here at what they are.

Most scientists assume (explicitly or otherwise) that observable facts or phenomena (including lawlike regularities) always have analyses in terms of lower-level constitutive processes or states of affairs. Of course, scientists will generally concede that *some* facts or phenomena in nature must be basic or unanalyzable. They recognize that vertical explanations, explanations by analysis—that is, in terms of constitutive lower-level processes—can't continue indefinitely and that sooner or later we must arrive at a point where those explanations can go no lower. At that point we'll have identified genuinely primitive phenomena, whose primitiveness is reflected in the fact that there will be no answer to the question *how* the phenomena at that ground level occur. The universe simply works in those ways, and no appeal to constitutive processes will explain why. Now *that* position is quite reasonable. But most scientists assume, further, that wherever explanation by analysis stops, wherever these fundamental phenomena occur, it will always be on the level of the very small—for example, the neurological, biochemical, atomic, or subatomic level. They assume, in other words, that there are no primitive phenomena at the observable level—for example, at the level of behavior. That's the small-is-beautiful assumption.

First of all, notice that this is only an assumption, not an empirically established fact. Moreover, antimechanists and antireductionists have mounted a very strong case against it. This isn't the place to present a detailed criticism of the assumption; that's actually one of the biggest topics in the philosophy of mind. So let me just mention briefly what sorts of problems one can point to. First, it's possible to show how the assumption fails in particular cases. For example (as I argued in chapter 1), the analysis of memory in terms of underlying memory traces rests on abstract and very deeply embedded philosophical assumptions that are literally unintelligible. And then one can show how to extrapolate from the case of memory to the domain of mental phenomena more generally. For instance, it's possible to show how mechanistic analyses of the mental rest generally on deeply flawed presuppositions—most notably, Platonic assumptions about the nature of properties or transparently false assumptions about the nature of similarity or representation. Now (as you might imagine) all this is a very complex story, there's no time for it here, and besides, this is well-trodden territory.

Here's another way to expose the poverty of the small-is-beautiful assumption. That assumption is one form of the view that nature has a preferred (or inherently fundamental) level of description, a level at which we can identify absolutely primitive phenomena and their basic properties. Most supporters of that view would maintain that the preferred level will be described in an adequate theory of physics. But no matter what the preferred level of description is taken to be, the small-is-beautiful assumption is committed to the view that statements true of observable phenomena are inherently superficial and that only statements true of the microcosm can be statements about primitive phenomena. That's why most adherents of the small-is-beautiful assumption would say that the physicist asks deeper questions than the psychologist, or interior decorator, or simply the average human being engrossed in everyday matters of psychological survival. But that position is bizarre. It's also a view an examination of whose defects would now take us too far afield. I'll simply note for now that I consider the view to be an insidious form of perspectival chauvinism. For example, to say that the physicist's description of nature is inherently privileged compared to that of (say) the interior decorator, insurance agent, or household mover is no more tenable than supposing there's a privileged answer to the question "How many things are in this room?" or "How many events occurred yesterday?"

So let me comment, finally, on the political reason for the pervasiveness of physics envy in the behavioral sciences. To put it bluntly, laypersons and behavioral scientists are often too easily impressed and intimidated by the physicist's command of imposing formalisms as well as the cognitive scientist's similar reliance on the specialized technical language of the neuroscientist, computer scientist, or engineer. This phenomenon is virtually identical to one witnessed quite often in my own field of philosophy, where perfectly competent professionals have been unjustifiably cowed by colleagues who rely heavily on the language of formal logic. (I ought to know; this is the game I played shamelessly for a long time. All I had to do was present my arguments in symbolic form and in an apparently sophisticated technical veneer, and I was guaranteed to discourage many from even attempting to argue against me. It would play right into their insecurities.) The problem is that many regard these specialized forms of expertise as surefire signs of high-powered profundity. But what they often illustrate instead is how technical facility can be nothing but a smokescreen for work that in other respects is shallow and conceptually unsophisticated. And unfortunately, although there are many who can intuit what's sometimes wrong with ideas presented in such impressive technical packages, they're afraid they're unqualified to comment because they lack the appropriate formal or technical skills. In most cases, I don't think that physical and cognitive scientists are consciously trying to con the world at large. In many cases, I believe they're also fooling themselves. But the truth, in my view, is that whether they realize it or not, physicists' knowledge and skills are generally irrelevant to the study of consciousness, and cognitive scientists' reliance on neurobiology, computerese, or other technical jargon is often little more than a trendy and fancy method for obscuring elementary philosophical errors. Memory-trace theory, again, is a perfect example. For instance, Karl Pribram's attempt to analyze memory in terms of holographic representational states of the brain is as simplistically mistaken as Plato's suggestion that memories are analogous to impressions in wax.[13]

So what I want to say to parapsychological naturalists, dissociation researchers, and some other groups of anomalists is this: your discriminatory abilities may differ in many ways from those of the physicist or chemist and probably also from those in other areas of the social, behavioral, or physical sciences. Don't be fooled by chauvinistic attempts to belittle your activities or the distinctive sensibilities you rely on when you take a motley domain of behavior or other phenomena and try to make it intelligible and systematic. Have faith in your sensitivity, perceptivity, and observational skills. Of course, you shouldn't go to the other extreme and become unself-critical. You shouldn't allow your own specialized professional community to degenerate into a club (or cult) insulated from outside criticisms and in which you simply reinforce one another's errors and confusions. So when you're feeling assailed by criticism directed at your field as a whole, it's important for you to remain vigilant, to see whether the criticisms are bogus and dishonest.

It's also be important for you to remember that there's more than one way to be scientific, that you *may* really see things your critics don't, and that your critics may be blinded by their own theoretical biases and constrained by their own cognitive and perceptual limitations. You need to cultivate your observational skills and refine your understanding of the inevitable subtleties of your domain of investigation. And you shouldn't apologize if you're engaging in a scientific enterprise different from most of the physical sciences. Nature has many different aspects; and no single approach to describing nature *can* be complete. If your domain of interest is some subset of human behavior, then as far as I'm concerned, what you do is no less significant *and no less fundamental* than what the physicist does. Once the small-is-beautiful assumption takes its rightful place in the philosophical dustbin, it should be clear that what we need is a healthy scientific pluralism, which acknowledges and values the different methodologies, perspectives, and distinctive sensibilities required for different scientific disciplines. Then it will be clear that when we look at all the various sciences together, what we find is not a hierarchy with physics at the top, nor even a single unified body, but rather a genuine community of equals.

REFERENCES

Aldridge-Morris, R. (1989). *Multiple personality: An exercise in deception.* Hillsdale, NJ: Erlbaum.
Bem, D. J. (1994). Response to Hyman. *Psychological Bulletin, 115*(1), 25–27.
Bem, D. J., & Honorton, C. (1994). Does psi exist? Replicable evidence for an anomalous process of information transfer. *Psychological Bulletin, 115*(1), 4–18.

Bem, D. J., Palmer, J., & Broughton, R. S. (2001). Updating the ganzfeld database: A victim of its own success? *Journal of Parapsychology, 65*(3), 207–218.
Braude, S. E. (1985). Review of Trevor H. Hall, The enigma of Daniel Home. *Journal of the Society for Psychical Research, 53*, 40–46.
Braude, S. E. (1995). *First person plural: Multiple personality and the philosophy of mind* (Rev. ed.). Lanham, MD: Rowman & Littlefield.
Braude, S. E. (1997). *The limits of influence: Psychokinesis and the philosophy of science* (Rev. ed.). Lanham, MD: University Press of America.
Braude, S. E. (1998). Commentary on "False memory syndrome and the authority of personal memory-claims." *Philosophy, Psychiatry, & Psychology, 5*, 299–304.
Braude, S. E. (2003). *Immortal remains: The evidence for life after death.* Lanham, MD: Rowman & Littlefield.
Braude, S. E. (2007). *The gold leaf lady and other parapsychological investigations.* Chicago: University of Chicago Press.
Elliotson, J. (1843). Numerous cases of surgical operations without pain in the mesmeric state: With remarks upon the opposition of many members of the Royal Medical and Chirurgical Society and others to the reception of the inestimable blessings of mesmerism. In F. Kaplan (Ed.), *John Elliotson on mesmerism* (pp. 227–282). New York: Da Capo.
Esdaile, J. (1846). *Mesmerism in India, and its practical applications in surgery and medicine.* London: Longman, Brown, Green & Longmans.
Esdaile, J. (1852). *Natural and mesmeric clairvoyance, with the practical application of mesmerism in surgery and medicine.* London: Hippolyte Bailliere.
Gauld, A. (1992). *A history of hypnotism.* Cambridge: Cambridge University Press.
Hall, T. H. (1984). *The enigma of Daniel Home.* Buffalo: Prometheus.
Inglis, B. (1977). *Natural and supernatural.* London: Hodder & Stoughton.
Ofshe, R., & Watters, E. (1993). Making monsters. *Society, 30*(3), 4–16.
Spanos, N. P. (1983). The hidden observer as an experimental creation. *Journal of Personality and Social Psychology, 44*, 170–176.
Spanos, N. P., & Chaves, J. F. (1989). Hypnotic analgesia and surgery: In defence of the social-psychological position. *British Journal of Experimental and Clinical Hypnosis, 6*, 131–139.
Spanos, N. P., & Hewitt, E. C. (1980). The hidden observer in hypnotic analgesia: Discovery or experimental creation? *Journal of Personality and Social Psychology, 39*, 1201–1214.
Spanos, N. P., Weekes, J. R., & Bertrand, L. D. (1985). Multiple personality: A social psychological perspective. *Journal of Abnormal Psychology, 94*, 362–376.

NOTES

1. Braude, 1995, 1998, 2003.
2. See, e.g., Spanos, 1983; Spanos & Chaves, 1989; Spanos & Hewitt, 1980; Spanos, Weekes, & Bertrand, 1985.
3. Esdaile, 1846, 1852. See also Elliotson, 1843 and the discussions in Braude, 1995 and Gauld, 1992.
4. Aldridge-Morris, 1989.
5. Ofshe & Watters, 1993.
6. For details, see Braude, 1995.
7. Braude, 1985, 2007; Hall, 1984.
8. For details, see Bem, 1994; Bem & Honorton, 1994; Bem, Palmer, & Broughton, 2001.
9. For details, see Braude, 1997. Also see Inglis, 1977.
10. For more on this, see Braude, 2007.
11. My thanks to Peter Barach for reminding me of this.
12. Braude, 1997.
13. See chapter 1.

Index

abilities, nature of, 96–98, 141–179n57; complex constitution of, 96–98, 147, 152–153, 169, 170; latent, xi, 125, 141, 153, 154, 156, 157, 158, 160, 161–162, 166, 168, 170–171, 171; relevance of practice, 148, 159–160, 163, 165, 167–169, 169, 210, 212
action vs movement, 36–37, 60
agent-regret, 106–107, 108
Alcock, James, 204
Aldridge-Morris, Ray, 203, 203–204
all-purpose-psi argument, 152–153
American Association for the Advancement of Science (AAAS), 173
amnesia, 119–120, 120–121, 121, 122, 203
anomalous monism, 6, 67, 76, 79n17
apparitions, 186, 196n5
argument from human bias, 206–207
Aristotle, 174
Armstrong, D.M., 54, 55, 57–58
attribute-distribution and attribute-depletion, 113, 125–126, 132
Augustine, Saint, 105–109, 109, 110, 111–112, 118, 137n6

Barach, Peter, xii, 216n11
Barnes, Gerald, xii
Basmajian, J., 191
Bayne, Tim, 137n3
behaviorism, 36, 59–61, 67, 211
Behnke, Stephen, 129

Bem, Daryl, 179n55
Bennett, M.R., 25n3
Bernheim, Hippolyte, 86–88, 95, 102n23
Bester, Alfred, 187
Bierman, Dick, xii
biofeedback, 189, 191
brain lesions, 75–76
Brown, Rosemary, 158–160
Bryant, Richard, 86, 102n16, 102n18, 102n22
Buridan's ass, 133
Bursen, Howard A., 25n3, 33
Byrne, J.H., 20
"The Case of ESP" (Nova/Horizon film), 153, 178n14

causation, x, 2, 3, 27–28, 28, 29–31, 31, 32, 41, 42, 43, 45, 50, 56, 57–58, 75–76, 77–79, 108, 114, 172, 174, 184, 186, 187, 188, 192, 194
causal nexus, 192–195
channeling. *See* mediumship
character traits, x, 53–54, 63, 64, 68–69, 70–71, 72, 91, 96–98, 113, 125, 132, 165, 199, 211–212
chess, 160, 172
clairvoyance, 172, 185, 186
Clarke, Randolph, 125, 126, 137n9, 138n38, 138n40
cognitive science, 1, 4, 8, 12, 14, 21, 44, 46, 50, 52, 53, 71, 72–73, 76, 78

217

coincidences. *See also* synchronicity
congruence, geometric, 9–11, 33, 34, 39, 41
Crabtree, Adam, 120
Crawford, W.J., 155
Crookes, William, 154, 203

Davidson, Donald, 67
Davison, Scott, xii
Demolished Man, The, 187
Dennett, Daniel, 130, 138n51
dissociation, ix, x–xi, xii, 81–102n35, 105, 109, 118, 120. *See also* dissociative identity disorder (DID)
dissociative anesthesia, 81–82, 84, 86. *See also* hypnotic anesthesia
dissociative identity disorder (DID), x, xi, 83, 88, 93–94, 96–97, 98, 100, 103–139n60, 141, 165, 170, 177n1, 197, 200, 201, 203, 204, 205, 206, 209, 210; multiple persons thesis, 129, 129–130, 131–132, 138n46; polyfragmented cases, 116, 129, 138n57–139n58; single person thesis, 129, 129–130, 131, 132, 133, 134, 138n46
dreaming, xi, 105–106, 107, 108, 109, 110, 111–112, 118, 128, 137n6, 146, 186
Dreifuss, F.E., 171
dualism, 29–30, 43, 50
Ducasse, C.J., 164–165

ectoplasm, 155
Eisenbud, Jule, 178n6, 179n57, 196n12
eliminative materialism, 70–71
Elise B., 86–88, 95
Esdaile, James, 202
essentialism, 18, 32, 37, 38–39, 44, 57, 63
ESP (extrasensory perception), xi, 22, 42, 147, 153, 156, 163, 165, 169, 172, 182, 184, 185–187, 187, 192, 204. *See also* clairvoyance; telepathy
Eva C., 155
evil eye, 185
experimental repeatability, 175–176
experimenter expectancy effects, 42, 155, 160, 187–188. *See also* Rosenthal effect

False Memory Syndrome Foundation, 203

fart factor, 147, 150, 178n8
fear of psi, 188–189
Flournoy, Theodore, 161–162
Fodor, Jerry, 53–54, 56, 58, 70, 71–72, 73
French, A.P., 115
Freud, Sigmund, 109–110, 111–112, 118, 208

ganzfeld experiments, 204
Gardner, Martin, 204
Gauld, Alan, xii, 83, 167, 169, 216n3
Gauss, Carl Friedrich, 168
Geley, Gustave, 155
ghost hunters, 173
Goldberg, Bruce, xii, 50, 79n1–79n2, 79n15–79n16
Goligher, Kathleen, 155
Grimsley case, 123, 124, 125

Hacker, P.M.S., 25n3
Hall, Trevor, 203
Halleck, Seymour, 110, 112, 116–118
hallucination, xi, 39, 81–87, 90–91, 93, 95, 96; doubled person, 85–86
Hamlet (the pig), 91–92, 95–96
Hansel, C.E.M., 153
hard-line approach to therapy, 124–125, 127–128
Heil, John, 4, 25n3, 79n2
hexing, 185
Hilgard, Ernest, 83, 85, 102n20
Hillside Strangler case, 203
Home, D.D., 151, 152, 153–154, 154, 203–204
Honorton, Charles, 204, 205
Humphrey, Nicholas, 130
Hyman, Ray, 203–204
hypnosis, x, 81, 81–88, 90, 96, 102n18, 102n22, 141, 142, 144, 154, 156, 160–161, 165, 166, 186, 189–190, 192, 202, 203, 204, 205; as social compliance, 202–203; hypnotic anesthesia, 202–203. *See also* systematized anesthesia; hypnotic blindness, 82, 85, 86, 102n18, 102n22; *See also* hallucination

identity, concept of, 10–11, 44, 106, 118, 119; personal identity, xi, 103–104,

105, 106, 106–109, 118–119, 121,
  128–129, 132–133, 133–134, 137n6
International Remote Viewing Association
  (IRVA), 142
isomorphism, 5, 7–8, 11–12, 14, 16, 19, 58,
  77. See also similarity

Janet, Pierre, 82, 102n5–102n6
Journal of Trauma and Dissociation, 210

Kantian ego, 100, 113, 134
Kelly, Ed, xii, 79n19
Kennett, Jeanette, 129, 130, 132, 137n2,
  138n44–138n46, 138n50,
  138n57–139n58
Kesner, Raymond, 20
Kluft, Richard, 88, 138n33
knowledge: *that* versus *how*, 158, 159,
  163–164
Köhler, Wolfgang, 5–7, 14, 16, 18, 19

Lamont, Peter, 203
Lashley, Karl, 22
latent abilities. See abilities
Liégeois, Jules, 87
linguistic facility, 161, 168–169, 170–171
living-agent psi explanation, 162–163,
  171, 172
Locke, John, 132
Loftus, Elizabeth, 203
luck, 183, 190–191
luck-of-the-draw strategy, 122–123
Luria, A.R., 156, 178n21

Malcolm, Norman, 25n3
Matthews, Steve, 129, 130, 132, 133, 134,
  136, 138n46, 138n57–139n58
McDaniel, Stan, xii, 48n19
McConkey, Kevin, 86, 102n16, 102n18,
  102n22
McHugh, Paul, 203–204
McMoneagle, Joe, 151
meaning, nature of, 5, 7, 13, 22, 52, 62, 70,
  115, 143
mechanistic theorizing, ix–x, 3, 22–23, 23,
  28, 31, 33, 43, 44, 46, 50, 70, 100, 176,
  211, 213
mediumship, 152–155, 157–160, 161–162,
  162–163, 164–165, 166–167, 168,
  170–173, 178n17, 183, 186, 203;
  interpreted as possession, 167; physical,
  152–155, 178n17, 183, 203
memory, x, xi, 1–26n32, 33, 38, 44, 46, 50,
  77, 88–94, 95, 95–96, 96, 98, 121, 122,
  145, 148, 150, 155–156, 157, 159, 161,
  162, 203, 213, 214; autobiographical
  tentacles, 91–93, 95–96; cellular, 22;
  dispositional nature of, 89–90, 92–93;
  false memories, 203; genetic, 22;
  holographic analysis, 3, 46, 214–215;
  mnemonists, 155–156; recorder view
  of, 203; trace theory of, x, 1–26n32, 33,
  38, 44, 50, 77, 213, 214
Milligan, Billy, 115–116, 122
motivated misperception, 206–207,
  208–209, 215
multiple personality. See dissociative
  identity disorder
Myers, F.W.H., 84

Nadel, Lynn, 20, 26n17, 26n20
Nader, Karim, 19–20, 26n8, 26n13
negative hallucination. See hallucination,
  dissociative anesthesia
Neppe, Vernon, 172

Oakley, David A., 82, 84, 102n7, 102n10,
  102n12, 102n14, 102n16
Ofshe, Richard, 203
O'Keefe, John, 20
Orne, Martin, 83, 86

Palladino, Eusapia, 152, 153–154,
  154–155, 178n17
Parapsychological Association (PA), 173
person, concept of. See identity: personal
  identity
personality traits. See character traits
physics envy, 23, 62, 211–214
Piper, Mrs., 151
placebo effects, 189–190
Plato, x, 3, 8, 18, 32, 38, 57, 63, 73, 77,
  77–79, 144, 181, 199, 213, 215
Pylyshyn, Zenon, 76, 79n18
poltergeist phenomena, 207
postmortem survival, xi, 1, 4, 22, 142, 151,
  153, 157–159, 162–164, 166, 167–173;
  Hungarian grand-master case, 172;

transplant cases, 22
posttraumatic stress disorder (PTSD), 94
precognition, 186
prayer, xii, 182, 192–195
Pribram, Karl, 3, 46, 214–215
Price, Pat, 147
prodigies, xi, 141, 151, 152, 158, 159, 162, 168. See also savants
protein kinase M-zeta (PKMζ), 19
psychic healing, 184, 185
psychokinesis (PK), xi–xii, 42, 149, 152, 171, 182, 183, 183–185, 186, 187, 190, 192, 196n2, 196n7
psychosomatic ailments, 190, 191, 192

Quinton, Anthony, 132, 133

Radden, Jennifer, 104, 121, 129, 137n9, 138n35
Raikov, Vladimir, 160–161
Randi, James "The Amazing", 204
reincarnation, 1, 22, 157–158, 168, 172; versus possession, 168. See also xenoglossy
Reich, Wilhelm, 99
representation, concept of, 2, 3, 5–7, 11, 12–14, 15, 16, 18, 19, 20–21, 22, 51–53, 56, 57, 57–59, 61, 64, 65, 67, 68, 69, 70, 73, 75, 76–78, 213, 215
repression, 98, 102n34
resistance to (fear of) psi, 185, 186–187, 188–189, 191
responsibility, xi, 103–139n60; legal versus moral, 104–105, 111, 112–116, 129, 130, 131, 133, 138n35; weak versus strong, 110–112, 118, 123, 127; causal responsibility versus taking responsibility, 127; versus accountability, 121–122
Rhine, J.B., 176, 183
Richet, Charles, 155
Roll, William, 22
Rosenthal effect, 187, 196n8
Ross, Colin, 88
Roussel, Albert, 144

Sacktor, Todd, 19
Saks, Elyn, 129

savants, xi, 141, 151–152, 155, 157, 158, 159, 162, 168–169. See also prodigies
Shechmeister, B. R., 115
Schiller, F.C.S., 162
Schmidt, Helmut, 196n2, 196n7
Schrenck-Notzing, Baron von, 155
Sheldrake, Rupert, x, 23, 25n2, 27–48n25, 196n11
shlemiel vs shlemazel, 190–191, 191. See also luck
similarity, 6, 7–11, 12, 16, 21, 22, 23, 32, 33, 34, 36, 39–41, 51, 52, 77, 107, 213
Sinnott-Armstrong, Walter, 129
Slovenko, Ralph, 104, 112–115, 115–116
small-is-beautiful assumption, 44–45, 72, 213, 215
Smith, Hélène, 154, 161–162
sneaky psi, 175, 186, 188, 189–192. See also source of psi problem
Society for Scientific Exploration (SSE), 173; Journal of, 210
sociobiology, 46
source of psi problem, 175, 184, 187
Spanos, Nicholas, 202–203, 203, 205
Stevenson, Ian, 164–165, 167, 169, 170, 171
Stroop effect, 84
super psi, 163, 172, 184, 185
"super-psi" alternative to postmortem survival. See living-agent psi
survival of bodily death. See postmortem survival
systematized anesthesia, xi, 86. See also dissociative anesthesia

telepathy, xi, 120, 171–172, 182, 185, 186, 187, 189, 192; telepathic deferment, 186; telepathic leakage, 172, 187, 192; telepathic transparency, 186–187, 189. See also ESP
trance logic, 86
Turkle, Sherry, 23, 211
Twilight Zone, 187

unlucky people. See luck, shlemiel vs shlemazel

vitalism, 28–29, 29, 30, 31

Watters, Ethan, 203
Wilkes, Kathleen, 129
Williams, Bernard, 106–107
Wiseman, Richard, 204
Wittgenstein, Ludwig, 50
Worth, Patience, 154, 166–167

xenoglossy, 158, 164, 166, 168–169, 170–172

Yalowitz, Steven, 48n25, 79n17
Young, Walter, 88